American
Literary Anecdotes

American
Literary Anecdotes

Robert Hendrickson

Facts On File
New York • Oxford • Sydney

American Literary Anecdotes

Facts On File, Inc.   Facts On File Limited   Facts On File Pty Ltd
460 Park Avenue South   Collins Street   Khartoum & Talavera Rds
New York NY 10016   Oxford OX4 1XJ   North Ryde NSW 2113
USA   Kingdom   Australia

Library of Congress Cataloging-in-Publication Data

Hendrickson, Robert, 1933–
    American literary anecdotes/Robert Hendrickson.
      p.   cm.
    Includes index.
    ISBN 0-8160-1599-6
      1. American literature—Anecdotes. 2. Authors, American— Anecdotes.
    I. Title.
PS138.H46   1990
    818′.02—dc20   88-34088

British and Australian CIP data available on request from Facts On File.

Facts On File books are available at special discounts when
purchased in bulk quantities for businesses, associations,
institutions or sales promotion. Please contact the Special Sales Department of
our New York office at 212/683-2244 (dial 800/322-8755 except in NY, AK or HI).

Text design by Ron Monteleone
Jacket design by Victore Design Works
Composition by Facts On File, Inc.
Manufactured by The Maple-Vail Book Manufacturing Group
Printed in the United States of America

10 9 8 7 6 5 4 3 2 1

This book is printed on acid-free paper.

For my grandson, Ross

CONTENTS

INTRODUCTION

I have tried to collect in these pages more American literary witticisms and curiosities than have ever been assembled before, reading over the past 10 years hundreds of books and hundreds of millions of words in order to do so. While I believe this is the widest-ranging book on the subject, it wouldn't be accurate to call it "complete" by any means. Though America is a young country she has a literary history old and vigorous enough to have yielded an abundance of literary anecdotes that can not possibly be covered in one book, or even in a set of encyclopedias. I'm sure, too, that the reader will agree that these thousands of bon mots, stories and curiosities are no less interesting than those of any other literature. Regarding witticisms, for example: Although America doesn't have the long tradition of literary wit justifiably associated with Great Britain (where it seems almost essential that every author and editor and publisher and critic be quick with the quip), the *best* American authorial wits compare favorably with the greatest literary wits in the world. In fact, Mark Twain and Dorothy Parker would be high up on my list of the 10 most formidable wits of all time, and Robert Benchley wouldn't be much further down.

The basic ground rules for this collection are the same as for its companion volumes, *British Literary Anecdotes* (which covers writers from Commonwealth nations) and *World Literary Anecdotes*. First, I've scrupulously tried to exclude anecdotes of living writers and anecdotes about deceased writers that could hurt anyone remaining behind. Writers and their relatives have troubles enough, and John Aubrey is generally right, I think, when he says of his marvelous "rude and hastie collection," *Brief Lives*, that before literary anecdotes are "fitt to lett flie abroad" the "author and the Persons...ought to be rotten first." Second, I should say that my collection too is "rude and hastie," though I hope hastier than rude; in any case I tried to be as brief as possible with each entry so that there would be space for more entries. This sometimes meant condensing or paraphrasing what I would have preferred to quote at length, but I hope that in most cases I've managed to get the essence of the author and anecdote. Third, I've tried to indicate when a story is doubtful or when it has been told about several writers, though I have doubtless missed some anecdotes I should have labeled apocryphal (despite checking one or more biographies for most stories). Finally, I've tried to include stories and very brief sketches of all the major American literary figures and represent all the noted literary wits among them with an ample selection of their bon mots. But I haven't hesitated to include literary anecdotes concerning people who weren't authors, or to include authors noteworthy, or remembered today, solely for one good anecdote, sometimes just for their last words or epitaphs. I hope in this last case that the stories may lead readers to the forgotten work of some very deserving writers.

It should be added that this book, which ranges from Colonial to present times, is arranged alphabetically by author, but has a place and name index, which includes writers who haven't an entry to themselves but are mentioned in other entries; as well as a topic index enabling readers to find one or more anecdotes about certain subjects, such as accidentally destroyed manuscripts, literary hoaxes, love affairs, hard-drinking authors, strange deaths etc. etc.

A number of writers represented here could have been included in the British or World literary ancedotes volumes, which forced me to adopt the rather arbitrary rule that a writer's last citizenship be the price of admission to a collection. The U.S. lost Henry James and T.S. Eliot this way, but gained Auden and Einstein, among others. (The only exception here was P.G. Wodehouse, an American citizen in his late years, who, along with his butler Jeeves, is so quintessentially British that I hadn't the heart to put him anywhere but in England.)

My thanks to my editor, Gerry Helferich, and copy editor, Paul A. Scaramazza, both of whom made valuable contributions to this work. I would also like to thank the many people, too numerous to mention here, who suggested anecdotes to me through the years, particularly those correspondents who wrote from all over the world (including one from Saudi Arabia whose address I've lost and whom I can't write to thank), providing me with more literary hors d'oeuvres after my *Literary Life and Other Curiosities* was published in 1980. But, of course, all of the errors herein are my responsibility. I can't even blame them on my wife, Marilyn, who worked as hard on this book as I did but who would be "she who hung the moon and stars" to me if she neither worked upon nor even read a word of my deathless prose.

Robert Hendrickson
Far Rockaway, New York

Dean Acheson (1893–1973)

It is said that the statesman and prominent writer on foreign affairs was asked by a distraught Lyndon Johnson why he wasn't popular. "Let's face it, Mr. President," Acheson replied, "you're not a very likeable man."

∇ ∇ ∇

Abigail Adams (1744–1818)

Her famous letters to her husband, published in several volumes, range from before John Adams became the second president of the United States to her death eight years preceding him. They are charming, wise and witty letters that illuminate the early years of the Republic, but can be gossipy and venomous, too. One time Abigail observed that the marriage of a certain young woman to a much older man was a union of "the Torrid and the Frigid Zones." John Adams, sixtyish himself, wrote back testily: "But how dare you hint or lisp a Word about Sixty Years of Age? If I were near, I would soon convince you that I am not above forty."

∇ ∇ ∇

Brooks Adams (1848–1927)

Henry Adams' brother, also an historian, accurately predicted in 1900 that within 50 years there would be only two world powers, the Soviet Union and the United States, with the latter possessing economic supremacy. The very shy Adams, an agnostic most of his life, in his last years both found religion and overcame his lifelong shyness, when he stood up at the Congregational church in Quincy, Massachusetts, and made a public confession of his faith.

∇ ∇ ∇

Franklin Pierce Adams (1881–1960)

F.P.A., as the humorist and Algonquin Round Table habitué was known, professed to dislike writing and considered it hard work. One time an interviewer told him of an author who was "terribly eager" to begin writing every day. Replied F.P.A.: "The only people who like to write terribly are those that do."

Adams was a punctual man. "Promptness is a worthy cause," he once told an editor, "but costly. You call the doctor and he says he'll be at your home between three and four to have a look at your wife. You wait. He arrives at seven. You have an appointment with the dentist for 3 P.M. sharp. At 3 P.M. sharp you are waiting in his receiption room. So are six other patients waiting their turn. You buy tickets for the theater. The curtain will rise on the dot of eight, or so the announcements say. Fifteen minutes earlier you are in your seat and already have memorized the pages of program notes. You also have read all the ads and decided on which sandwich you'll order later at Sardi's. At 8:17 the curtain rises. Slowly. I have wasted a year and a half of my life waiting for curtains to rise, and seven years waiting for people who were late."

Alexander Woollcott asked that his friends give him a shower when he moved into his new apartment. "I'd actually appreciate your bringing china, linen and silver," he made it known. Accordingly, F.P.A. brought him a moustache cup, a handkerchief and a dime.

"Ah what is so rare as a Woollcott first edition?" The impossibly vain Woollcott enthused while signing a first edition copy of his *Shouts and Murmurs*. F.P.A., standing next to him, replied: "A Woollcott second edition."

New York World editor Herbert Bayard Swope was questioning a foreign visitor at his home about German poetry when the name of Henrich von Kleist came up. "Who's Kleist?" Swope demanded. F.P.A., seated nearby, answered, "The Chinese messiah."

Adams wasn't noted for his good looks. One morning humorist Irvin Cobb entered a room where a moosehead was mounted over the mantel. "My God, they've shot F.P.A.!" he cried.

After watching young Helen Hayes play Cleopatra on Broadway in *Caesar and Cleopatra*, F.P.A. remarked to a friend that she appeared to be suffering from "fallen archness."

Adams and his wife doted on their white angora cat Miztah, with whom *New Yorker* editor Harold Ross planned to mate his cat Missus—until she mysteriously disappeared one spring night. The two Adams often went so far as to spell out words in front of their cat to keep him from becoming conceited: "See how H-A-N-D-S-O-M-E he is!"

Adams, Harpo Marx and other members of the Thanatopsis Poker Playing and Inside Straight Club were playing in a hotel room when a waiter entered in the middle of a big hand, tripped, and fell, spilling a mess of food all over the table. Nobody stopped cursing until Harpo Marx quipped, "Well, the waiter drops out," and F.P.A. added, "Yeah, he only had a tray."

An interminable bore went on and on with a story until he came to the inevitable point where he said, "Well, to cut a long story short…"

"Too late," F.P.A. advised.

▽ ▽ ▽

Hannah Adams (1755–1831)

Hannah Adams was forced through family misfortune to make a living for herself from the time she was 17. Though her mainly historical works yielded a meager income, they provided Adams with enough to support herself and become the first professional woman author in America.

▽ ▽ ▽

Henry Brooks Adams (1838–1918)

Unlike many writers, Adams was always enchanted by his art and craft. In one letter he wrote: "The fascination of the silent midnight, the veiled lamp, the smouldering fire, the white paper asking to be covered with elusive words; the thoughts grouping themselves into architectural forms, and slowly rising into dreamy structures, constantly changing, shifting, beautifying their outlines—this is the subtlest of solidary temptations, and the loftiest of the intoxications of genius."

The eminent historian's little nephew was told that his uncle was a brilliant man who knew everything. All through lunch the boy sat silent, in awe of the distinguished man of letters, until finally, during a lull in the adult conversation, he could bear it no longer and blurted out, "Uncle Henry, how do you feed a chameleon?"

Adams was one of the few authors who privately printed his books before allowing his publisher to print and sell them to the general public. He would have several copies of a book printed and distribute them to friends whose literary opinions he valued, making changes whenever he found their criticisms valid.

He said of himself in his later years: "I want to look like an American Voltaire or Gibbon, but am settling down to be a third-rate Boswell hunting for a Dr. Johnson."

In his autobiography, *The Education of Henry Adams*, which he wrote in the third person, Adams describes his formal education as useless and even harmful. Sending a copy to Henry James, he claimed in his letter that it was better for a writer to reveal everything about himself than have someone else do it. Better to commit suicide by writing your own autobiography, he said, than to be murdered by someone writing your biography.

$$\nabla \ \nabla \ \nabla$$

John Quincy Adams (1767–1848)
A prolific author, the sixth president of the United States produced over 10 large volumes of work, not including his diaries and correspondence. He is the only U.S. president who might be considered a professional poet, having published a 108-page book of poetry in 1832.

$$\nabla \ \nabla \ \nabla$$

Louisa Catherine Adams (1775–1852)
President John Quincy Adams's wife was a talented woman whose autobiographical books *Record of a Life, or My Story* and *Adventures of a Nobody* are filled with sharp, amusing observations. An early feminist, she was well aware of the dangers of marriage for a woman in her day, once remarking that "hanging and marriage...[are] strongly assimilated."

$$\nabla \ \nabla \ \nabla$$

George Ade (1866–1944)
One afternoon the Indiana humorist was sitting with a little girl of eight at a friend's house.

"Mr. Ade," she said, looking up from her storybook, "does m-i-r-a-g-e spell marriage?"

"Yes, my child," Ade softly replied.

A prominent attorney tried to match wits with Ade after the author had given a hilarious speech. Hands in his pockets, he drawled, "Doesn't it strike the company as a little unusual that a professional humorist should be funny?" When the laughter subsided, Ade replied, "Doesn't it strike the company as a little unusual that a lawyer should have his hands in his own pockets?"

$$\nabla \ \nabla \ \nabla$$

James Agee (1909–1955)
While a struggling young writer the novelist and film critic lived with his wife on a Stockton, New Jersey, farm they rented for $25 a month. There was no bathroom in the decrepit house and when visitors complained, Agee would tell them, "Why, all God's outdoors is a toilet!"

Jean Louis Rodolphe Agassiz (1807–1873)

The Swiss-born naturalist, author and educator taught for 25 years at Harvard, and in that time had more offers to give public lectures than he had time for—without detracting from his scientific studies. One lyceum repeatedly asked him to speak and, when he kept refusing, assured him that he would be very well paid for his lecture. "That is no inducement to me," Agassiz replied. "I cannot afford to waste my time making money."

At the start of each year at Harvard, Agassiz would tell his classes: "Gentlemen, the world is older than we have been taught to think. Its age is as if one were gently to rub a silk hankerchief across Plymouth Rock once a year until it were reduced to a pebble."

∇ ∇ ∇

Conrad Aiken (1889–1973)

The poet, novelist and short story writer lost both his parents when a young boy in Savannah. As he later put it: "... after the desultory early-morning quarrel came the half-stifled scream, and then the sound of his father's voice counting three, and the two loud pistol shots; and he [the child] had tiptoed into the dark room, where the two bodies lay motionless and apart, and, finding them dead, found himself possessed of them forever."

Aiken became one of the most masterful and neglected of American writers, in part because he never compromised, as he said on his deathbed, and partly because from the beginning he panicked at being in the limelight. When Aiken was elected Harvard's class poet in 1911, for example, he refused the honor, leaving school, and he never in his long career appeared in public to read his poems or accept one of his many awards. "He [the poet] had known, instantly," he later explained, "that this kind of public appearance, and for such an occasion, was precisely what the flaw in his inheritance would not, in all likelihood, be strong enough to bear ... It was his decision that his life was to be lived *off-stage*, behind the scenes, out of view."

In 1972 Malcolm Cowley wrote him saying he and other friends had celebrated Aiken's 83rd birthday with a party at which he recited the poet's sadly neglected poem "Thee." Aiken replied that Cowley's letter had arrived in the same mail as a royalty statement advising that "Thee" had been remaindered.

Louisa May Alcott (1832–1888)

Though few of her readers knew it, the author of the warm, gentle *Little Women* (1868) was a manic-depressive who suffered terribly from nightmares and hallucinations and frequently contemplated suicide. Much of her illness can be traced to her years as a nurse during the Civil War, when she contracted typhoid and then mercury poisoning in the treatment of that disease, but she had suffered manic depression as a child, when she was forced to work to help support her family. In her late years her condition improved, though she was never completely free from it.

The author's father, Bronson Alcott, was a venerable Don Quixote, as Carlyle termed him, a thoroughly impractical philosopher who was "all bent on saving the world by a return to acorns and the golden age." Many of his educational theories are accepted today, but in his time his rigid adherence to his principles made more suffering for his wife and four children than for himself, so much so that later in life Louisa May Alcott defined a philosopher as "a man up in a balloon, with his family and friends holding the ropes which confine him to earth and trying to haul him down."

As a lover of all living things—including mosquitoes, which he would brush aside but never kill even if they were gorged on his blood, and potato bugs that he collected and dumped over the fence into the tax collector's garden (he did not like his taxes supporting slavery)—Bronson Alcott believed in helping animals by not eating them. But he was a vegetarian with a sense of humor. Once Emerson was carving a roast for his guests, all the while lecturing them on the barbaric practice of cannibalism. Suppressing a smile, Alcott turned to him and said, "But Mr. Emerson, if we are to eat meat at all why should we not eat the best."

Despite his impractical nature Bronson Alcott remained a good friend of Ralph Waldo Emerson's all his life. Though Emerson recognized Alcott's limitations, he visited his Concord neighbor frequently and Alcott and his family reciprocated. Louisa May Alcott developed a schoolgirl crush on Emerson, writing him long, romantic letters that she never mailed, softly singing love songs at night under his window, and anonymously leaving flowers at his door. In fact, only one magazine article is listed in her journal without an accompanying dollar sign to record the sale—an article on Emerson noted as "a labour of love." As for Emerson, he never learned of her infatuation, not even after she became famous and Bronson Alcott became known as "the grandfather of *Little Women*."

The inscription over the mantel in Alcott House was a couplet by William Ellery Channing:

The hills are reared, the seas are
  scooped in vain
If learnings' altar vanish from the
  plain.

"Stick to your teaching," publisher James T. Field told her when she submitted a youthful effort, "you can't write."

Alcott once branded *Little Women* "moral pap" and told a friend at another time, "I think my natural ambition is for the lurid style." On still another occasion she confessed to a friend that she intended to write a "blood and thunder tale as they are easier to compose and are better paid than moral and elaborate works." In fact, for 15 years, from 1854 to 1869, she published pseudonymous thrillers and Gothic romances (including "The Abbot's Ghost" and "Pauline's Passion and Punishment") in popular magazines to earn a living. She was an established Gothic writer before turning to her moralistic stories for children.

∇ ∇ ∇

Thomas Bailey Aldrich (1836–1907)
His novels were never favored by many academics, but then neither did novelist Thomas Bailey Aldrich particularly care for academic prose. In reply to a letter from an erudite professor, he wrote: "It was very pleasant ... to get a letter from you the other day. Perhaps I should have found it pleasanter if I had been able to decipher it. I don't think that I mastered anything beyond the date (which I knew) and the signature (which I guessed at). There's a singular and a perpetual charm in a letter of yours; it never grows old, it never loses novelty...Other letters are read and thrown away and forgotten, but yours are kept forever—unread. One of them will last a reasonable man a lifetime."

∇ ∇ ∇

Sholom Aleichem (Solomon Rabinowitz; 1859–1916)
The Russian-born Yiddish author took his pen name from the traditional greeting of Jews, meaning "peace unto you." Aleichem suffered from triskaidekaphobia, fear of the number 13, and his manuscripts never had a page 13. Ironically, he died on a May 13, but the date on his headstone in Mount Carmel Cemetery, Glendale, New York, reads "May 12a, 1916." According to one tale, Aleichem, called "the Jewish Mark Twain," chanced to meet Mark Twain in New York. "I am the American *Sholom Aleichem*," Twain modestly told him.

Horatio Alger Jr. (1832–1899)

Before he became the author of his vastly successful rags-to-riches "Horatio Alger" tales, which sold well over twenty million copies, Alger was a Unitarian preacher in Brewster, Massachusetts. Accused of pederasty with at least two of the boys in his parish, the creator of Ragged Dick and Tattered Tom admitted his guilt and was discharged from the pulpit, fleeing to New York, where he began his writing career.

"Holy Horatio," as he was known at Harvard Divinity School, lost his virginity to a cafe singer in Paris in 1855. "I was a fool to have waited so long," he wrote in his diary. "It was not nearly so vile as I had thought."

∇ ∇ ∇

Fred Allen (John Florence Sullivan; 1894–1956)

The American radio comedian and author of *Treadmill to Oblivion* and *Much Ado About Me*, was a morose-looking man who believed that "the world is grindstone and life is your nose." Allen once saved a little boy from being hit by a truck. Pulling the boy to safety, he shouted, "What's the matter, son! Don't you want to grow up and have troubles?"

All of the scripts for Allen's long-running radio show—39 a year—were bound by the comedian and stacked on 10 feet of shelves beside a one-volume copy of the collected works of Shakespeare, which occupied a mere 3 1/2 inches of space. "I did that as a corrective," Allen explained, "just in case I start thinking a ton of cobblestone is worth as much as a few diamonds."

James Thurber said that one of Allen's off-the-cuff remarks was among the funniest he had ever heard. It was made in the early days when Allen earned his living as a vaudeville comedy juggler. Night after night Allen noticed a musician in the pit who never smiled and always wore a blank expression. Finally one evening he stopped his act, leaned over the pit and asked the man, "How much would you charge to haunt a house?"

"You finally do so well in your career, all you can drink is buttermilk," Allen told an interviewer toward the end of his life. "When they start feeding me intravenously, I'll know I've made it to the top."

∇ ∇ ∇

Maxwell Anderson (1888–1959)

After the critics panned his play *Truckline Cafe*, the Pulitzer Prize-winning playwright took out an ad in the *New York Times* calling the critics the "Jukes

family of journalism, who bring to the theatre nothing but their own hopeless-
ness, recklessnss and despair."

▽ ▽ ▽

Sherwood Anderson (1876–1941)

On November 27, 1912, Anderson, who had been a drifter and served in the
Spanish-American War before marrying and settling down, was dictating a letter
to his secretary in the paint manufacturing plant he managed in Elyria, Ohio. In
the midst of a sentence he stopped, walked quickly from the room, and wasn't
seen again for four days, when he was found in a Cleveland drugstore. Neither
Anderson nor anyone else was ever able to explain how the apparent victim of
amnesia got there or what had happened over the four days. In any case,
Anderson was through with the paint business and moved on to Chicago, where
he became an advertising copywriter and published his first book, *Windy
McPherson's Son*, in 1916. The novel deals with "a boy's life in a drab town, his
rise to success as a manufacturer, and his renunciation of this life to 'find truth.'"

Horace Liveright, Anderson's publisher, had a reputation as a philanderer, so
Anderson wasn't surprised to see him with still another attractive woman when
he bumped into Liveright in New Orleans. "I want you to meet my wife," the
publisher said. Anderson sarcastically replied, "Oh, yeah, sure, Horace." After
a vast silence he realized that, this time, the lady *was* Mrs. Liveright.

Publisher Liveright decided to subsidize Anderson with $75 a week while he
was writing a novel in Greenwich Village. But the money disrupted Anderson;
he found himself with so much security that he was unable to write. Bursting
into Liveright's office one morning, he cried, "Horace, Horace, please stop those
checks! *Give me back my poverty!*"

The wife of a midwestern banker had once sat beside Anderson at a dinner.
Later he received a letter from her advising him that, having read his then daring
Winesburg, Ohio and having sat next to him, "she felt that she could never, while
she lived, be clean."

Anderson was a victim of a 20th-century invention, the literary cocktail party.
The American author died of peritonitis and complications after swallowing a
toothpick with an hors d'oeuvre at a cocktail party given by his publisher.

On Anderson's death his hometown paper, the *Elyria* (Ohio) *Chronicle-Telegram*
headlined: SHERWOOD ANDERSON, FORMER ELYRIA MANUFACTURER,
DIES.

Anonymous

An 18th-century colonial printer with a penchant for puns wrote a punning epitaph for himself:

> Here lies a *form*—place no *imposing stone*
>   To mark the *head*, where weary it is lain;
> 'Tis *matter dead!*—its mission being done,
>   To be *distributed* to dust again.
> The *body's* but the *type*, at best, of man,
>   Whose *impress* is the spirit's deathless *page*;
> *Worn out*, the *type* is thrown to *pi* again,
>   The *impression* lives through an eternal age.

For all his working career the editor of a small-town New England paper had saved an old-fashioned wooden scarehead type of about 60-point size, never using it no matter how much he was implored. But one summer he went off on a fishing trip and while he was gone a terrible cyclone hit the town, nearly devastating it. Figuring that this disaster rated the 60-point scarehead, his assistants got it down and set up a sensational front-page headline. But the editor was hardly happy when he returned and saw the result. "Balls of fire!" he cried. "What d'ye mean by taking down that type for a cyclone! All these years I've been savin' that type for the Second Coming of Christ!"

An old story from the Texas Panhandle tells of a winter so cold that spoken words froze in the air, fell entangled on the ground, and had to be fried up in a skillet before the letters would reform and any sense could be made of them. The idea is an ancient one, used by Rabelais and familiar to the Greek dramatist Antiphanes, who is said to have used it in praising the work of Plato: "As the cold of certain cities is so intense that it freezes the very words we utter, which remain congealed till heat of summer thaws them, so the mind of youth is so thoughtless that the wisdom of Plato lies there frozen, as it were, till it is thawed by the refined judgment of mature age."

Among the most unusually named of all the American magazines published over the last three centuries is *Smith's*. It was some anonymous genius's idea to so name the magazine in the mid-19th century, not in honor of anyone but to attract a readership from among the myriad of Americans named Smith.

Using the wrong punctuation can be costly. In the 1890s a congressional clerk was supposed to write: "All foreign fruit-plants are free from duty" in transcribing a recently passed bill. But he changed the hyphen to a comma and wrote: "All foreign fruit, plants are free from duty." Before Congress could correct his error with a new law the government lost over $2 million in taxes.

The most costly grammatical error in history occurred when the American space probe *Mariner I,* bound for Venus, headed off course and had to be destroyed at a cost of $18.5 million. The rocket had responded erratically because an anonymous flight computer programmer had left out a comma from *Mariner's* computer program.

A newspaper editor in upstate New York at the turn of the century was criticized at a town meeting for his bad grammar and diction. "So I been criticized somewhat for grammar," he replied. "Well, I got three good reasons for it. To begin with, I don't know any better. If I did, none of you would know the difference; and more than that, if I spoke and wrote any better than I do, I'd be managing editor of a big New York paper at a decent salary and you farmers would lose the best damned editor in Herkimer County."

"Punning is the lowest form of wit," an irate critic told an inveterate punster.
"Yes," the punster replied, "for it is the foundation of all wit."

When the *New York Post* and *New York Sun* were feuding early in this century, an editor on the *Post* called the *Sun* "a yellow dog." Answered a *Post* editor, most aloofly, "The *Post* calls the *Sun* 'a yellow dog.' The attitude of the *Sun,* however, will continue to be that of any dog toward any post."

Possibly the most embarrassing modern-day typographical error—due to the slip of the unknown editor or typesetter—appeared in the *Washington Post* in 1915. In a news story it was noted that President Wilson had taken his fiancée Edith Galt to the theater the previous night and, rather than watching the play, "spent most of his time entering [instead of "entertaining"] Mrs. Galt."

As far back as Roman times Seneca laughed at those who brought books for ostentatious display and never read them, but one American millionaire in the 1920s bought almost half a million dollar's worth of books by the yard. "Measure those bookshelves with a yardstick and buy enough books to fill 'em," he told his secretary while furnishing his Chicago apartment on Lake Shore Drive. "Get plenty of snappy red and green books with plenty of gilt lettering. I want a swell showing." At least more original is the advice *Lady Gough's Book of Etiquette* gave library owners in Victorian times: Don't place books by married male authors next to those by female authors and vice versa.

The cub reporter asked a friend, "How do you spell pinochle?" The next day the friend read the lead of the reporter's story: "An inspired Illinois team yesterday reached the pinochle of success."

"The relation of the agent to the publisher," claimed one anonymous agent, "is the same as that of the knife to the throat."

No one knows who invented this common definition of publishing, but almost everyone in the business agrees with it: "The largest floating crap game in the world."

A would-be humorist sent a batch of jokes to a magazine. A few months later he got the following letter from the editor: "Dear sir: Your jokes received. Some we have seen before, some we have not seen yet."

Umbrage derives from the Latin *umbra* (shadow or shade), the same root that gives us "umbrella." The expression means to take offense, suggesting someone "shadowed in offended pride, retreating into the darkness of proud indignation." There is a story about the editor of a small newspaper who quickly read a wire service story during World War II stating that the Russians had *taken umbrage* at something, as they often did. Not knowing what the phrase meant, he headlined the story: "Russians Capture Umbrage."

An aspiring poet read some pallid verses to a friend in his very cold apartment. "I won't be able to stand here much longer," the friend said, "unless you put some fire into your verses or some of your verses into the fire."

No one has determined who conceived the following "Rejection from a Chinese Eitor," but he or she must have been an editor:

> Illustrious brother of the sun and moon—Behold thy servant prostrate before thy feet. I kow-tow to thee and beg of thy graciousness thou mayest grant that I may speak and live. Thy honored manuscript has deigned to cast the light of its august countenance upon me. With raptures I have perused it. By the bones of my ancestry, never have I encountered such wit, such pathos, such lofty thoughts. With fear and trembling I return the writing. Were I to publish the treasure you sent me, the Emperor would order that it should be made the standard, and that none be published except such as equaled it. Knowing literature as I do, and that it would be impossible in ten thousand years to equal what you have done, I send your writing back. Ten thousand times I crave your pardon. Behold my head is at your feet. Do what you will.
>
> Your servant's servant,
> The Editor

"You know how it is in the kids' book world," observed a children's book editor: "It's just bunny eat bunny."

An editor-in-chief at a leading publishing house was told that two editors at another house had had four and five wives respectively. "Acquisitions editors acquire," he replied.

"Ta-ra-ra-bom-der-e," a hit popular song in 1892 and later the basis for the Howdy Doody children's T.V. program in 1950, originated with an anonymous piano player in a St. Louis brothel.

"In America only the successful writer is important, in France all writers are important, in England no writer is important, in Australia you have to explain what a writer is." (This observation is also attributed to Geoffrey Cotterell.)

The editors of an American science fiction magazine received the following letter in 1952: "Please cancel immediately the subscription and forward refund for the nine copies still due the subscriber to the agent listed below. Mr._____ was killed while trying an experiment in the magazine."

An anonymous critic reviewing *The Snakes of Hawaii*, published by the Honolulu Zoo, hailed it as the most definitive work on the subject, one "Completely devoid of zoological, grammatical, and typographical errors." All the book's 20 pages are blank, for there are no snakes in Hawaii.

No library can charge a patron more than the cost of replacing a lost or overdue book, or its estimated fair market value, but the waived fine on the world's longest overdue book—taken out from the University of Cincinnati library in 1832 and returned 145 years later in 1968 by the borrower's great-grandson—was calculated at $22,646. That, however, was just *one* book. A 58-year-old New York attorney—who didn't even have a library card—had over *15,000* books overdue from the New York Public Library. In 1973 firemen accidentally discovered the mountains of books in the man's apartment while making an inspection tour after putting out a fire on the floor below. When asked why he had hoarded so many books, the attorney replied, "I like to read."

A 1978 newsletter from a branch of Mensa, an organization for high-IQ people, had the spellings "recieved," "attornies" and, of course, "intelligense."

Isaac Asimov tells the story of the anonymous author whose agent told him his books weren't selling because there wasn't enough sex in them. "Not sexy enough?" the writer shouted. "What are you talking about? Look, right here on the first page the courtesan dashes out of the room stark naked and runs out into the street with the hero following her just as naked and in an explicitly described state of sexual arousal."

"Yes, yes," said the agent, "but look how *far down* the first page!"

Replied an American high school student when asked for a definition of poetry: "It's that stuff in books that doesn't reach the margins."

During a long American writers' strike against television producers in 1981, producers, actors and even secretaries and stagehands churned out scripts for the voracious daytime soap operas. One actor on a popular soap knew his character would soon be killed off and volunteered to be the show's head writer during the strike. Not only did his character live, he also became the lead—and any actor who protested this sudden turn of events saw his or her character killed off.

At the 50th anniversary dinner party of the New York Drama Critics Circle in 1985 attendance was poor for no apparent reason, only two writers of all the past award winners accepting their invitations. A critic mentioned the poor attendance to one of the playwrights, who replied: "Why should anyone want to have dinner with critics?"

∇ ∇ ∇

Michael Arlen (Dikran Kuyumjian; 1895–1956)

Born in Bulgaria of Armenian descent, Arlen was educated in England and eventually settled in the United States. One of the most popular novelists of the 1920s, the author of the then-titillating *The Green Hat* (1924) was mobbed by admirers when he sailed from London to New York in 1925. At the time he became probably the only author ever to have the buttons ripped from his fly by adoring, souvenir-hunting fans.

Arlen regretted ever meeting English author Rebecca West, who cracked, "He is every other inch a gentleman." American humorist Irvin Cobb, however, approved of him. "I like Mike," said Cobb. "He's the only Armenian I ever met who never tried to sell me a rug."

"Why, Mr. Arlen, you look almost like a woman," purred Edna Ferber on first meeting the impeccable dandy. Arlen bowed deeply. "Miss Ferber, so do you!" he replied. (The riposte has been attributed to several other authors as well.)

∇ ∇ ∇

Timothy Shay Arthur (1809–1885)
Arthur, the author of some 100 moral tales and tracts, let William W. Pratt dramatize his melodramatic story *Ten Nights in a Barroom and What I Saw There* (1854) in 1858. Since then it has become the longest-running American play, in production for over a century with at least four films made from the script.

∇ ∇ ∇

Penelope Ashe (fl. 1969)
You will find no Penelope Ashe in any biographical dictionary, for she doesn't exist. Penelope Ashe is the pseudonym of the myriad authors of the "round-robin" novel *Naked Came the Stranger* (1969), mentioned here because it probably had more collaborators under one pen name than any other book in history. Twenty-five *Newsday* writers published this spoof on sex novels but did not reveal their secret until after the book was reviewed. There have been a number of collaborations involving five or more authors, but *Naked Came the Stranger* holds the record. Among the noted writers who have participated in such projects in the last century or so are Henry James, W.D. Howells, Harriet Beecher Stowe, Theophile Gautier, Alexander Woollcott, Louis Bromfield, Agatha Christie, Dorothy Sayers and G.K. Chesterton.

∇ ∇ ∇

W.H. (Wystan Hugh) Auden (1907–1973)
In one of his poems the British-born Auden, who became a U.S. citizen in 1946, writes that he had no wish to be a poet until an afternoon in March when he was 15 and he was walking in a ploughed field with a friend. "Tell me, do you write poetry?" the friend asked. "I never had, and said so," Auden later remembered, "but I knew from that very moment what I wished to do."

Although he was a homosexual, the poet married Erika Mann, daughter of German author Thomas Mann, in 1935 so that she could escape from Nazi Germany on his British passport. His friend Christopher Isherwood proposed the union to Auden, who cabled back a simple "Delighted" and the couple first met on their wedding day. Erika and Auden never spent a night together, the poet living with Chester Kellman from 1946 until the end of his life, but his legal marriage to Erika Mann lasted until her death in 1969.

He refused to allow friends to attend one of his poetry readings. "I never allow anyone I know to come to those things," he explained. "First of all I want to keep all my tricks to myself, and second, I'm always afraid someone in the back of the hall is going to shout something like 'We've heard all that before' or 'Get her!'"

Someone described his amazingly furrowed face as "like a wedding cake left out in the rain." As he aged his face became so layered with lines that composer Igor Stravinsky quipped, "Soon we will have to smooth him out to see who he is."

"We can't stand it a minute longer," two Yale students said in a note they wrote to the poet after staring at him throughout a long train ride from New York to New Haven: "Are you Carl Sandburg?"
He wrote back in reply: "You have spoiled mother's day."

Auden, in his later years, said that when he was 20 he wrote a line "which, had I intended it to be a caption for a Thurber cartoon, I should today be very proud of." With "a blush" he recalled the line: "And Isobel who with her leaping breasts pursued me through a summer."

∇ ∇ ∇ ∇ ∇ ∇ ∇ ∇

Benjamin Franklin Bache (1769–1798)
Ben Franklin's grandson, proud to be called Lightning Rod Jr., bitterly attacked President Washington and Federalist policies in his *Philadelphia Aurora*. Angered by one of Bache's editorials, veterans of Washington's army wrecked the newspaper office. When Bache said that compared to any of the great generals of European history Washington wasn't fit to lead a sergeant's guard, he was arrested by American authorities under the Alien and Sedition Acts, though he died before he could be tried. The infamous Alien and Sedition Acts were, in fact, partly aimed at Bache and his *Aurora*.

∇ ∇ ∇

Delia Salter Bacon (1811–1859)
The Ohio-born schoolteacher, who wrote several long-forgotten novels, is remembered for her theory, expounded in *The Philosophy of the Plays of Shakespeare*

Unfolded (1857), that Shakespeare's plays were written by a group of men headed by Francis Bacon and including Sir Walter Raleigh and Edmund Spenser. They had, she said, concealed a great philosophic system within the plays by the use of ciphers, which she had discovered. Nathaniel Hawthorne said that her devotion to this single idea "had thrown her off balance" and when she traveled to England to research her theory more she went entirely out of her mind. For the last two years of her life she was violently insane.

∇ ∇ ∇

Joel Barlow (1754–1812)
One of the Hartford Wits, the poet spent much of his life in Europe, where he was made a French citizen in 1792. It was in France that he wrote his charming poem "The Hasty Pudding," which is better remembered today than any of his more pompous poems. Barlow wrote the poem after the New England pudding was unexpectedly served to him in a Savoyard inn, bringing back memories of home. As American minister to France in 1812, Barlow was instructed to conclude a commercial treaty with Napoleon. On his way to meet Napoleon, the poet became involved in the retreat of the French army from Russia and died of exposure at the Polish village of Zarnowiec on Christmas Eve.

∇ ∇ ∇

Djuna Barnes (1892–1982)
In his biography of the avant-garde author, Andrew Field writes of Barnes' sexual attractiveness in her early years: "A tall and handsome young European from Harvard named Putzi Hanfstaengl [later a Hitler confidant] courted her most intensely. A subsequent lover told me that Putzi once suffered an extremely painful burst blood vessel in his penis while dancing with Djuna."

Said Djuna to a very hyperactive member of her set in Paris: "You would be marvelous company slightly stunned."

∇ ∇ ∇

P.T. (Phineas Taylor) Barnum (1810–1891)
Barnum was actually a kind, gentle man with a vivid imagaination and a whimsical turn of mind, which his books, including his autobiography and *Humbugs of the World* (1865), clearly show. The great showman, who began his career as a shopkeeper and newspaper editor, was swindled by investments made from bad advice, far more disastrously than he ever swindled anyone else. He was suckered worst when he lost $500,000 in a mismanaged clock company, had to declare bankruptcy and considered ending his life. Barnum's last words were said to be: "How are the receipts today at Madison Square Garden?"

As Barnum lay on his deathbed the *New York Evening Sun* asked his publicity agent if the showman would object to having his obituary published before he died. Barnum so loved publicity that he gave his permission and read the obit with relish the next day.

▽ ▽ ▽

Ethel Barrymore (1879–1956)

The celebrated actress is probably the only performer ever to obtain permission from a playwright to add a last line to his play. She added and spoke as the curtain line of Thomas Raceward's *Sunday* (1904) the famous words: "That's all there is: There isn't any more."

▽ ▽ ▽

John Barrymore (1882–1942)

Annoyed with a row of people coughing in the audience, the actor sent out for a fish during intermission and threw it at them when he came back on stage. "Busy yourself with that, you damned walruses," he cried, "and let the rest of us proceed with the play."

"A footnote," he observed, "is like running downstairs to answer the doorbell during the first night of marriage." (See MARK TWAIN on the parenthesis).

The great Russian director Konstantin Stanislavski held up a pin and told Barrymore that he selected his actors by means of it. Making Barrymore leave the room, he hid the pin and asked Barrymore to return. "Please look for the pin," he said. Barrymore searched everywhere and finally found it. "Excellent!" Stanislavski said, "I can tell you are a real actor. I can tell a real actor by the way he looks for a pin. If he prances around the room, striking attitudes, pretending to think very hard, looking in ridiculous places—exaggerating—then he is not good."

▽ ▽ ▽

Black Bart (Charles E. Boles; fl. late-19th century)

Black Bart was the nom de plume of Charles E. Boles, a daring American robber who held up stagecoaches in the 1870s, and did it alone, *on foot* (he had no use for horses) and *with an unloaded shotgun*! A consummate artist at his chosen work, Black Bart wasn't a bad poet, either. He wrote many poems, the following sample certainly his rationalization for his crimes.

> I've labored long and hard for bred
> For honor and for riches

But on my corns too long you've tred
You fine-haired Sons of Bitches

Black Bart will have to do until America produces a Villon. Unfortunately, little is known of him. The man who signed his poems PO-8 seems to have disappeared after being released from jail in 1888.

▽ ▽ ▽

John Bartlett (1820–1905)
Bartlett's *Familiar Quotations* has been a standard American reference work since its publication in 1855. Its compiler was born in Plymouth, Massachusetts, and for many years owned the University Book Store in Cambridge. Harvard professors and students made the store a meeting place and Bartlett's encyclopedic knowledge made "Ask John Bartlett" the customary advice to anyone who wanted the source of a quotation. This reliability was justified with the appearance of his book, which has gone through many editions and revisions.

▽ ▽ ▽

Ralph Barton (d. 1931)
Bored with it all, the artist and satirist committed suicide, leaving behind a note saying that he was tired of devising strategies "for getting through 24 hours of every day" and specifying that his remains should be left "to any medical school that fancies them, or soap can be made of them. In them I haven't the slightest interest except that I want them to cause as little bother as possible."

▽ ▽ ▽

Bernard Mannes Baruch (1870–1965)
The renowned financier, government adviser and author often operated off of a park bench in downtown New York. One day in 1946 he found this usual bench occupied. "Oh, oh," he said, "someone's taken the office."

▽ ▽ ▽

L. (Lyman) Frank Baum (1856–1919)
The author of *The Wonderful Wizard of Oz* (1900) always had a big cigar stuck in his mouth, though he never seemed to light it up. One summer day at the seashore, he confided that he couldn't smoke because of his heart. The only time he lit up, he said, was when he went in the water. "I can't swim," he explained, "so when the cigar goes out, I know I'm getting out of my depth."

Rex Beach (1877–1949)

This adventure novelist started out as a gold prospector in the Klondike. "When I decided to write," he told an interviewer, "I didn't have any of the background or equipment that was considered necessary then. I thought all authors were Englishmen."

∇ ∇ ∇

Henry Ward Beecher (1813–1887)

The great preacher and author, brother of Harriet Beecher Stowe, was a complex man whose interests ranged from involvement in antislavery movements to involvement with female members of his congregation. Beecher's Bibles, for example, were Sharp repeater rifles that the Reverend, one of America's most famous and controversial preachers, raised money for at his Brooklyn Heights church in New York and shipped to "Bloody Kansas" in crates labeled "Bibles." Beecher encouraged his parishioners to join the "underground railroad" and even held mock slave auctions at Plymouth Congregational Church to illustrate the evils of slavery. The church, still in use, was called "The Church of the Holy Rifles" and is now a national historic shrine. Beecher once wrote that "the Sharp rifle was a truly moral agency...[had] more moral power...than a hundred Bibles."

Beecher was involved in the most sensational American sex scandal of the 19th century when in 1854 he was accused by his parishioner Theodore Tilton of committing adultery with Tilton's wife, Elizabeth, in Beecher's Plymouth Church study, seducing her by telling her God had ordained that they have sexual relations. Though the trial resulted in a hung jury the once vastly respected Beecher became a notorious figure for several years.

Someone tried to insult Beecher by sending him an envelope containing a single sheet of paper with the word FOOL scrawled across it. The next Sunday the preacher exhibited the letter in church, observing, "I have known many an instance of a man writing letters and forgetting to sign his name, but this is the only instance I have known of a man signing his name and forgetting to write his letter."

Beecher was making an impassioned antislavery speech when a heckler in the rear of the auditorium interrupted him by crowing like a rooster and convulsing the audience. Beecher remained calm until the crowing ceased and the crowd stopped laughing. Then he took out his pocket watch. "That's strange," he said. "My watch says it is only ten o'clock. But there can't be any mistake about it. It must be morning, for the instincts of the lower animals are absolutely infallible."

Robert Benchley (1889–1945)

During his Harvard days, the humorist and drama critic took a final examination in which he was asked to "discuss the arbitration of the international fisheries problem in respect to hatcheries, protocol, and dragnet and travel procedure as it affects (a) the point of view of the United States and (b) the point of view of Great Britain."

Benchley answered as follows: "I know nothing about the point of view of Great Britain in the arbitration of the international fisheries problem and nothing about the point of view of the United States. Therefore, I shall discuss the question from the point of view of the fish."

Benchley was known to drink; in fact, he was known to drink more and to be able to hold more than anyone else in his circle.

"What do you drink so much for?" Scott Fitzgerald, of all people, once lectured him. "Don't you know alcohol is slow poison?"

"So who's in a hurry?" Benchley replied.

For the title of a 1928 book the master of low comedy chose *20,000 Leagues Under the Sea, or David Copperfield*.

Standing on the balcony of Delmonico's restaurant and looking out at Fifth Avenue, one spring evening in 1923, Marc Connelly suddenly pointed to Benchley and shouted to the pedestrians below: "People, people! Your new prince!" As Connelly put it in his autobiography: "Without a flicker of hesitation, Benchley stepped forward to the balustrade. He lifted his hands to silence unshouted cheers, then, as smoothly as though he had gone over the speech with an equerry, he assured his listeners in broken German that he did not want them as a conquered people to feel like slaves under a yoke but as chastened human beings aware that their future depended on the acceptance of a regime which they might resent but that would do its best to govern them in a kindly fashion. Benchley promised that as soon as they evidenced self-restraint, he would order curfews lifted, begin freeing political prisoners, and in time restore to qualified Americans the right to vote for local officials. 'And now,' he concluded, 'my prime minister and I will retire to discuss matters of state. And you have all been so cute, next Saturday night I will permit fireworks and dancing in the streets.'"

His son wrote that he liked to collect books with odd titles. These he kept on a special shelf, books such as: *Talks on Manure; Keeping a Single Cow; Forty Thousand Sublime and Beautiful Thoughts; In and Out with Mary Ann; Perverse Pussys...*

Neither Alexander Woollcot, Dorothy Parker nor Franklin P. Adams uttered the famous bon mot "Let's get out of these wet clothes and into a dry martini," as various sources have claimed. Benchley made the witticism after running into the Algonquin, having just been caught in a rainstorm after leaving a press reception at the Plaza Hotel.

An efficiency expert hired by Condé Nast decreed that any employee late for work at *Vanity Fair* had to fill out a form explaining his or her tardiness. In minute handwriting Benchley filled out a form one morning, explaining that all the elephants at the Hippodrome had escaped and had been attempting to board a steamship leaving for Boston. To prevent a terrible marine disaster he had had to round them up and herd them back to the Hippodrome, this explaining why he was 11 minutes late for work.

Vanity Fair issued a directive ordering members of its editorial staff under no circumstances to discuss their salaries with other staff members. Benchley and Dorothy Parker responded by marching throughout the building wearing billboards specifying exactly how much they made.

Dorothy Parker asked Benchley why he didn't leave the office at *Vanity Fair* and review plays himself, since he was so fond of drama. "No, I'll stay at the desk," Benchley said. "I do most of my work sitting down— that's where I shine."

Dorothy Parker and Benchley set up business together as free-lance writers after leaving *Vanity Fair*, renting a small office and marking the door "The Utica Drop Forge and Tool Company, Benchley and Parker, Presidents." Their cable address was "Parkbench." Benchley later described the tiny office: "One cubic foot less of space and it would have constituted adultery."

In the margin of one of Benchley's manuscripts *New Yorker* editor Harold Ross (who had a "profound ignorance," according to Dorothy Parker), wrote "Who he?" opposite Andromache (the wife of Hector in Greek mythology). Benchley wrote below: "You keep out of this."

During a session of charades at a friend's house Benchley was given the name of Hungarian playwright Ladislaus Busfekete to act out. Snorting he dropped to the floor, circled the room on all fours, crawled out the French doors and out the front door, got up, brushed himself off, and hailed a cab to take him home.

The first time he visited Venice, Benchley was on assignment for the *New Yorker*. "Streets full of water," he wired Harold Ross, "please advise."

Alexander Woollcott told the story of Benchley leaving a Manhattan eatery and asking a uniformed man in the doorway to hail him a taxi. "I'm not a doorman," came the indignant reply, "I'm a rear admiral in the United States Navy!" "In that case," Benchley countered, "get me a battleship."

During a stay in Paris a doorman gave Benchley, a generous tipper, very poor attention. But as the writer left on his last day the man fawned all over him, finally opening the door of Benchley's taxi, holding out his hand, and saying, "You're not going to forget me, sir?"
Benchley grabbed his hand and shook it heartily.
"No," he promised. "I'll write you every day."

The Broadway and Hollywood actor Charles Butterworth was a little man with a deadpan delivery. Once he, Benchley and friends were watching a tennis tournament at a woman's nudist camp in California. All eyes remained glued on the action, and not a word was said until Butterworth, breaking up even Benchley, turned and asked, "Who's winning?"

James Thurber told the story of the time the proud owner of an "indestructible" watch showed it to Benchley and Dorothy Parker. They banged it on the table, threw it on the floor and stomped on it. Finally, the owner picked it up and held it to his ear. "I can't believe it—it has stopped!" he said incredulously.
"Maybe you wound it too tight," Benchley and Parker said in unison.

Leaving a party on Riverside Drive early in the morning, Benchley wandered over to Grant's Tomb, not realizing that several friends were following him. After a while his friends saw him pick something up, write a few words on a slip of paper and then place the object back on the ground again. When he left, his friends came closer. There, outside the tomb, stood an empty milk bottle with a note in it reading: "One milk, no cream—U.S. Grant."

Benchley attended the premiere of *The Squall*, a turkey about gypsies who spoke in broken English. He bore the pain as long as he could, until a young gypsy girl came on stage and delivered the immortal lines, "Me Nubi. Nubi good girl. Nubi stay."
Benchley immediately rose.
"Me Bobby," he said. "Bobby bad boy. Bobby go." And he left the theater.

"Some laughter was heard in the back rows," he reported after attending the opening of a decidedly unfunny stage comedy. "Someone must have been telling jokes back there."

Usually a man of impeccable judgment, Benchley made a bad mistake as theater adviser to millionaire John Hay Whitney. "I could smell it when the postman came whistling down the lane," he told the millionaire about a play he had received that was based on several popular *New Yorker* magazine stories. "Don't put a dime in it." Luckily, Whitney decided to back *Life With Father* anyway, and it ran for seven and a half years.

"It took me fifteen years to discover I had no talent for writing," he remarked, "but I couldn't give it up because by that time I was famous."

Toward the end of a Hollywood party in the late 1930s, Benchley began backing away from playwright Robert Sherwood and suddenly cried, "Those eyes—I can't stand those eyes looking at me!" Everyone thought a joke was coming, but the humorist was dead serious. Pointing at Sherwood, he said, "He's looking at me and thinking of how he knew me when I was going to be a great writer...And he's thinking *now* look at what I am!"

Though he was bored by Hollywood, Benchley is the only author ever to win an Academy Award for a film he starred in. His *How to Sleep*, which he wrote and solely performed, won the 1936 Academy Award for the best live-action short subject.

At the end of his career, when he was no longer reviewing plays, Benchley went to a Broadway opening with a friend. He fell asleep during the first act, but when a telephone rang on stage he awoke with a start, shouting, "Will someone please answer that—I think it's for me!" The next day one review read, "Show terrible but Benchley superb in small part."

The first time Dorothy Parker attempted suicide, swallowing a bottle of barbiturates, Benchley visited her in the hospital to try and cheer her up. "Dottie," he said, looking at her sadly, "if you don't stop this sort of thing, you'll make yourself sick."

Benchley's columns sometimes reflected his darker side, as in this tragic 1930 bit: "I would like to protest the killing by a taxicab, on December 10th of Wesley Hill, the Angel Gabriel of *Green Pastures*...There was really no sense in that, Lord, and you know it as well as I do."

For his own mock epitaph he wrote:
   This is all over my head

"I can hear him laughing now," Benchley's wife said upon reaching the Nantucket graveyard where his ashes were to be buried—and then inspecting the open burial urn she was transporting. As a kind of cosmic farewell joke, the ashes in the urn had blown away en route and she had been driving for miles with an empty vessel.

∇ ∇ ∇

James Gordon Bennett (1795–1872)

Bennett and his sensational *New York Herald* had no friend in the young, immoderate editor of the *New York Aurora*. Walt Whitman wrote this short description in 1842: "A reptile marking his path with slime wherever he goes, and breathing mildew at everything fresh and fragrant; a midnight ghoul, preying on rottenness and repulsive filth; a creature, hated by his nearest intimates, and bearing the consciousness thereof upon his distorted features, and upon his despicable soul; one whom men avoid as a blot to his nature—whom all despise, and whom no one blesses—all this is James Gordon Bennett."

∇ ∇ ∇

James Gordon Bennett (1841–1918)

The son of the founder of the *New York Herald* was an eccentric who ran the paper well but had little or no regard for money. Once he gave the guard on a train a $14,000 tip. Another time he threw a batch of money into a roaring fireplace to watch it burn and was angry when a young man salvaged the notes, flinging them back into the flames. When he found someone seated at his favorite table in a Monte Carlo restaurant, he bought the place for $40,000, evicted the diners, sat down to eat—and when he left gave the restaurant back to its original owners as a tip.

An anonymous "Old Philadelphia Lady" living in Paris wrote Bennett one of the most famous letters in newspaper history:

> To the Editor of the *Herald*:
> I am anxious to find out the way to figure the temperature from centigrade to Fahrenheit and vice versa. In other words, I want to know, whenever I see the temperature designated on the centigrade thermometer, how to find out what it would be on Fahrenheit's thermometer.
>
> Old Philadelphia Lady
> Paris, December 24, 1899

The letter became famous after it was unintentionally reprinted the next day, a mishap that made the eccentric Bennett so mad that he published it every day until he died. Readers cancelled their subscriptions, even threatened to kill the old woman, but Bennett nevertheless ran her letter for the next 18 years and five months, for a total of 6,718 continuous days in all.

∇ ∇ ∇

Bernard Berenson (1865–1959)

The distinguished art historian, who often put on airs, had a long visit with American novelist Edith Wharton, who often put on airs herself. "I feel as if I had just been let out of school," said Berenson with a sigh of relief as he got into his car and was driven away. Meanwhile, back on the terrace, waving, Edith Wharton sighed, "Now I can take off my stays."

∇ ∇ ∇

Eddie Bernays (b. 1891)

It is said that this publicity writer, a nephew of Sigmund Freud, coined the term "public relations" in May 1920, as a respectable way to describe his profession—in the wedding announcements heralding his marriage. He had previously established the first firm doing such work.

∇ ∇ ∇

Theodore Bernstein (1904–1979)

In the Winners & Sinners bulletin he distributed to *The New York Times* staff, Bernstein criticized a *Times* headline that read, ELM BEETLE INFESTATION RAVISHING THOUSANDS OF TREES IN GREENWICH. "Keep your mind on your work, buster," the editor wrote. "The word you want is 'ravaging.'" He titled the piece "Insex."

∇ ∇ ∇

John Berryman   See ANNE BRADSTREET.

∇ ∇ ∇

Ambrose Bierce (1842–1914?)

Unsuccessful in selling his brilliant but grim collection of stories, *Tales of Soldiers and Civilians*, to a major American book publisher, "Bitter Bierce" finally self-published it under the imprint of a San Francisco merchant and friend of his. As a dedication he wrote: "Denied existence by the chief publishing houses of this country, this book owes itself to Mr. E.L.G. Steele, of this city…."

"Bierce," Jack London once remarked of him, "would bury his best friend with a sigh of relief, and express satisfaction that he was done with him."

Bierce's Union service in the Civil War was the most horrible experience in his life and he never forgot the futility of it. Some 38 years after the war, in September 1903, there was found in West Virginia the skeleton of a fellow soldier in rags. In a letter to a friend he wrote: "They found a Confederate soldier over there the other day, with his rifle alongside. I'm going over to beg his pardon."

It is said that after serving in the Union army as a volunteer, being twice severely wounded and brevetted a major for bravery, he went to San Francisco and decided his vocation in an odd way. He tossed a coin to determine whether he would become a prospector or a writer.

He suggested the following epitaph for newspaper editor Frank Pixley: *Here lies Frank Pixley, as usual.*

In early 1890 Kentucky's Governor-elect William Goebel was shot and killed as a result of feuding over the state election. Bierce wrote a quatrain about the shooting that appeared in William Randolph Hearst's *New York Journal* on February 4, 1900:

> The bullet that pierced Goebel's breast
> Can not be found in all the west;
> Good reason, it is speeding here
> To stretch McKinley on his bier.

The distasteful poem attracted little notice until seven months later when anarchist assassin Leon Czolgosz shot President McKinley, who died on September 14th. Some went so far as to blame Bierce's prophetic poem for inciting Czolgosz. But it developed that the assassin had never read the poem and wasn't carrying a copy of Hearst's inflammatory anti-McKinley *Journal* in his pocket when he shot the President. Instead, Czolgosz told reporters that a lecture given by anarchist leader Emma Goldman had inflamed him. For his part, Bierce rather lamely claimed that his quatrain had been written as a warning against the inadequate security measures taken to protect American presidents at the time.

▽ ▽ ▽

Nelly Bly (Elizabeth C. Seaman; 1867–1922)

Journalist Elizabeth Cochrane Seaman adopted the pen name "Nelly Bly" from a song by Stephen Foster. She is said to have taken it when an editor insisted that she use a pseudonym and an office boy happened to walk by whistling the tune. One of the first female reporters, Nelly Bly began her career when only 18. Her forte became exposés, such as her account in *Ten Days in a Madhouse* (1887) of the horrible conditions on New York's Blackwell's Island, where she was an inmate for 10 days after feigning insanity. In 1889 the *New York World* sponsored her famous trip around the globe, which she completed in the record time of 72 days, six hours and 11 minutes and which brought her international fame far exceeding that of any other woman of her day. Flowers, trains and racehorses were named for Nelly Bly and songs were written in her honor.

∇ ∇ ∇

Maxwell Bodenheim (1892–1954)

Some, perhaps most, of the world's greatest poems have been published without the poets receiving a farthing, cent or sou; and a great number weren't published at all, until years after the poets had died. Such has been the market for literature, always and everywhere. But what about famous poems that have been paid for with a pittance, quality not considered here? Vachel Lindsay's pamphlet "Rhymes to Be Traded for Bread," which he took on the road with him and did just that with, has to qualify, as does Julia Ward Howe's "The Battle Hymn of the Republic," for which the *Atlantic Monthly* paid $4.00. But perhaps Maxwell Bodenheim's "Strange Lady" sets some kind of a standard. The bohemian poet, addicted to alcohol, drugs and sex, not necessarily in that order, wrote just about anything before his life ended in a sordid murder. The novels *Replenishing Jessica* (1925) and *Naked on Roller Skates* (1931) were among his masterworks. His poem "Strange Lady" originally sold for 25 cents. This was paid in the late 1920s by a passerby in Greenwich Village who spotted the verse pinned to the public toilet door that served as Max's showcase for his wares when he was flat broke.

Bodenheim and Hecht held a literary debate in Chicago in 1917, the topic: "Resolved—That People Who Attend Literary Debates Are Imbeciles." Hecht, after studying the audience, quickly began and ended with, "The affirmative rests." Bodenheim, scrutinizing the crowd just as carefully, simply announced, "You win."

A notorious sponger, Bodenheim once stayed at poet William Carlos Williams' house in Paterson, New Jersey, for several months, faking a broken arm, cast and all. Finally, Williams, a doctor, lost his patience. He examined Bodenheim, found no break and kicked him out.

"Thank you for inviting me to dine at your house," Bodenheim wrote to a rich Chicago lady with literary pretensions who was in the habit of having a variety of writers and artists for dinner. "But I prefer to dine in the Greek restaurant at Wabash Avenue and 12th Street where I will be limited to finding dead flies in my soup."

The dissolute poet and his alcoholic mistress Ruth Fagin, a 29-year-old honors graduate of the University of Michigan, let a 25-year-old dishwasher named Harold, who had been in and out of asylums all his life, share their sordid five- dollar-a-week room on New York's Third Avenue. One night Bodenheim awoke to find the man trying to rape Ruth. When he interfered, Harold reached for a .22 rifle and fatally shot him. The psychotic dishwasher then stabbed Ruth to death with a kitchen knife, got drunk and turned himself in to police.

∇ ∇ ∇

John B. Bogart (1845–1921)
This crusty *New York Sun* city editor is said by some to have originated, in conversation, the old saw: "When a dog bites a man, that is not news, because it happens so often. But if a man bites a dog, that is news." However, the adage may be based on an old story.

∇ ∇ ∇

Nathaniel Bowditch (1773–1838)
The Salem, Massachusetts, navigator and mathematician found over 8,000 errors in *Moore's Practical Navigator*, the best English book on navigation, and substantially revised it, issuing it as the *New American Practical Navigator* (1802). *Bowditch's Navigator*, as it is generally known, is still in print. As Van Wyck Brooks has pointed out, it was a good answer to the common British taunt "Who reads an American book?" for it saved many British as well as American lives and all British seamen who wanted to keep up with Yankee skippers had to read it.

∇ ∇ ∇

Samuel Bowles (1826–1878)
A newspaper editor and author, Bowles devoted most of his life to the *Springfield Republican* in Massachusetts, making it a virtual school for the "new journalism" of the time. His advice to a young reporter became a maxim for conciseness, pungency and the importance of the lead in a newspaper story. "Put it all in the first paragraph," he told the young man.

∇ ∇ ∇

Ernest Boyd (1887–1946)
The Irish-born author became an important literary figure after immigrating to the United States in 1913. His essay "Aesthete: Model 1924," which appeared in the first issue of H.L. Mencken's *The American Mercury* that year, attacked the

young idealists of Greenwich Village and launched what was called the Battle of the Aesthetes. Before it was over a terrified Boyd suffered insulted aesthetes picketing his apartment house, throwing stink bombs through his window, jamming his doorbell with pins and making obscene phone calls to him in the early hours of the morning.

∇ ∇ ∇

Hal Boyle (1911–1974)
Boyle, as a columnist for the Associated Press, drove into Tunis soon after it fell to the Allies in World War II shouting: "Vote for Boyle, a son of the soil: Honest Hal, the Arab's Pal." Arabs picked up the former part of the phrase, without having any idea what it meant, and kept repeating it as a greeting to puzzled new troops from 1943 through 1944.

∇ ∇ ∇

Anne Bradstreet (1612?–1672)
According to one critic, "the beginnings of feminine influence in the United States" can be traced to Mrs. Bradstreet, whose father and husband were both governors of the Masschusetts Bay Colony. Despite the responsibilities of her eight children and high position, America's "first woman poet" wrote thousands of verses. John Berryman's remarkable ode "Homage to Mistress Bradstreet" (1956) is said to have been inspired by both Anne Bradstreet and author Eileen Simpson, Berryman's first wife. Recalled Simpson years after the poem was written: "Her life was so intertwined with ours it was sometimes difficult for him to distinguish between her and himself, between her and me."

∇ ∇ ∇

William Cowper Brann (1855–1898)
Brann's violent treatment of the moral and social problems of his day as editor of the *Iconoclast* in Waco, Texas, made him a notorious national figure. He finally became involved in a dispute with the local religious college and was killed in a pistol duel with one of its supporters.

∇ ∇ ∇

Jim Bridger (1804–1881)
The fabled American frontiersman is said to have been illiterate, but one story has him reading *Richard III* and suddenly throwing the play down in disgust, shouting, "I won't listen any more to the talk of a man who was mean enough to kill his mother."

Louis Bromfield (1896–1956)

In his *What Became of Anna Bolton*? (1945) the novelist based his eponymous character on society hostess Laura Corrigan, the wife of an American millionaire climbing the social ladder in London. Though a generous, warmhearted person, Mrs. Corrigan was well known for her vanity and social gaffes. On one occasion she was asked if she had seen the Dardanelles on her Mediterranean cruise. "No," she said, "but I did have a letter of introduction to them."

∇ ∇ ∇

Heywood Broun (1888–1939)

While serving in 1915 as drama critic for the *New York Tribune* Broun panned his share of plays, writing of *Just Outside the Door* that "wherever the long arm of coincidence intrudes, the author seizes it and shakes hands." But his most memorable review began with his description of a performance by actor Geoffrey Steyne as "the worst to be seen in the contemporary theatre." Steyne sued for damages to his professional reputation. While the suit was pending he chanced to appear in another play that Broun reviewed. Broun noted this time that "Mr. Steyne's performance was not up to his usual standard." (The suit was eventually dismissed.)

As a cub reporter for the *New York World* Broun was sent to interview Utah's Senator Smoot, but Smoot refused, telling him, "I'm sorry, I have nothing to say."

"I know," Broun replied, "now let's get down to the interview."

Broun was a sloppy dresser well known among his friends for the carelessness and disarray of his personal appearance. But he could alarm strangers. One time he and a number of war correspondents were presented to General Pershing. Eyeing him with some concern, the general inquired, "Have you fallen down, Mr. Broun?"

Caught in a downpour and soaked to the skin Broun ran into the Algonquin, where he ordered a glass of wine to warm himself. He tasted the wine, didn't like it, but quickly downed the liquid, quipping, "Oh, well, any port in a storm."

"Don't look now," he told Tallulah Bankhead on one of her opening nights, "but your show's slipping."

His bad jokes came to be expected by his friends. Here's a sample: "If a philosopher lectured on Descartes in a bordello what would I say?—I would say the philosopher was putting Descrates before de whores."

Morris Ernst, who knew Broun from when he was a boy, and was well aware of his hypochondria, once described his friend as "A one-man art show of cardiograms."

Before undergoing an operation for a hernia the confirmed hypochondriac wrote the following limerick while waiting in his hospital bed:

> There was a young man with a hernia
> Who said to his surgeon "Gol-dernya,
> When carving my middle
> Be sure you don't fiddle
> With matters that do not concernya."

∇ ∇ ∇

Charles Brockden Brown (1771–1810)

Brown has been called America's "first professional writer," as well as "the first American novelist," and his Gothic novels influenced Poe and Shelley, among other authors. Beginning his adult life as a lawyer in Philadelphia, he soon moved to New York, where he devoted himself exclusively to writing. He turned out five novels in about three years but couldn't make a go of it and had to take a job, although he continued writing and editing. His was the lot of most freelance writers, whose main job benefit is the right to starve in freedom, and he eventually died of consumption. The first novelist to address womens' rights and to introduce the Indian into fiction, Brown lived in "a dismal room in a dismal street," wearing a shabby great coat and "shoes run down at the heel," thus setting the style for American writers to come. He claimed he didn't need good clothes or a good view, however. All he needed was "Good pens, thick paper and ink well-diluted..."

∇ ∇ ∇

Solyman Brown (fl. ca. 1840)

This New York dentist published in 1840 a long ode on tooth diseases entitled *Dentologia: A Poem on the Diseases of the Teeth in Five Cantos.* One of the strangest of literary works, it gives after the poem a list of 300 American dentists of the time. No one knows if any of them paid for the "ad."

William Hill Brown (1765–1793)

William Hill Brown wrote the first American novel, *The Power of Sympathy* (1789), an epistolary romance that dealt with seduction and suicide in the family of Sarah W. Morton, his next-door neighbor. Because the story dealt with events in her life the novel was long attributed to Mrs. Morton, who in fact bought and burned as many copies of *The Power of Sympathy* as she could find.

∇ ∇ ∇

William Cullen Bryant (1794–1878)

America's precocious poet of nature read the entire New Testament in Greek two months after beginning his study of the language. In 1808 Bryant published his first work, *The Embargo, or Sketches of the Times; A Satire by a Youth of Thirteen*, indignant satires on Jefferson's administration. When only 17 he wrote his *Thanatopsis*, of which one critic says, "American poetry may be said to have commenced in 1817 [with the publication of] Bryant's *Thanatopsis*…" His literary career, however, lasted for nearly 70 years, until the year of his death, when he was still editor of the *New York Evening Post*.

His celebrated "Thanatopsis" would never have been published if the poet's father hadn't rescued it from the desk drawer to which William had relegated it—full six years after Bryant wrote the poem.

Bryant wrote lovingly, with his usual nobility and dignity, of the month of June in his poem of the same name. In the poem he concluded that he wanted to die in June of the year, and he did, 10 years later.

∇ ∇ ∇

Ned Buntline (Edward Zane Carroll Judson; 1823–1886)

A founder of the "patriotic" anti-Catholic Know-Nothing Party and coiner of its name, a leader of the bloody Astor Place riots in New York's theatrical district and an accused murderer, Judson was a fascinating if often contemptible character. He singlehandedly created the dime novel phenomenon when he met William F. Cody, dubbed him Buffalo Bill and made him the hero of his first adventure novels, which were based, however, on Judson's own experiences as a trapper and soldier in the Far West. "Buntline" even starred Buffalo Bill in his play, *The Scouts of the Plain* (1873). Judson wrote all of his more than 400 novels under the pseudonym Ned Buntline. He wrote one of them, 610 pages, in 62 straight hours, not even taking time off to eat or sleep. (See EDWIN FORREST.)

Luther Burbank (1849–1926)

The renowned horticulturist and garden writer was working in his experimental garden when approached by an obnoxious neighbor.

"Well, what on earth are you working on now?" the man asked.

"I'm trying to cross an eggplant and milkweed," Burbank said.

"What in heaven do you expect to get from that?" asked the neighbor.

"Custard pie," said Burbank calmly.

∇ ∇ ∇

Robert Jones Burdette (1844–1914)

This Iowa-born humorist wrote perhaps the least affected preface to a book in his *The Rise and Fall of the Moustache* (1877), on which subject he gave over 5,000 lectures:

> The appearance of a new book is an indication that another man has found a mission, has entered upon the performance of a hefty duty, activated by the noblest impulses that can spur the soul of man to action. It is the proudest boast of the profession of literature, that no man ever published a book for selfish purposes or with ignoble aim. Books have been published for the consolidation of the distressed; for the guidance of the wandering; for the relief of the destitute; for the hope of the penitent; for uplifting the burdened soul above its sorrows and fears; for the general amelioration of the condition of all mankind; for the right against wrong; for the good against bad; for the truth. This book is published for two dollars per volume.

∇ ∇ ∇

Gelett Burgess (1866–1951)

Burgess, author of the immortal "Purple Cow" verse, invented the expression *blurb* with the publication of his *Are You a Bromide?* in 1907. His publisher, B.W. Huebsch, told the story:

> It is the custom of [American] publishers to present copies of a conspicuous current book to booksellers attending the annual dinner of their trade association, and as this little book was in its heyday when the meeting took place I gave it to 500 guests. These copies were differentiated from the regular edition by the addition of a comic bookplate drawn by the author and by a special jacket which he devised. It was the common practice to print the picture of a damsel—languishing heroic, or coquettish…on the jacket of every novel, so Burgess lifted from a Lydia Pinkham or tooth-powder advertisement the portrait of a sickly sweet young woman, painted in some gleaming teeth, and otherwise enhanced her pulchritude, and placed her in the center of the jacket. His accompanying text was some nonsense about "Miss Belinda Blurb," and thus the term supplied a real need and became a fixture in our language.

Edward L. Burlingame (d. 1922)

The noted editor of *Scribner's Magazine* from 1887 to 1914, Burlingame rejected probably the most notorious rejected author in American literary history. In June 1881, Charles Guiteau stormed into the Scribner offices screaming that he would kill Burlingame for rejecting his manuscript. Staffers managed to eject Guiteau, who a month later assassinated President Garfield.

Burlingame once received a batch of poetry with the following note attached: "My husband has always been a successful blacksmith. Now he is old, and his mind is slowly weakening so he has taken to writing poems, several of which I enclose herein."

∇ ∇ ∇

Elihu Burritt (1810–1879)

Burritt, "the learned American blacksmith" who "forged metal and Greek verbs with equal ease," was a self-educated man who worked at the anvil all day and taught himself more than 40 languages at night, translating Longfellow's poems into Sanskrit. In addition to these labors, he also gave lectures frequently, often walking 100 miles to fill an engagement.

∇ ∇ ∇

Edgar Rice Burroughs (1875–1950)

Burroughs's novels about Tarzan, the son of a British aristocrat abandoned in the jungle as baby and raised by apes, began with *Tarzan of the Apes* (1914). It is said that the novelist's apeman may have been inspired by William Milden, earl of Streatham, who was shipwrecked off Africa in 1868 when barely 11 and supposedly lived with apes for 15 years before being found and returned home.

The old story that Burroughs's Tarzan books were banned because the Lord of the Apes was living in sin with Jane is true. In 1929 the Los Angeles County library system removed all Tarzan books from its shelves because Tarzan and Jane weren't married—although, in fact, they were wed, at the end of the first sequel, *The Return of Tarzan*.

Among the greatest of popular adventure writers, he saw himself this way: "I am sorry that I have not led a more exciting existence, so that I might offer a more interesting biographical sketch; but I am one of those fellows who has few adventures and always gets to the fire after it is out."

Nicholas Murray Butler (1862–1947)

The author and later president of Columbia Unviersity was discussing stories with author Brander Matthews. "In the case of the first man to use an anecdote there is originality," Matthews said; "in the case of the second there is plagiarism; with the third, it is the lack of originality; and with the fourth, it is drawing from a common stock…"

"Yes," Butler interrupted, "and in the case of the fifth, it is research."

▽ ▽ ▽

William Allen Butler (1825–1902)

This New York lawyer had no idea of what he had started when he wrote his satirical poem "Nothing to Wear" (1857), a satire of Flora M'Flimsy, a society lady who claimed she had nothing to wear to parties. Butler published his poem anonymously in *Harper's Weekly*, but in an era of social climbing it quickly caught the public's imagination and was published in book form without his permission. Several people claimed to have written it and the poem was widely reprinted, imitated and parodied in America and abroad. The "Nothing to Wear" craze inspired a good number of books, including the society satire *Nothing to Do* by Horatio Alger Jr., of all people, and even a satire by Mortimer Thompson entitled *Nothing to Say: A Slight Slap at Mobocratic Snobbery, Which Has "Nothing to Do" with "Nothing to Wear."* (See also HORACE GREELEY.)

▽ ▽ ▽

Mather Byles (1706–1788)

Byles flowered in a rather barren time patch for American poetry, but he is remembered today for his repartee rather than his poems. The ready wit, a granson of Increase Mather, was tried by his Congregational church in 1777 and sentenced to deportation for his Tory views. The sentence was reduced to imprisonment in his house, where a guard was stationed outside to enforce it. "Who is that outside your house?" asked a visitor, unaware of the trial and sentence. "Oh," Byles replied, "that is my observe-a-Tory."

▽ ▽ ▽

Harold Witter Bynner (1881–1968)

In their book *Spectra* (1916) the poet and his friend, poet A.D. Ficke, parodied the technique and diction of modern poetry. Writing under the pseudonyms "Emmanuel Morgan and Anne Knish," they represented their book as the founding of a new movement in American poetry. For a time their hoax was taken seriously by most critics (Bynner himself reviewed the book favorably for a prestigious magazine), and Spectric poems were all the rage with poetry editors everywhere, despite examples in *Spectra* like:

> A Madagascar crab once
> Lifted blue claws at me
> and rattled long black eyes
> That would have got me
> Had I not been gay.

∇ ∇ ∇

William Byrd (1674–1744)
Byrd's library of 4,000 books was the largest in America at the time. The Virginia tobacco planter, author and colonial official kept a secret diary in shorthand as an avocation, never intending for it to be published. In several entries he explores his sexual nature, condemning his lust for "another man's wife" and his attempt (successful) "to pick up a woman." He had no inhibitions about married love, judging by his entry for July 30, 1710: "In the afternoon my wife and I had a little quarrel which I reconciled with a flourish. Then she read a sermon in Dr. Tillitson to me. It is to be observed that the flourish was performed on the billiard table."

∇ ∇ ∇ ∇ ∇ ∇ ∇ ∇

James Branch Cabell (1879–1958)
The Southern novelist was very reticent about his personal life, perhaps in part due to the notoriety his novel *Jurgen* (1918) received when Comstocks tried to suppress it because of its transparent sexual imagery. But Cabell did like to tell the story of a letter he received from a would-be fan, apparently a young student with a paper to write. "Dear Mr. Cabell," it read, "I have chosen you as my favorite author. Please write to me immediately and tell me why."

The author of scores of novels and collections of short stories, which kept him busy all the time, Cabell was fond of saying even in his old age that he was in the midst of writing a book and that "an author won't die in the middle of a book."

James M. Cain (1892–1977)

When an interviewer from a literary magazine commiserated with the novelist, noting that Hollywood had ruined *Double Indemnity, The Postman Always Rings Twice* and all his other books, Cain sat up and studied a shelf in his library. "No, they are all still right there," he said.

∇ ∇ ∇

Erskine Caldwell (1903–1988)

Maxwell Perkins wanted to buy two of the struggling young writer's stories for *Scribner's Magazine*. "Would two-fifty be all right? For both of them?" he asked. "Two-fifty?" Caldwell said. "I don't know. I thought maybe a little more than that." "You did?" Perkins replied. "Well what would you say to three-fifty then? That's about as much as we can pay, for both of them. In these times magazine circulation is not climbing the way it was, and we have to watch our costs. I don't think times will get any better soon, and maybe worse yet. Economic life isn't very healthy now. That's why we have to figure our costs so closely at a time like this." Caldwell sighed resignedly. "I guess that'll be all right," he said. "I'd thought I'd get a little more than three dollars and a half, though, for both of them."

∇ ∇ ∇

John C. Calhoun (1782–1850)

This great Southern statesman and author had handwriting so bad that a correspondent once sent back one of his letters because he couldn't read it. And Calhoun agreed with the man. "I know what I think on this subject," he told him, "but cannot deciper what I wrote."

∇ ∇ ∇

Truman Capote (1924–1984)

Capote was told that novelist Jack Kerouac had boasted that he never rewrote a manuscript after putting the words on paper. "That's not writing," he remarked, "that's typing."

One of Capote's earliest sexual encounters occurred when he was only six and a half and involved a family of passing gypsies. After giving a gypsy woman a bucketful of water, Truman was asked if he wanted to see the gold at the end of the rainbow. He skeptically handed over a few coins to pay for this miraculous exhibition. The woman promptly pulled up her skirts beyond her waist. She was stark naked and her pubic hair had been dyed a stunning gold. After displaying herself for several moments, she finally instructed him that he should not complain because he had truly seen the real thing.

"Of course no writers ever forget their first acceptance," the author told an inteviewer. "One fine day when I was seventeen I had my first, second and third, all in the same morning's mail. Oh, I'm here to tell you, dizzy with excitement is no mere phrase!"

In *Here at the New Yorker* Brendan Gill tells the story of Capote working as "a sort of self-appointed art editor" when he was a young assistant at the magazine. According to the possibly apocryphal tale, Gill says, when Capote opened the mail, if he "didn't like a drawing, he dropped it over the far edge of the big table at which he worked." Years later the table was moved and "behind it were found hundreds of drawings that Capote had peremptorily rejected…"

∇ ∇ ∇

Henry Guy Carlton (1856–1910)

This popular playwright and humorist was a stutterer who liked to joke about his affliction. Meeting a friend one day, he asked, "N-N-Nat, c-c-an you g-g-give m-m-me f-f-fifteen m-m-minutes?"

"Why certainly," his friend said. "What is it?"

"I w-w-want to have a f-f-five-minute c-c- conversation with you," Carlton advised.

∇ ∇ ∇

Hoagy Carmichael (1899–1981)

The author-composer of "Stardust" and other great favorites, also wrote possibly the world's longest song title: "I'm A Cranky Old Yank In A Clanky Old Tank On The Streets Of Yokahama With My Honolulu Mama Doin' Those Beat-O, Flat-On-My-Seat-O, Hirohito Blues."

∇ ∇ ∇

Rachel Carson (1907–1964)

After watching a fall migration of monarch butterflies the naturalist author wrote in her diary:

It occurred to me this aftenoon, remembering, that it had been a happy spectacle, that we had felt no sadness when we spoke of the fact that there would be no return. And rightly—for when any living thing has come to the end of its cycle we accept that end as natural. For the monarch butterfly, that cycle is measured in a known span of months. For ourselves, the measure is something else, the span of which we cannot know. But the thought is the same: When that intangible cycle has run its course, it is a natural and not unhappy thing that a life comes to its end.

Raymond Carver (1938–1988)
Raymond Carver had already written many excellent short stories before his untimely death at the age of 50. The American poet and short story writer generally wrote stories that imitated or were largely based upon his life, but the last story he wrote reversed this process. The author felt "in the pink of health" when in 1987 he wrote "Errand," a short story about Russian author Anton Chekhov's death from tuberculosis. A few months later, Carver, like Chekhov in his story, began spitting up blood and learned that he had lung cancer.

∇ ∇ ∇

Alice Cary (1820–1871) and Phoebe Cary (1824–1871)
The American "poet sisters" often collaborated, when they weren't presiding over their popular Sunday-evening literary salon in Manhattan's Gramercy Park neighborhood during the 1860s. The sisters entertained American authors and visiting celebrities, including William Makepeace Thackeray. Brought to New York from Ohio by Greeley, they were very close all their lives and even died in the same year.

∇ ∇ ∇

Frank Case (1870–1946)
Even Frank Case, the manager and eventually the owner of the Algonquin Hotel where the Round Table wits held forth in the twenties, managed a quip that compares well with almost anything uttered by Parker, Benchley, Connelly et al. "Time wounds all heels," he once observed.

∇ ∇ ∇

Willa Cather (1873–1947)
The Nebraska-reared author based her short story "The Birthmark" on a close friend's disfigurement. When editors of the magazine that had agreed to publish the story learned that its main character was very similar to a living person and that that person might be hurt by the story, possibly enough so to commit suicide (as the character in the story did), they asked the author to free them from their commitment to publish the tale. Miss Cather refused. "My art," she said, "is more important than my friend." (Fortunately her friend never read the story.)

So incensed was Cather about the Hollywood film made from her novel *A Lost Lady* (1923) that she stipulated in her will that her work could never again be adapted for the screen, stage, radio, television or any new medium "which hereafter may be discovered or perfected."

Bennett Cerf (1898–1971)

The publisher and anthologist told the story of a book called *The Ten Command-ments* that was to be published for the armed services during World War II but was too long. "How about using only five of them," quipped one of his editors, "and calling it *A Treasury of the World's Best Commandments*?" (See also GERTRUDE STEIN.)

∇ ∇ ∇

Raymond Chandler (1888–1959)

The Chicago-born mystery novelist, raised from the age of seven in England, refused to finish the screenplay of his *The Blue Dahlia* unless he were allowed to write the entire treatment while drunk; he explained that this was the only way he could calm his nerves and cope with Hollywood interference and insults. Producer John Houseman reluctantly agreed, providing several safeguards to protect Chandler's health and safety, and within a week or so the script was completed.

Complaining to his publisher about the editing of one of his books, he wrote: "When I split an infinitive, God damn it, I split it so that it will stay split, and when I interrupt the velvety smoothness of my more or less literate syntax with a few sudden words of bar-room vernacular that is done with the eyes wide open and the mind relaxed."

He had a sure-fire method for speeding up a story. "When the plot flags," he advised an interviewer, "bring in a man with a gun."

According to S.J. Perelman, Chandler "had the most bitter reluctance to commit anything to paper." When stuck he would dictate the "utmost nonsense" into a tape recorder, using the transcript as his basis for a first draft.

∇ ∇ ∇

William Ellery Channing (1780–1842)

Channing ruined his health as a young man by his "stoic desire for self-improve-ment," which included sleeping on a bare floor, rising early, subjecting himself to a rigid diet and studying until three o'clock in the morning. The preacher and author is said to have really made his break with Calvinism and its view of an essentially depraved humanity when as a boy he had heard his father preach a fire and brimstone sermon on infant damnation and then begin to whistle as he left the church.

John Jay Chapman (1862–1933)

This American literary critic and essayist, a close friend of William James, was a fiery man given to impulsive acts that at least once bordered on insanity. While a student at Harvard a drunken Chapman savagely horsewhipped a student who he believed had insulted his fiancée. So ashamed was Chapman of his behavior the next day that he punished himself by holding his left hand in the flames of an open fireplace, burning it so severely that it had to be amputated.

∇ ∇ ∇

John Cheever (1912–1982)

American novelist and short story master John Cheever could afford only one suit in his early years as a writer. Cheever liked to work away from home and left the family apartment every morning, even though his office was in the same building. "In the morning," he once told an interviewer, "I dressed in my one suit and took the elevator to a windowless room in the basement where I worked. I hung my suit on a hanger, wrote until nightfall, when I dressed and returned to our apartment. I wrote many of my stories in boxer shorts."

"My definition of a good editor," he said, "is a man who I think charming, who sends me large checks, praises my work, my physical beauty, and my sexual prowess, and who has a stranglehold on the publisher and the bank."

∇ ∇ ∇

Henry Clapp (1814–1875)

The New England-born Clapp traveled to Paris and came back, it has been said, hating respectability as much as he had hated sin. Settling in New York, he became a journalist, writing under the pen name Figaro, and reigned as "the king of Bohemia" at Pfaff's Cellar near Bleeker Street, the intellectual water hole of the 1850s, where Whitman, Fitz-James O'Brien, Ada Clare (Clapp's mistress) and many others could be seen. One time a group of artists was discussing Horace Greeley when Clapp interrupted. "Greeley," he said, "was a self-made man who worshipped his creator."

∇ ∇ ∇

MacDonald Clarke (1798–1842)

As evidenced by his book of verse, *Elixir of Moonshine by the Mad Poet* (1822), Clarke was known as "the Mad Poet of Broadway." The New York poet, perhaps the first of American bohemians, drowned in the East River, possibly a suicide. Author of "The Rum Hole" (1835), in which a groghouse is "the horrible Light-House of Hell...built on a ledge of human bones, whose cement is of human blood," he was eulogized by Walt Whitman.

The Mad Poet of Broadway had no illusions about achieving fame while he lived, as this epigram of his shows:

'Tis vain for present fame to wish.
Our persons first must be forgotten;
For poets are like stinking fish,
They never shine until they're rotten.

∇ ∇ ∇

Grover Cleveland (1837–1908)

The 22nd and 24th U.S. president's *Presidential Problems* (1904) was a defense of his policies while in office. Whatever their success, he was an honest man who offended the spoilsmen. Cleveland told the story of Timothy J. Campbell, a New York Tammany Hall politician who asked him to support a certain bill. I can't, Cleveland said, the bill is clearly unconstitutional. "What's the Constitution between friends?" Campbell replied.

∇ ∇ ∇

Irvin S. Cobb (1876–1944)

Though Cobb made frequent reference to his ample girth, the American humorist was totally unprepared for the lady who approached him at a party and asked, "Are you Irvin Cobb, the outstanding writer?"

When told that his editor on the *New York World* was ill, Cobb remarked, "I hope it's nothing trivial."

Toward the end of his career he confessed: "I couldn't write the things they publish now, with no beginning and no end, and a little incest in the middle."

Another time Cobb quipped, "If writers were good businessmen, they'd have too much sense to be writers."

He quietly walked down Fifth Avenue for six blocks directly behind Fannie Hurst, whom he hadn't seen for some time. The novelist, who had put on a lot of weight, finally turned to him and asked, "Well, are you going to say hello to me or not?" "Don't tell me you're Fannie Hurst," said Cobb. "The same Fannie Hurst," she replied. "No, no," Cobb said. "The same Hurst I will concede—but definitely *not* the same fanny."

He left a Letter of Instructions to be opened after his death:

I charge my family…that they shall put on none of the bogus habiliments of so-called mourning. Folds of black crepe never ministered to the memory of the departed...Lay my ashes at the roots of a dogwood tree in Paducah at the proper planting season. Should the tree live, that will be monument enough for me.

∇ ∇ ∇

George M. Cohan (1878–1942)
The actor, songwriter and playwright had perhaps the most expensive work habits of any author past or present. Cohan often rented an entire Pullman car drawing room and kept traveling until he finished whatever he was working on. He could turn out 140 pages a night this way.

The original title of his "You're a Grand Old Flag" (1906) was "You're a Grand Old Rag." Cohan (who pronounced his name Cohen) changed the title when critics protested that he was profaning the Stars and Stripes.

∇ ∇ ∇

Harry Cohn (1891–1958)
The head of Columbia Pictures in its heyday, Cohn's reputation ranged somewhere between skunk and rat. But directors, actors and writers turned out in force for his funeral. Noting the unusually large attendance, comedian Red Skelton remarked, "Well, it only proves what they always say—give the public something they want to see, and they'll come out for it."

∇ ∇ ∇

Mary Colum   See ERNEST HEMINGWAY.

∇ ∇ ∇

Anthony Comstock (1844–1915)
About 160 tons of books, stereotyped plates, magazines and pictures were destroyed by Anthony Comstock, founder of the New York Society for the Suppression of Vice, in his long career as a self-appointed crusader against immorality in literature. As chief special agent for the society, he is said to have arrested 3,000 persons over a forty-odd-year career, destroying some 50 tons of books alone that he deemed obscene. The Comstock Postal Act, in Mencken's words, "greatly stimulated the search for euphemisms," pregnant being translated as "enceinte," syphilis and gonorrhea as "social diseases," and so on. Comstock had the power of an inquisitor, "comstockery" becoming a synonym for narrow-minded, bigoted and self-righteous moral censorship. The crusader particularly objected to Shaw's play *Mrs. Warren's Profession*, and Shaw coined "comstockery," making good clean fun of his name.

Stuck with millions of lithographs of a painting of a nude woman bathing, a Manhattan art dealer hired press agent Harry Reichenbach to help him sell them. Reichenbach boldly displayed the prints in the gallery window and hired a group of children to stand and stare at them. Then he called Comstock and hysterically demanded that he investigate this sordid exhibition. Comstock campaigned against the store, the story made the front pages, and seven million lithographs were sold.

One story had the rotund Comstock hauling a woman before a judge and crying, "Your Honor, this woman gave birth to a naked child!" But this was the caption of a 1915 cartoon in *The Masses*.

∇ ∇ ∇

Marc Connelly (1890–1980)
A friend came up in back of Connelly while he was lunching at the famed Algonquin Round Table and playfully rubbed the author's bald head. "Ah, that feels as smooth and soft as my wife's ass," he said. Connelly quickly ran his own hand over the same area. "So it does," he said, "so it does."

It was for a *Vanity Fair* series called "Artists Write Their Own Epitaphs" that the Algonquin wits fashioned the famous mock epitaphs on themselves that include Dorothy Parker's "PARDON MY DUST."
Connelly's contribution read:

HERE LIES MARC CONNELLY
    WHO?

∇ ∇ ∇

Robert Bernard Considine (1906–1975)
Among the most prolific of reporters over his distinguished 45-year career, Bob Considine could write anywhere—he typed at least one story in a descending elevator—and almost always accurately. However, covering the dying Pope Pius XII in Rome he filed a story based on wrong information in which, he later recalled, "I ended Pius's noble life 48 hours earlier than God chose, which may have seemed presumptious to both." He was immeasurably relieved when the story was killed before being printed. "I did not go directly to the bar on the floor below," he remembered. "I paused on a marble step at the head of the staircase, knelt down and breathed a Hail Mary. *Then* I went to the bar."

"Be kind to copy boys," was his rule, "for you'll meet them on the way down, when they are editors."

Calvin Coolidge (1872–1933)

Coolidge, who retired from the presidency to write his autobiography and newspaper and magazine articles, was the least animated of presidents and authors. "How did they know?" Dorothy Parker quipped when informed of Calvin Coolidge's death, and Alice Roosevelt Longworth observed that the President "looks like he had been weaned on a pickle." Aside from these bon mots and his succinct "I do not choose to run [for a second term]" Coolidge is primarily remembered for sleeping a full 10 hours a night and saying nothing while he was awake. Generally, his idea of humor was to hide in the bushes by the White House and suddenly leap out, scaring the hell out of unsuspecting Secret Service agents, but in an attempt to change his image I tried to find some genuine Coolidge ripostes. At last I came up with one. It seems that the President was told that headstrong Senator Borah went horseback riding every day. "It's hard to image Borah going in the same direction as his horse," Coolidge quipped. The world awaits more Coolidge witticisms.

According to a probably apocryphal story, after he left office the notoriously tight-fisted Coolidge began negotiations to write a two-part series on his White House years for $25,000. Meeting an editor from Colliers in his hotel room to clinch the deal on a bitterly cold night, he gave the man a shot of whiskey. Soon after, another editor arrived frozen to the bone and the former president offered him a drink. As Coolidge poured, the first editor pushed his glass forward to be refilled. "You've had yours!" snapped Coolidge and he recapped the bottle without another word.

∇ ∇ ∇

James Fenimore Cooper (1789–1851)

Cooper was nothing if not a pugnaciously determined man. He wrote his first novel in 1819, when he was 30 years old, and he hated writing—even letters. Cooper had been reading aloud to his wife a novel of English society when he threw the book down and declared, "I could write you a better book than that myself!" His wife dared him to try and the result was *Precaution* (1820), a conventional tale of genteel English society. No matter that it was, according to William Lyon Phelps, "one of the worst novels in history, hopelessly bad in style, structure and characters, and disfigured by typographical errors." As Phelps observed, Cooper was "inspired by failure" and, in Browning's words, "made the stumbling block a stepping stone" and went on to write his acclaimed novels.

He may have written "more than thirty novels and tons of polemics," but his was not the philosophy of a hack writer. His ideals never wavered. Once Cooper wrote to the editor of a new magazine who had boasted about the size of his periodical and the large sums he paid contributors. "I never asked or took a dollar in my life, for any personal service, except as an officer in the navy, and for full-grown books," he advised. "Do you think size as important in a journal as quality? We have so much mediocrity in this country, that excuse me for saying it, I think distinction might better now be sought in excellence."

John Jay had told Cooper the plot of his second novel, *The Spy* (1821). After Cooper began writing it, his publisher expressed concern about the growing size of the manuscript. So Cooper sat down and wrote the last chapter, telling the publisher "to have the book set up, printed and the pages numbered, so that he, Cooper, might know the extreme limit of the book." He then sat down and filled in the intervening space that had been allotted him.

Though even Cooper's kindest critic admits that "he came to the gates of immortality with a vast amount of excess baggage," he was a pathmaker who founded two great American schools of fiction: the frontier story and the sea story. Of *The Pilot* (1823), his first sea story, he once remarked: "Not a single individual among all those who discussed the project, within the range of the author's knowledge, either spoke or looked encouragingly. It is probable that all these persons anticipated a signal failure."

Mark Twain hated the work of Cooper second only to that of Sir Walter Scott, but then he charged that Scott's work was a cause of the Civil War! Twain reviewed "two-thirds of a page" of Cooper and said he had "scored 114 offenses against literary art out of a possible 115. It breaks the record."

∇ ∇ ∇

Charles Townsend Copeland (1860–1952)
The waspish Professor Copeland taught English at Harvard for many years beginning in 1893, influencing numerous authors (including John Reed and John Dos Passos). Copeland was noted for his beautiful reading voice and brilliant wit. On the subject of a career in journalism for a writer he commented: "Get in, get wise, get out." Observed lean little "Copey" of copulation: "The sensation is momentary and the position ridiculous."

∇ ∇ ∇

James Corbett (1866–1933)
The world heavyweight boxing champion was a witty man who wrote several books after retiring from the ring. Wit apparently ran in the family. It's said that Steve Brodie once angered Corbett's father by predicting that John L. Sullivan would knock his son out. "So you're the fellow who jumped over the Brooklyn Bridge," the elder Corbett said when the two met for the first time. "No, I jumped

off of it," Brodie corrected him. "Oh," replied Corbett, "I thought you jumped *over* it. Any damn fool can jump off it."

▽ ▽ ▽

Malcolm Cowley (1898–1989)

"Authors are sometimes like tomcats," the literary critic told an interviewer, recalling his many friendships with writers over his long career. "They distrust all the other toms but they are kind to kittens."

In his delightful *And I Worked at the Writer's Trade* (1988) Malcolm Cowley tells the story of the now defunct Macaulay Publishing Company, headed by Lee Furman, who "believed in the magic of titles." At one editorial meeting in 1933, Furman urged his staff, "Let's have a big novel written to order and let's give it a tremendous title—you know, something that will make people think of *The Good Earth* or *All Quiet on the Western Front*. Any bright ideas?" Replied poet Isidor Schneider, serving as the company's advertising manager: "What about *All Noisy on the Eastern Behind*?"

▽ ▽ ▽

Jacob Sechler Coxey (1854–1951)

Over his long life—he died when 97—activist author Jacob Sechler Coxey lived through everything from the Civil War to the atomic bomb. His Coxey's Army was one of the first and best remembered groups to march on Washington, D.C., to demand change of some kind, following the panic of 1893. It was their leader's plan to have Congress authorize money for public construction, which would provide widespread employment, an idea to be implemented during the great depression in the 1930s. But his highly publicized march from Massillon, Ohio, on Easter Sunday failed to accomplish its purpose. This quixotic character was a perennial candidate for public office, and was elected mayor of Massillon, 1931–33. He wrote three books on monetary problems, which so fascinated him that he named one of his sons Legal Tender.

▽ ▽ ▽

Hart Crane (1899–1932)

It was the Ohio-born poet's habit to prowl the waterfront at night and pick up sailors or, failing that, any man available. While staying with Harry and Caresse Crosby in Paris he outdid himself. One morning, after he and his lover had left, Mrs. Crosby found "On the wallpaper and across the pale pink spread, up and down the curtains and over the white chenille rug...the blackest footprints and handprints I have ever seen, hundreds of them." He had picked up a chimney-sweep.

Recognized as an outstanding poet of his day despite having published only two slim books in his lifetime, Crane was an alcoholic who often threatened to kill himself and finally threw himself from a ship returning from Mexico to the United States. It is possible that he was brooding over a beating he had taken after trying to pick up a man in the sailor's quarters the previous evening. In any case, early that morning he took off his coat, walked to the railing, vaulted it and jumped into the sea as stunned passengers watched. He was seen swimming strongly away from the ship before he went under.

Amateur psychoanalysts have made much of the fact that the father of this poet who drowned himself was the inventor and manufacturer of Life Savers candy. Hart Crane never did benefit from the family fortune. He died in debt, owing his publisher $210.

"Someone told me," John Dos Passos confided, "that when Hart finally met his end by jumping overboard from the Havana boat the last his friends on deck saw of him was a cheerful wave of the hand before he sank and drowned. That last friendly wave was very like Hart Crane."

∇ ∇ ∇

Stephen Crane (1871–1900)

Crane always thought that the world treated ministers' sons unfairly. "Have you ever observed how the envious laity exult when we are overtaken by misfortune?" he asked an interviewer who had confided that he, too, was the son of a minister. "This is the point of view: The bartender's boy falls from the Waldorf roof. The minister's son falls from a park bench. They both hit the earth with the same velocity, mutilated beyond recognition."

Crane's objections to hazing when he joined Delta Upsilon at Lafayette College in 1890 were the most extreme in the history of the fraternity. When frat members broke into his room one night to haze him, they turned tail and fled on finding him waiting in a corner with a revolver in his hand.

He published at his own expense his first novel, *Maggie: A Girl of the Streets* (1893), borrowing the money from his brother and issuing it under the pseudonym Johnston Smith (the two most frequently listed names in the New York telephone book). The grim paperbound novel, set in a New York neighborhood called Rum Alley, sold just two copies. However, Crane, who shared a small rundown studio apartment with three young artists, was practical enough to put the unsold copies to some use. One cold winter's night he used a pile of them to start a fire in his room.

In his first few years as a writer Crane often turned up at novelist Hamlin Garland's house for a meal, with a rolled manuscript crammed in the pockets of his shabby clothes. Once the manuscript proved to be a batch of excellent poems, and Garland asked him if he had any more. "I have four or five," said Crane, trapping his temple, "up here, all in a little row." And to prove it, he sat down and wrote one off in finished form.

Another dinnertime Garland found half the manuscript of a Civil War novel rolled in Crane's pocket. "Where's the rest of it?" he asked, convinced that he was reading a masterpiece. "In hock to the typist," Crane said, and Garland gave him $15 to redeem the rest of *The Red Badge of Courage.*

Cora Stewart, Crane's common-law wife, was the madam of a combination bordello and nightclub in Jacksonville, Florida, when he met her. Crane was enchanted by the name of her establishment: the Hotel de Dream.

Crane covered the Spanish-American War for Joseph Pulitzer's *World*. He was fearless and seemed, in the words of one biographer, to be "a man who courted death in order not to be a victim of life." Early one morning he strolled beyond the American lines and into the little town of Juana Diaz in Puerto Rico, and the mayor surrenderd the town to him. Wherever he went he tempted the rifles of the enemy, but never out of bravado. Once he strode along the battle lines, snipers targeting in on the strange figure in a white raincoat. Get down, the others kept shouting, but he ignored them. Correspondent Richard Harding Davis finally figured out how to save his life. "You're not impressing anyone by doing that, Crane!" he shouted, and Crane immediately took cover, not wanting to be taken for a show-off.

American author Willa Cather believed that all of Crane's short life was "a preparation for sudden departure." She remembered Crane writing a letter one time and suddenly stopping. "[He] asked me about the spelling of a word," she recalled, "saying carelessly, 'I haven't time to learn to spell.' Then, glancing down at his attire, he added with an absent-minded smile, 'I haven't time to dress either; it takes an awful slice out of a fellow's life.'" (He died not long after of tuberculosis in Germany, where he had gone to seek a cure.)

"Robert," he said to a friend as his last words, "when you come to the hedge that we must all go over, it isn't so bad. You feel sleepy and you don't care. Just a little drowsy anxiety, which world you're really in, that's all."

Davy Crockett (1786–1836)

Davy Crockett was a real person, but whether he was a writer or not is disputable. David Crockett, as the song goes, was "a son of the wild frontier" from his earliest years. Born in 1786 in Limestone, Tennessee, Davy was hired out to a passing cattle driver by his Irish immigrant father when ony 12; he wandered the frontier until he turned 15, before finally returning home. He became a colonel in the Tennessee militia, fought under Andrew Jackson during the Creek War and, after serving as a justice of the peace and state legislator, acted on a humorous suggestion that he run for Congress in 1827. Much to his surprise, he won the election. Crockett served two terms in Congress, and was noted in Washington for his backwoods dress and shrewd native humor, though many of the commens often attributed to him are largely apocryphal. His motto was "Be sure you are right, then go ahead." When defeated for relection in 1835—mainly because he opposed Jacksonian banking and Indian policies—he moved to Texas, where he joined the Texas war for independence from Mexico. On March 6, 1836, Colonel Crockett was killed along with the other defenders of the Alamo. The folk hero's famous autobiography, *A Narrative of the Life of David Crockett of the State of Tennessee* (1834), was probably dictated, but is written in his robust style, complete with many examples of the tall tale. A score of books appeared under his name during his lifetime—and he may have had a hand in some of them—but for the most part they were by journalists taking advantage of his popularity in contemporary folklore, as did the 50 or so almanacs published in his name.

∇ ∇ ∇

Harry Crosby (1898–1929)

The wealthy expatriate American poet and publisher, a friend of Hemingway and other writers, shot himself to death in Paris toward the end of the Lost Generation era. Crosby lived life to the fullest no matter what it cost. Even his practical jokes were expensive. One time he surreptitiously stocked bookstalls along the Seine with rare first editions, priced ridiculously low, just to witness the chaos he created when patrons tried to buy the rare volumes from the booksellers.

∇ ∇ ∇

e.e. (Edward Estlin) cummings (1884–1962)

When E(dward E(stlin) Cummings wrote his name, he wrote it e.e. cummings, refusing to capitalize it, as if to divorce himself from vanity and selfhood. He felt the same about the word *I*, never using the first person perpendicular, always writing it as *i*, even in the title of his book of poems *i* (1953). Cummings's poetry actually depended to a great degree on typographical distortion—unconventional punctuation, spacing, run-on words. While he was serving in France with an American ambulance corps during the First World War, one of his letters written in this special style aroused the suspicion of a censor, and he was thrown into a French concentration camp for three months on an unfounded charge of treasonable correspondence, an experience that resulted in his book *The Enormous Room*. But Cummings's use of *i* for *I* wasn't original. Modest English author Benjamin Stillingfleet (1702–71) did the same thing long before Cummings. In fact, before the introduction of printing the nominative for the person speaking could be written as either a lowercase letter or as a capital. Printers standardized the capitalized form because a little *i* was easily dropped from lines in typesetting. That this was probably a matter of convenience, not egotism, can also be seen by the fact that *me* and *my* weren't capitalized.

Borrowing money from his mother, Cummings self-published a much-rejected book of poetry in 1935. Its dedication went: "No Thanks to: Farrar & Rinehart, Simon & Schuster, Coward-McCann, Limited Editions, Harcourt, Brace, Random House, Equinox Press, Smith & Haas, Viking Press, Knopf, Dutton, Harper's, Scribner's, Covici, Friede."—all publishers who had rejected his manuscript.

A publisher's note to the Modern Library edition of *The Enormous Room* described him as "the terror of typesetters, an enigma to book reviewers, and the special target of all the world's literary philistines."

The poet believed in flying saucers. After he gave a friend the opportunity to view a strange distant light through the telescope in his New Hampshire farmhouse and the friend opined that it seemed to be a meteorological balloon, Cummings treated him with some disdain. Aggravated, his friend demanded, "What do *you* think it was if not meteorological instruments?" Replied the poet, matter of factly: "Little men from another planet."

∇ ∇ ∇

Will Cuppy (fl. 1920s)

The eccentric author, born in Chicago, lived for a time like a hermit on what is now Jones Beach on New York's Long Island, a place then accessible only by boat. Cuppy's shack housed a large library of works on psychology and psychoanalysis and he would brag to his infrequent visitors. "I have every symptom mentioned in those books."

H.D. (Hilda Doolittle; 1886–1961)

H.D., as the poet signed her work, was Ezra Pound's first love; the two were childhood sweethearts when he was 16 and she 15, until her father put an end to their affair. Like Pound, she immigrated to Europe, also becoming a member of the Imagist movement. When H.D. first began writing her poems she fought a repression that she felt prevented her from doing her best work. One of her strategies, according to a lifelong friend, poet William Carlos Williams, was to symbolically deny her repression and feel free when she sat down to write, by splashing ink all over her clothes.

∇ ∇ ∇

Richard Henry Dana (1815–1882)

Early New England schools were often Gehennas of discipline in which flogging and pulling pupils by the ears was the rule rather than the exception. It is said that Dana, who attended such a school, "had his mind made up in regard to floggers" long before he went to sea and saw the cruel floggings of sailors that he recorded in *Two Years Before the Mast* (1840).

∇ ∇ ∇

Clarence Darrow (1857–1938)

The legendary lawyer and author was approached by a reporter who asked him for a prepared copy of a speech Darrow was scheduled to make that night. Darrow, annoyed by the young man, handed him a blank piece of paper and turned to go. "But Mr. Darrow," the reporter said quickly, "this is the same speech you gave last week."

Another reporter asked Darrow if murderers were limited to certain types of people. "Everybody is a potential murderer," Darrow replied. "I've never killed anyone, but I frequently get satisfaction reading the obituary notices."

Darrow ran into an old friend who had become a doctor.

"If you'd listened to me, you'd be a doctor now, too," the man told him.

"What's wrong with being a lawyer?" Darrow asked.

"Well, I don't say lawyers are all crooks," the doctor said, "but you've got to admit your profession doesn't exactly make angels of men."

"No," Darrow replied, "you doctors have us beat there."

"Lord" Timothy Dexter (Timothy Dwight; 1747–1806)

The English are most famous for eccentric writers, but American author Timothy Dwight of Newburyport, Massachusetts, can hold his own with the most outré of them. "Lord" Dexter, as he called himself, spent his considerable fortune—which he made by odd but shrewd business transactions such as trading woolen mittens and warming pans in the West Indies—on a curious Georgian mansion in Newburyport complete with his own royal court consisting of a fishmonger poet laureate, a huge witless jester, and an African princess housekeeper, among others. Dexter's autobiography, *A Pickle for the Knowing Ones* (1802), included the names of the men he wanted to serve as his pallbearers. The pamphlet became famous for the complete lack of punctuation throughout its 24 pages. Stung by criticism, however, Dexter repented in the second edition, providing an extra page filled with all kinds of punctuation marks. Readers had complained that there were no stops, he noted, so he had "put in A nuf here and thay may pepper and solt it as they plese."

∇ ∇ ∇

Pierre Samuel Dupont de Nemours (1739–1817)

Founding the Dupont Company wasn't enough for this eccentric French aristocrat who had immigrated to the United States. An avid naturalist and birdwatcher he also compiled two dictionaries in 1807, which he entitled *Crow-French* and *Nightingale-French*. In them he gave what he called the French translations of the various calls of the crow and nightingale.

The cat, claimed the French-American author, is a better speaker than the dog. "The cat," he explained, "has the advantage of a language which has the same vowels as pronounced by the dog with six consonants in addition: m, n, g, h, v and f. Consequently the cat has a greater number of words."

∇ ∇ ∇

Chauncey M. Depew (1834–1928)

No one ever wanted to speak at a dinner after Mark Twain, an impossible act to follow. But raconteur Chauncey M. Depew managed to survive the experience. Twain had given an uproarious after-dinner speech aboard ship, speaking for about half an hour. Finally Depew had to stand up.

"Mr. Toastmaster and Ladies and Gentlemen," he said. "Before this dinner Mark Twain and myself agreed to trade speeches. He has just delivered my speech, and I am gratified for the pleasant way in which you received it. I regret to say that I have lost the notes of *his* speech and cannot remember anything he was to say. Thank you."

∇ ∇ ∇

Emily Dickinson (1830–1886)

Sometimes the reclusive poet would let little children into her house to give them treats of candy or cookies. But she usually avoided them, tying her treats to a long string and lowering the surprises to the children out of her bedroom window.

In one of her letters the poet explained, "If I feel physically as if the top of my head were taken off, I know that is poetry."

Only six of some 1,700 Dickinson poems, not counting an early verse valentine, were published in her lifetime.

While attending Amherst Academy she was, of all things, known as one of the two "wits of the school" and even wrote comic articles for the school magazine, in which she conducted the "comic column." One such piece was largely composed of burlesque sermons taken from a series that had regularly been appearing in New York newspapers.

In 1860 Charles Wadsworth, the Presbyterian minister she fell in love with after hearing him preach a sermon, suddenly left to start a new life in California. From then until her death 26 years later she refused to wear colors, dressing only in white—her "white election," as she called it.

Calvin Coolidge was taken on a privileged tour of the Dickinson house in Amherst and allowed to see relics withheld from the general public. Before he left he was permitted to hold a packet of holograph manuscripts of Emily Dickinson's poems. Silent Cal looked at them quickly and made his only comment of the entire tour: "Wrote with a pen, eh? I dictate."

According to one account her last words were "Oh, is that all, is it?" Another version has "I must go in, the fog is rising."

∇ ∇ ∇

Walt Disney (1901–1966)

One would think Disney's Mickey Mouse among the most innocuous, least objectionable characters in literature, but in truth Disney's creation was banned over a dozen times. In 1933, for example, Mickey Mouse was banned in Nazi Germany, and three years later he was banned in the Soviet Union. In 1937, Mickey was banned in Yugoslavia because a cartoon he starred in depicted a revolution against a monarchy; in 1938 Fascist Italy banned the mouse; and in 1954 East Germany banned Mickey as an anti-Red rebel. In the United States one Mickey Mouse syndicated comic strip was suppressed in 1932 because it depicted a cow in a pasture reading Elinor Glyn's then-controversial *Three Weeks*.

Disney patterned Mickey Mouse on a real mouse named Mortimer that he had trapped in a wastebasket and kept as a pet during his early days at the Newman Laugh O'Gram studio in Kansas City. When he proposed Mortimer as a name for his cartoon mouse, however, his wife disagreed and the artist came up with Mickey instead. Disney was always to be the squeaky voice of the mouse in sound films and he once told reporters that his "first born" was "the means by which I ultimately achieved all the other things I ever did—from Snow White to Disneyland."

Late in life he told an interviewer, "I love Mickey Mouse more than any woman I've ever known."

∇ ∇ ∇

Thomas Dixon (1864–1946)
Dixon's racist novel *The Clansman* (1905), favoring the activities of the Ku Klux Klan, was used by director D.W. Griffith as the basis for *The Birth of a Nation*, Hollywood's first great screen spectacle. The Baptist minister was disappointed when Griffith wasn't able to pay the $7,500 he owed him for his story; he very reluctantly accepted a 25 percent interest in Griffith's film, having no other choice. Over the years his 25 percent translated into several million dollars.

∇ ∇ ∇

Thomas Aloysius Dorgan (1877–1929)
TAD, as the *New York Journal* reporter and cartoonist was known (after the initials of his name), may well have been the most prolific of American word and phrase coiners. He is credited with originating many expressions, including, "The first hundred years are the hardest," "As busy as a one-armed paper hanger with the hives," "23 skiddoo," "Yes, we have no bananas," "hot dog" and "yes man," among numerous others.

Gordon Dorrance (1890–1957)

"In all the proof that has reached me," the author wrote to his publishers, "windrow has been spelled window. If, in the bound book, windrow still appears as window, then neither rain nor hail nor gloom of night nor fleets of riot squads will prevent me from assassinating the man who is responsible. If the coward hides behind my finding, I shall step into Scribner's and merely shoot up the place Southern style."

∇ ∇ ∇

John Dos Passos (1896–1970)

In the early days in Paris the American novelist and Ernest Hemingway visited the race track at Auteuil, planning to make a stake that each writer could live on that winter. Dos Passos had heard that Hemingway had an infallible way to pick winners: He would go down to the paddock and *smell out* the victor of each race. The two men pooled all their money and proceeded. Unfortunately, that day marked the end of Hemingway's infallible nose—he was unable to sniff out a single winner all afternoon, and was, in fact, never able to again. Without a sou remaining in their pockets the two friends had to walk back to the Left Bank.

e.e. cummings asked him if he ever dreamed about sex. When he replied in the negative, the poet explained that sex often enters dreams in many disguises. "Tell me what did you dream last night, for example?" Cummings insisted. Dos Passos, by now bored with the entire conversation, finally told him, "Why, I dweamed I had a bunch of aspawagus and was twying to give it to you."

∇ ∇ ∇

Frederick Douglass (1817–1895)

The son of a white man and a black woman—a slave fieldhand noted for her brilliant mind—Douglass was separated from his mother as a child, though she would walk 24 miles roundtrip at night to see him whenever she could. Douglass in effect had no mother or father from the age of eight on, but nothing broke his spirit. He bought his first book with money he secretly earned polishing boots. The book, *The Columbian Orator*, helped make him in later years among the greatest speakers of his time. After he escaped to the North he wrote his first book, the famous *Narrative of the Life of Frederick Douglass, an American Slave* (1845), writing the book mainly to prove that he wasn't an impostor making speeches about an invented life.

Patrick Doyle (1924–1987)

This New York City police reporter, who (according to the *Guinness Book of World Records*) covered more homicides (20,000) over his career than any reporter in the world, was a "Front Page" type who got a story any way he could. Often Doyle posed as a police inspector to get on the scene of a crime. One time he fooled a young policeman posted at the front door of a Manhattan townhouse where a murder had taken place. But just as he was entering he spotted reporters from other papers rushing down the street to ruin his exclusive. "Son," he said to the rookie cop, "those guys are reporters. Let them in here and they'll send you so far out in Staten Island the woodpeckers will be pecking on your nightstick."

∇ ∇ ∇

Joseph Rodman Drake (1795–1820)

Among the first, if not the very first, of American poets who died too young, Drake published only one work, the satirical *Croaker Papers*, on which he collaborated with Fitz-Greene Halleck under the pseudonyms "Croaker" and "Croaker, Jr." Dying of consumption when only 25, he asked his wife on his deathbed to burn all his manuscripts, but she refused to do so. Though Poe ridiculed Drake's work, a compensating tribute came from his friend Halleck, whose "On The Death of Joseph Rodman Drake" contained the famous lines "Green be the turf above thee" and is considered one of the finest American elegies.

∇ ∇ ∇

Theodore Dreiser (1871–1945)

The old story that his publisher's wife suppressed the sale of *Sister Carrie* (1900) because she was shocked by the novel's frankness was in reality a myth created by Dreiser, who was stung by the book's bad reviews and poor sales. Doubleday withdrew it from circulation after only 456 copies had sold and in 1901 gave Dreiser a royalty check—for $68.40.

Dreiser's *An American Tragedy* (1925) was inspired by newspaper accounts of the murder of Grace "Billie" Brown in 1906. Miss Brown had been seduced and then killed by the social-climbing nephew of the man who owned the New York factory where she worked as a secretary.

Dreiser's poem "Tandy" was so similar to Sherwood Anderson's earlier poem "The Beautiful" that Franklin P. Adams printed the poems side by side in his *New York Sun* "Conning Tower" column to draw attention to the similarities, deeply embarrassing Dreiser.

It is said that Dreiser would have sailed on the *Titanic* in 1912, and possibly gone down with it, if he hadn't been so cheap. He thought the fare on the *Titanic* outrageous and sailed aboard the *Kroonland* instead.

He gave one recorded party, a glum affair at which he served no drinks to a congregation of confirmed guzzlers like Mencken, Scott Fitzgerald and Ernest Boyd. Fitzgerald, in fact, brought as a gift a magnum of champagne, but Dreiser put it in the icebox, never to remove it that evening, and the dour party resumed.

His story "Glory Be, McGlathery" was written and published after magazine editor Arthur Vance challenged him, "I'll make you a proposition, Theodore! If you will write a story that hasn't a prostitute or a kept woman in it, I promise to buy it and pay our top price."

Ribbing Dreiser about his belief in omens, H.L. Mencken remarked in a letter to him: "The other day a dog peed on me. A bad sign." Dreiser, however, knew of Mencken's custom of taking friends to Poe's grave in Baltimore after a night of beer drinking and then as a sign of respect, urinating on the poet's grave. By return mail he advised Mencken: "A spirit message informs me that the dog who so offended you now houses the migrated soul of Edgar Allan Poe, who thus retaliates."

Dreiser's older brother Paul was the author of such popular songs as "On the Banks of the Wabash Far Away" (on which Theodore collaborated), "The Blue and the Gray" and "My Gal Sal." It is said that he changed the *i* in his name to an *s*, becoming Paul Dresser, because he didn't want to be associated with the "amoral" novel, *Sister Carrie*, that his brother had written.

The truth he found was so repugnant to so many that he and his books were condemned even in the obituary columns. In an obituary of the realistic French author Emile Zola the *New York Times* noted that "[Zola] died in his own vomit; it would be well for an American writer named Dreiser, a disciple of Zola, to take note."

When Dreiser was asked for his credo in 1928, he replied: "As I see him the utterly infinitesimal individual weaves among the mysteries a floss-like and wholly meaningless course—if course it be. In short I catch no meaning from all I have been, and pass quite as I came, confused and dismayed."

"The most suppressed and insuppressible writer in America" always had a high opinion of himself. Many years before he died he selected the last words he would speak on his deathbed: "Shakespeare, here I come!" Unfortunately, circumstances prevented him from delivering them.

∇ ∇ ∇

Will Durant (1885–1981)
When he was a teacher in New York City, Durant, 27, fell in love with a 14-year-old pupil of his, Ida Kaufman, whom he named Ariel; he married her a year later. The couple collaborated on their vast *Story of Civilization*, for the 68 years they were married. They had vowed to die together, but Ariel died suddenly while Durant was seriously ill and he died two weeks later without knowing of her death.

∇ ∇ ∇

Timothy Dwight (1752–1817)
Dwight had a remarkable mind. Like Lincoln after him he could proceed with two trains of thought simultaneously, and it is said that he could dictate three letters at the same time or break off from dictating a letter and complete it a week later, after his secretary read him just the last few words he had left off with. The Congregational divine, author and later president of Yale University, was as industrious as he was precocious. Entering Yale at only 13 he embarked on a learning schedule so disciplined that it eventually broke his health and he had to recuperate with the hiking trips that resulted in his *Travels in New England and New York* (1821). One way he saved more time for learning in college was to consume only 12 small mouthfuls of food for lunch, which was his main meal of the day. This practice reduced him almost to a skeleton.

∇ ∇ ∇ ∇ ∇ ∇ ∇ ∇

Max Eastman (1883–1969)
Artist John Sloan had a falling out with Eastman, when he edited *The Masses*, and resigned from the magazine. Wrote editor Eastman to his former colleague: "Dear Sloan: I shall regret the loss of your wit and artistic genius as much as I shall enjoy the absence of your cooperation."

"A poet in history is divine," he once remarked, "but a poet in the next room is a joke." (See also ERNEST HEMINGWAY.)

Irwin Edman
The American philosopher and author was an albino who could read only with
a magnifying glass. But his memory was so prodigious that he could learn an
article by heart in one reading. "When you can only see a little, you must really
look at that little," he explained.

▽ ▽ ▽

Albert Einstein (1879–1955)
Einstein was unquestionably one of the greatest thinkers of all time, but his
genius wasn't apparent in his early years. Born in Ulm, Germany, he may have
been regarded as a dullard and even "slow, perhaps retarded" in his first years
at school there (accounts of his progress vary). The same opinion may have been
shared by his parents, for he did not learn to walk until a relatively late age, nor
begin to talk until he was past three. Einstein was graduated from the Polytechnic
Institute of Zurich and took employment with the Swiss Patent Office, devoting
all his spare time to pure science. In 1905, at 26, his genius suddenly, inexplicably,
burst into full bloom with three discoveries in theoretical physics that included
his revolutionary theory of relativity, which reshaped the modern world.

It took him five weeks to get on paper his theory of relativity, which appeared
as the 30-page article, "On the Electrodynamics of Bodies in Motion," in a 1905
issue of *Annalen der Physik*. After finishing the article he was so mentally and
physically exhausted that he had to go to bed for a full two weeks.

Pointing to a star in the heavens, a lady friend of Einstein's confided, "I can
spot Venus anytime. It always shines like a beautiful woman."
   "I'm sorry," Einstein said, "but the star you're pointing at is Jupiter."
   "Oh, Dr. Einstein," the young woman gushed, "you're just amazing. You can
tell the sex of a star that far away!"

Einstein told an interviewer what he considered the best "scientific formula"
for a successful life: "If a is success in life, I should say the formula is a equals x
plus z, x being work and y being play."
   "But what is z," the interviewer asked.
   "Keeping your mouth shut," Einstein answered.

Many German intellectuals signed a document entitled "Manifesto to the
Civilized World," written by novelist Hermann Sudermann in 1914. The
chauvinistic manifesto stated in essence that German militarism and German
culture were interwoven and inseparable. Someone asked Einstein if he didn't

think Sudermann's work was an epic. "Hah, it's an epic," he replied. "An epic in lunacy."

In 1930 he was a dedicated pacifist and made a speech declaring that "If only two percent of those assigned to military service would announce their refusal to fight...governments would be powerless. They would not dare to send such a large number of people to jail." He was soon affectionately dubbed "Two Per Cent Einstein" by a pacifist group, which made its slogan "Two Per Cent to Glory."

He was by nature a placid man. When out in his beloved sailboat he was known to wait three or more hours for a breeze to take him into shore, refusing all offers of assistance from motorized craft.

Finally, in America in his late years, the great mind met its match. "The hardest thing in the world to understand," he confessed, "is the income tax."

In 1953 William Frauenglass was subpoenaed to testify before the U.S. Senate Internal Security Subcommittee. Einstein, who had fled to America to escape the Nazis in 1933 and became a U.S. citizen, wrote him the following letter, which was published in the *New York Times*:

> Every intellectual who is called before one of the committees ought to refuse to testify, i.e., he must be prepared...for the sacrifice of his personal welfare in the interest of the cultural welfare of his country...This kind of inquisition violates the spirit of the Constitution. If enough people are ready to take the grave step they will be successful. If not, then the intellectuals of this country deserve nothing better than the slavery which is intended for them.

∇ ∇ ∇

Dwight David Eisenhower (1890–1969)

Eisenhower, though an author, was hardly considered among the most intellectual of American presidents. Yet "Ike" championed several liberal progressive ideas. When, for example, Senator McCarthy charged that the U.S. Information Agency had communist books in its European libraries, Eisenhower counseled students at Dartmouth: "Don't join the bookburners...Don't be afraid to go to the library and read every book."

John Eliot (1604–1690)

The American "Apostle to the Indians" established 14 villages of "Praying Indians" numbering 1,100 converts. With the aid of John Printer, the first native printer in the New World, he published in 1661 the first complete Bible printed in the English colonies—a translation into the language of the Massachusetts Indians (the Natick-Algonquin language).

∇ ∇ ∇

T.S. Eliot (1888–1965)

Eliot became a British subject in 1927 and is thus covered at length in *British Literary Anecdotes*, but because he was more than half of his life a U.S. citizen, he deserves at least one story here. It seems that when lunching with Eliot in the spring of 1946, American publisher Robert Giroux, then an editor at Harcourt Brace, asked the poet if he agreed with the old saw that most editors are failed writers. "Perhaps," Eliot replied, "but so are most writers."

∇ ∇ ∇

Ralph Waldo Emerson (1803–1882)

It is said that only Plato taught Emerson more than his aunt, Mary Moody Emerson, who took his education in hand when he was two years old and guided him until he entered Harvard at 14. Yet she was a strange woman, "odd Aunt Mary," and not so much because she was a dwarf. Obsessed with death, frequently speaking of the worms that would consume her body, she always wore a shroud that she had made herself, wore it as a nightgown and wore it wherever she went in Concord, no matter who might see her, being as bold as Emerson himself would become.

In a day when $15,000 lecture fees are paid celebrity authors it is interesting to note that in the 1880s Emerson, America's first lecturer known to receive a fee, got $5 for himself and oats for his horse as payment. After finishing a lecture, he had to argue whether the oats were part of the bargain.

He lent a Yankee neighbor his copy of Plato's *Dialogues*, which the man returned in a week or so. "Did you enjoy reading the book?" Emerson asked him. "Yup," the neighbor said. "Liked it very much. That fellow Plato has got a lot of my ideas."

Emerson thought little of Daniel Webster. In his diary he gives what he considers Webster's "three rules of living":

1) Never to pay any debt that can by any possibility be avoided
2) Never to do anything today that can be put off till tomorrow

3)   Never to do anything himself which he can get anybody else to do for him...

He may not have originated the expression "make a better mousetrap and the world will make a beaten path to your door" (as Sara Yule and Mary S. Keene reported in 1889), but the editors of his *Journal* felt that he did make a similar statement to an audience of one or more, a remark that a hearer recorded: "I trust a good deal to the common fame, as we all must. If a man has good corn or wood, or boards, or pigs, to sell, or can make better chairs or knives, crucibles or church organs, than anybody else, you will find a broad hard-beaten road to his house, though it be in the woods."

When he heard that American lawyer and Senator Rufus Choate had sneered that the ideas of the Declaration of Independence were "glittering generalities," Emerson remarked: "Glittering generalities! They are blazing ubiquities!"

By the time he reached the age of 65 Emerson's exquisite mind had tragically deteriorated to the point where he could not remember the simplest things. At the funeral of his famous contemporary Henry Wadsworth Longfellow in 1882, he whispered to his daughter, "The gentleman we have just been burying was a sweet and beautiful soul; but I forget his name."

On the boulder marking his grave in Concord's Sleepy Hollow Cemetery are lines from his poem "The Problem":

> The passive Master lent his hand
> To the vast soul that o'er him planned.

∇ ∇ ∇

Daniel D. Emmett (1815–1904)
Emmett, according to a biographer, composed his famous song "Away Down South in Dixie" (1859), the favorite marching song of the Confederacy, on his violin "while looking out on the cold dreary streets of New York City and wishing he were in Dixie." Ironically, his song was sung by troops abroad the *Star of the West* on their futile mission to relieve Fort Sumter early in 1861. Thus it could be said that *Northern* not Southern troops first sang the song in the Civil War.

∇ ∇ ∇

Morris Ernst   See HEYWOOD BROUN.

John Erskine (1879–1951)

The novelist, critic and scholar was met at the railroad station by the president of a unversity at which Erskine was to lecture. "I had trouble finding you," his host said. "I asked one gentleman if he were Dr. Erskine, and he said emphatically, 'I should say not!' I asked another and he said, 'I wish I were!' That proves that at least one of them had read your books."

"Yes," Erskine agreed. "But which one!"

∇ ∇ ∇ ∇ ∇ ∇ ∇ ∇ ∇

William Cuthbert Falkner (1825–1889)

William Faulkner's great-grandfather, Colonel William Falkner, who wrote the very popular novel *The White Rose of Memphis* (1880) and a reply to *Uncle Tom's Cabin* called *The Little Brick Church* (1882), among other works, was the inspiration for the violent Colonel John Sartoris in his grandson's *Sartoris* and *The Unvanquished*. Also an army officer, builder and lawyer, he died the way his grandson had Sartoris die—shot by his partner on the street in Ridley, Mississippi.

∇ ∇ ∇

William Faulkner (1897–1962)

The Nobel Prize-winning author was known as Count No Count to his neighbors in Oxford, Mississippi, during the early years. No one thought he would amount to much, this strange, lazy, rather seedy little man dressed in greasy khakis and a tweed sports jacket that had seen better days. The rumor spread that his intellectual friend, lawyer Phil Stone, must really be writing the stories that Faulkner signed his own named to.

He did not make much of an impression on his mentors when he attended classes as a special student at the University of Mississippi. "Mr. Faulkner, what did Shakespeare have in mind when he put those words in the mouth of Othello?" an English professor once asked him. "How should I know?" he replied.

While employed as postmaster at the Oxford, Mississippi, post office Faulkner wrote more on his own than he performed his duties and, judging by official charges against him, was lucky to have lasted three years at the job. About the only thing he did right was the letter he wrote in 1924 severing his ties with the post office. "As long as I live under the capitalistic system I expect to have my life influenced by the demands of moneyed people," he wrote. "But I will be damned if I propose to be at the beck and call of every itinerant scoundrel who has two cents to invest in a postage stamp. This, sir, is my resignation."

He briefly worked in a New York bookstore in 1921. According to his employer: "He was an excellent book salesman, almost insulting customers who picked up what he considered worthless books, and pressing better books upon them with the words, 'Don't read that trash; read this.'"

Eudora Welty once evoked his career as Oxford postmaster:

> Let us imagine that here and now, we're all in the old university post office and living in the '20s. We've come up to the stamp window to buy a 2-cent stamp, but we see nobody there. We knock and then we pound, and then we pound again and there's not a sound back there. So we holler his name, and at last here he is, William Faulkner. We interrupted him…When he should have been putting up the mail and selling stamps at the window up front, he was out of sight in the back writing lyric poems.

When Faulkner and the artist William Spratling shared the same garret in New Orleans' French Quarter early in 1926, the two men amused themselves by leaning out the window and shooting pedestrians in the buttocks with a BB gun. A running score was kept, and thus did the man who became arguably America's greatest novelist fight off depression and ennui.

Faulkner told this story about the publication of his first book: "At once I found that writing was fun. I even forgot I hadn't seen Sherwood Anderson for three weeks until he walked in my door, the first time he ever came to see me, and said 'What's wrong? Are you mad at me?' I told him I was writing a book. He said, 'My God,' and walked out. When I finished the book—it was *Soldier's Pay*—I met Mrs. Anderson on the street. She asked how the book was coming, and I said I'd finished it. She said, 'Sherwood says that he will make a trade with you. If he doesn't have to read your manuscript he will tell his publisher to accept it.' I said, 'Done,' and that's how I became a writer."

After Malcolm Cowley told him of "Hawthorne's complaint that the Devil got into his inkpot," Faulkner told him, "I listen to the voices, and when I put down what the voices say, it's right. Sometimes I don't like what they say, but I don't change it."

Faulkner was certainly not above writing for the movies or turning out a potboiler to make a living, but like Shaw he claimed all he did was for art's sake.

"If a writer has to rob his mother, he will not hesitate," he once told an interviewer. "The 'Ode on a Grecian Urn' is worth any number of old ladies."

Film director Howard Hawks was taking Clark Gable and William Faulkner on a hunting expedition to California's Imperial Valley when the conversation turned to literature. The actor, not noted as a literary man, asked Hawks' distinguished friend to name some good writers. "Thomas Mann, Willa Cather, John Dos Passos, Ernest Hermingway, and myself," Faulkner replied. "Oh, do you write, Mr. Faulkner?" Gable asked. "Yeah," Faulkner said. "And what do *you* do, Mr. Gable?"

A lady in Faulkner's hometown of Oxford, Mississippi, had just bought Faulkner's latest book and waved it in his face. "Mr. Faulkner, I want you to tell me something before I read your latest book," she said. "Do you think I'll like it?" "Why yes," an amazed Faulkner replied, "I do think you'll like that book. It's trash."

Cleaning out his desk after he left the Warner Brothers writing factory in Hollywood, coworkers found the fruits of his labor: an empty whiskey bottle and a piece of paper on which he had written, 500 times, "Boy meets girl."

To a critic who had written a book analyzing his work Faulkner wrote: "You found implications which I had missed. I wish that I had consciously intended them. I will certainly believe that I did it subconsciously and not by accident."

"The tools I need for my work," he told an inteviewer, "are paper, tobacco, food, and a little whiskey."

Emulating the unrepressed pair in D.H. Lawrence's *Lady Chatterley's Lover* (originally entitled *John Thomas*), Faulkner and one of his lovers gave names to their sexual parts—hers Mrs. Bowen and his Mr. Bowen. Faulkner even went so far as to register as Mr. and Mrs. Bowen when they stayed at a Santa Monica hotel.

"Read, read, read," Faulkner advised a young writer. "Read everything—trash, classics, good and bad, and see how they do it. Just like a carpenter who works as an apprentice and studies the master. Read! You'll absorb it. Then write. If it is good, you'll find out. If it's not, throw it out the window."

In a letter to his agent, Harold Ober, Faulkner unloaded his frustrations as the main financial support for an extended family consisting largely of women, with whom he said he had nothing in common. But toward the end of his diatribe he regained his sense of humor. "Incidentally," he added, "I believe I have discovered the reason inherent in human nature why warfare will never be abolished: it's the only condition under which the man who is not a scoundrel can escape for a while from his female kin."

"My brother is the most even-tempered man in the world," the novelist's brother John once confided. "Mad as a hornet all the time."

"You know, I think Albert [Erskine] is the best book editor I know," Faulkner told Random House publisher Bennett Cerf over luncheon at 21.
"Golly, Bill, coming from William Faulkner that's quite an encomium," Cerf said. "Have you told Albert?"
"No, I haven't, Bennett," Faulkner replied after a moment. "When I've got a horse that's running good, I don't stop to give him some sugar."

Faulkner disliked people gushing about his work. One time an avid fan questioned him about *Sanctuary* (1930), in which Temple Drake is raped with a corncob by the vicious criminal Popeye. "Mr. Faulkner," the breathless woman said, "I understand that an author always puts himself in his book. Which character are you in *Sanctuary*?" "Madam," Faulkner replied, "I was the corncob."

When he taught a writing class at Chapel Hill in 1931 an elderly woman who had slipped into the class got up and read an involved passage from one of his books. "Now, Mr. Faulkner," she asked on finishing, "what were you thinking of when you wrote that?" "Money," Faulkner replied.

The large number of compound words (manvoice, womansmelling etc.) in Faulkner's *Light in August* upset the copy editor and the book's galleys are full of editorial questions about them. Next to the inquiries are Faulkner's invariably angry replies: "Stet"; "O.K. damn it"; "O.K. as set, goddamn it"; and "O.K. as set/and written/Jesus Christ!"

Faulkner insisted that the only way he could cure a bad case of hiccups was to fly upside-down. Publisher Milton A. Abernathy, along for the ride, remembered Faulkner hiring a biplane and pilot and instructing the pilot to climb to 3,000 feet: "The next thing I knew, we were flying upside-down over some marshes. When we landed, Faulkner's hiccups were gone."

While writing his difficult novel *A Fable* (1954) Faulkner accumulated over 400 pages of manuscript and did not feel that he was nearly done. His perspective completely distorted by the size of the manuscript, he wondered if he would ever finish. "It's like standing close to an elephant," he quipped. "After a while you can't see the elephant anymore."

"I've got to feel the pencil and see the words at the end of the pencil," Faulkner once said, in explaining why he had to write in longhand. Yet his handwriting was so small and illegible that he had to type his work—often 13 hours' worth—at the end of a day. Otherwise, he would not be able to read his own handwriting the next morning.

To a University of Virginia student who asked him if he minded being misunderstood by the critics, he replied: "I don't read the critics. I don't know any literary people. The people I know are farmers and horse people and hunters, and we talk about horses and dogs and guns and what to do about this hay crop or this cotton crop, not about literature!"

The romantic Faulkner lured a young woman out for a night ride by promising her a look at a lovely bride in her wedding dress. Heading deep into the country he parked in an orchard and turned his headlights on an apple tree in full bloom.

When in 1946 Faulkner's editor at Random House suggested that Hemingway might write the introduction to a new edition of *The Sound and the Fury*, Faulkner firmly rejected the idea, saying, "It's like asking one race horse in the middle of a race to broadcast a blurb on another horse in the same running field."

Faulkner's relationship with Hemingway deteriorated soon after he placed Hemingway only fourth in a ranking of American writers, a judgment he delivered while lecturing at the University of Mississippi in the spring of 1947. Hemingway had been too careful, Faulkner said, hadn't risked enough, unlike Thomas Wolfe, his first choice, and himself, the runner-up, who were "grand failures" with the great courage to "attempt the impossible." Hemingway was incensed on hearing that his courage was impugned and Faulkner apologized, explaining that his thoughts hadn't been meant for publication. But a few years later he managed to insult Hemingway again (probably unintentionally) and the two men never reconciled, Hemingway caustically calling Faulkner the creator of "Onomatopoeia County." However, Faulkner had the last word when Hemingway shot himself in 1961—and he was bitterly unsparing: "I don't like a man that takes the short way home."

To a friend who wrote asking for permission to do a magazine profile on him, he scrawled in reply: "Oh hell no! Come down and visit whenever you can, but no piece in any paper about me as I am working tooth and nail at my lifetime ambition to be the last private individual on earth and expect every success since apparently there is no competition for the place."

While he was en route to receive the Nobel Prize in 1950 a reporter asked him what he considered the most decadent aspect of American life. "The invasion of privacy," he told her. "It's this running people down and getting interviews and pictures of them just because something's happened to them."

"One of the saddest things," he told an interviewer, "is that the only thing a man can do for eight hours, is work. You can't eat eight hours a day, nor drink for eight hours a day, nor make love for eight hours."

"I felt a terrible torment in the man," Tennessee Williams said after meeting him. "He always kept his eyes down. We tried to carry on a conversation but he would never participate. Finally he lifted his eyes once to a direct question from me, and the look in his eyes was so terrible, so sad, that I began to cry."

Late in his career, when he felt he had lost his powers, he marveled at the literary gift he once possessed. "I don't know where it came from," he said. "I don't know why God or gods or whoever it was, selected me to be the vessel."

In 1962 Faulkner declined an invitation from President Kennedy to a dinner for artists at the White House, explaining, "I'm too old at my age to travel that far to eat with strangers."

∇ ∇ ∇

Edna Ferber (1887–1968)
Disgusted with her first novel, *Dawn O'Hara* (1911), she threw the completed manuscript in the fire. But her mother rescued it from the flames and the first publisher she submitted it to sent back a letter of acceptance.

Her first best-seller, *So Big* (1924), which sold over 300,000 copies, was written like all of her books—last line first. She had absolutely no faith in the book. "I thought that I had not written a bestseller, but a worst seller," she later recalled. "Not that alone, I thought I had written a *non*-seller."

She was proud of her Jewish heritage. To a bigot who protested that, no, she simply couldn't be Jewish, Ferber replied, "Only on my mother's and father's side."

As a personal dedication in her own copy of her autobiography *A Peculiar Treasure* (1939) she wrote: "To Adolf Hitler who has made of me a better Jew and a more understanding and tolerant human being, as he has of millions of other Jews, this book is dedicated in loathing and contempt."

Ferber found beautiful scenery distracting while she was writing. "The ideal view for daily writing, hour on hour," she insisted, "is the blank brick wall of a cold-storage warehouse. Failing this, a stretch of sky will do, cloudless if possible."

Noël Coward thought he had put down the spinsterly Miss Ferber, dressed in a tailored suit, when he greeted her at the Algonquin Round Table and quipped, "Edna, why it's you! You look almost like a man."

"So do you," Miss Ferber replied.

(In some versions of the tale novelist Michael Arlen is the antagonist.)

$$\nabla \ \nabla \ \nabla$$

Richard Feynman (1918–1987)

The Nobel Prize-winning physicist and author visited his old hometown of Far Rockaway, New York, to take a look at his high school records. Afterwards he told his wife that, according to his file, his IQ was only 124, "just above average." His wife later recalled that he was nonetheless delighted with the results of his investigation: "He said to win a Nobel Prize was no big deal. But to win it with an IQ of 124—*that* was something."

$$\nabla \ \nabla \ \nabla$$

Eugene Field (1850–1895)

After making a name for himself in Denver, the humorist, who wrote "Wynken, Blynken, and Nod" (or "The Dutch Lullaby"), was offered a two-year contract by the *Chicago Daily News* at $50 a week.

"I'll take fifty dollrs for the first year," Field said, "but I want fifty cents more for the second year."

"Why?" his editor asked.

"I just want people to know that I'm on the way up."

When Field edited the *Daily News* column "Sharps and Flats" a fledgling poet sent him a long, tedious poem entitled "Why Do I Live?" Wrote Field on the rejection slip: "Because you send your poem by mail."

Field carried a lifelong grudge against proofreaders, whose ineptness, he felt, had marred too much of his work. While working for the *Denver Tribune* he hung a sign on the wall over his desk, reading: GOD BLESS OUR PROOFREADER. HE CAN'T CALL FOR HIM TOO SOON.

Though generally regarded as a whimsical, sentimental writer, the author of "Wynken, Blynken, and Nod" and "Little Boy Blue" sometimes strayed off that plain domestic path. Field's book *Only a Boy* (c. 1890) is considered one of the most erotic novels ever written, ranking with *Fanny Hill* and *The Satyricon*.

The English author Mrs. Humphry Ward had a sense of high moral purpose, exacting even for a member of the Arnold family. Once she told Field that Chicago was too crude a place for him. "Really, Mrs. Ward," Field replied, "I do not consider myself competent to give an opinion on the matter. Please bear in mind that up to the time Barnum captured me and took me to Chicago to be civilized I had always lived up in a tree in the wilds of Missouri."

∇ ∇ ∇

W.C. Fields (1879–1946)

The renowned comedian and screenwriter began his working life, appropriately enough, as a "drowner." As a young man, Fields was hired by concessionaires to pretend that he was drowning so that crowds would gather and they would sell more food.

At a Friar's Club banquet to honor W.C. Fields' 40th year in show business, Leo Rosten, the author of *The Joys of Yiddish*, among many humorous books, rose to introduce the comedian. In the course of his remarks Rosten ad-libbed, "Any man who hates dogs and children can't be all bad," inventing the famous line that is persistently attributed to Fields.

"May I fix you a Bromo-Seltzer?" a waiter asked Fields when he was suffering from one of his famous hangovers.
"Ye gods, no!" Fields moaned. "I couldn't stand the noise!"

Found reading a Bible on his deathbed Fields is said to have explained, "I'm looking for a loophole."

After his death on Christmas Day it was found that Fields, who had trusted no one ever since associates swindled him early in his career, had established bank accounts under various pseudonyms all over the country. But as he kept no records of these names or account numbers, his heirs were never able to recover any of this small fortune.

∇ ∇ ∇

F. Scott Fitzgerald (1896–1940)

Bathing naked in a public fountain, chewing up 100-franc notes and spitting them out a cab window, standing on their hands, turning cartwheels and somersaults down crowded city streets, stripping while sitting in the audience at the *Scandals*, falling drunkenly asleep over their plates at a formal dinner, stealing all the women's purses at a party and boiling them together in a large pot—there was no end to the crazy antics of Scott and Zelda Fitzgerald. Among the craziest was their drunken pursuit one night of the handsome author John Monk Saunders, considered by Zelda to be too much of a ladies' man. Finally finding Saunders' Hollywood home, the pair, accompanied by two friends, knocked on the door and the hospitable Saunders let them in, getting them all drinks. Zelda proceeded to sit down beside him on the couch, pull open his robe, sniff deeply and invite Scott over to do the same because, "John smells lovely!" Both of them sat on opposite sides of Saunders, noses sunk in his chest hair, sniffing. Zelda then took up a pair of scissors and urged Saunders to let her castrate him, explaining that then all his women problems would be over. Saunders, with patience deserving of a Pulitzer, merely smiled and politely refused.

Fitzgerald's career was almost nipped in the bud when Scribners sent a copy of his first novel *This Side of Paradise* to its sales manager, who had a great reputation for spotting potential best-sellers. The man's method was to let his sister pass judgment on all new books. This time the lady not only disliked the book but despised it so much that she used a pair of tongs to throw it into the fire! Luckily, cooler heads prevailed at Scribners.

When Fitzgerald inscribed a copy of *This Side of Paradise* (1920) to H.L. Mencken he wrote: "This is a bad book full of good things." Whatever its merits and demerits the book sold 20,000 copies in its first *week* of publication.

Franklin Pierce Adams missed the lyricism and promise in Fitzgerald's *This Side of Paradise* (1920) and devoted one of his "Conning Tower" newspaper columns to a listing of the over-100 spelling and grammatical errors he found in the novel. For his part, Fitzgerald never forgave F.P.A. and referred to him as "that horse's ass" for the rest of his life.

Fitzgerald claimed that French aviator Édouard Jozan had an affair with his wife, Zelda, in 1925 on the Riviera and that he challenged him to a duel. According to the novelist, both men fired one shot each and both missed by wide margins. For his part, Jozan, who later became an admiral in the French navy, claimed that his affair with Zelda came to nothing and he never commented about a duel. In any case, Fitzgerald modeled Tommy Barban in *Tender Is the Night* (1934) on him.

In "The Snows of Kilimanjaro" (1936) Hemingway told of "Scott Fitzgerald" beginning a story with "The very rich are different from you and me" and someone telling "Scott," "Yes, they have more money." This canard (see HEMINGWAY) hurt Fitzgerald deeply, and Hemingway or his editor Maxwell Perkins later changed "Scott Fitzgerald" to "Julian" in the story. Hemingway claimed in *A Moveable Feast* (1964) that he had helped Fitzgerald in another way. When Fitzgerald confided that his wife Zelda had charged "that the way I was built I could never make any woman happy," Hemingway escorted him into "Le water," took a look and pronounced him "perfectly fine." He then walked Fitzgerald over to the Louvre and showed him that the statues there were no different. "It is not basically a question of size in repose," he explained in Hemingway fashion. "It is the size that it becomes…"

Fitzgerald preserved this true Hollywood success story in his notebook. A famous producer was asked a favor by a man he hardly knew: He had only to call the man by his first name and slap him on the back while they stood in the studio commissary. Having the man's record traced and finding nothing amiss, the producer obliged him. "The man ascended into Heaven," Fitzgerald noted. "Almost literally, for he was taken into one of the best agencies—which is what George Gershwin referred to when he said, 'It's nice work if you can get it.' He sits there today, with a picture of his wife and children on the wall, and has his nails manicured at the Beverly Hills Hotel. His life is one long happy dream."

In his notes for *The Last Tycoon* (1941) he explained the origin of the expression "off the cuff." In the early days of film, "the director was supposed to have the plot on his cuff. There wasn't any script. Writers were all called gag-men—usually reporters and all souses. They stood behind the director and made suggestions, and if he liked it and it fitted what was on his cuff, he staged it and took his footage."

Also among the unused notes for Fitzgerald's *The Last Tycoon* is the true story of "a really appalling woman" and how she failed in her attempt to give damaging court testimony against "X," a Hollywood producer. A day before his case came to trial X rounded up a dwarf and two nondescript performers and sent them to the woman—each of them delivering outlandish messages to her about the case. The next day X had his attorney open his defense by stating that the woman was mentally unbalanced. Sure enough, when she was called to the stand she quickly launched into the story of her strange visitors and their messages. X won his case. As Fitzgerald put it, "the jury shook their heads, winked at each other and acquitted."

On meeting American novelist Edith Wharton, he said to her, quite abruptly, "Mrs. Wharton, do you know what's the matter with you? You don't know anything about life."

He once confided: "My stories written when sober are stupid."

"An author," he said "ought to write for the youth of his own generation, the critics of the next, and schoolmasters of ever after."

"All good writing," he wrote to a friend, "is swimming under water and holding your breath."

Late at night, after the partying was over for everyone else on the Riviera, Scott and Zelda Fitzgerald would stay up, diving into the sea from 35-foot-high rocks. When their hostess, Sara Murphy, scolded them for this, Zelda innocently replied, "But, Sara, didn't you know? We don't believe in conservation."

Fitzgerald sometimes exhibited what has most charitably been called an "odd, juvenile" sense of humor, which his sophisticated friends never appreciated. Once, as he surreptitiously slithered across the floor trying to remove a loose leg from a chair one of Gerald and Sara Murphy's guests sat in, playwright Philip Barry called out to him, "Oh, for God's sake, Scott, get up from there and stop crawling around!" Another time, when he pretended to fall asleep on a nightclub floor, Murphy controlled him by shouting, "Scott, this is *not* Princeton and I am *not* your roommate. Get up!"

Sometimes his sense of humor puzzled everyone. In Antibes one afternoon, deep in their cups as usual, he and Zelda knocked over a street vendor's cart of fruits and nuts, finding that hilarious. When no one else in their party laughed, he kept asking, "Wasn't that funny, wasn't that funny?" Still no one laughed and he handed the vendor a banknote to pay for the damages. "There, I've given him 500 francs," he insisted. "Now wasn't that funny? Now wasn't that funny?"

Even at the beginning he knew that his drinking was a problem and often tried to quit. One time he boasted of being on the wagon for eight full days. Said a friend to whom he confided this: "He talks as if it were a century."

He and Zelda were gracious, generous hosts, often tipping the whole amount of the check when taking friends to dinner—and giving glittering parties at their Great Neck, New York, home. But a feeling that some guests were taking advantage of their hospitality led to the mostly facetious house rules they posted one night:

Visitors are requested not to break down doors in search of liquor, even when authorized to do so by host and hostess.

Week-end guests are respectfully notified that invitations to stay over Monday, issued by host and hostess during the small hours of Sunday morning, must not be taken seriously.

It is hard to say whether Scott or Zelda was the worse driver. Weaving their secondhand Rolls-Royce home to Great Neck after a long night of partying in Manhattan speakeasies, Scott once drove off the road and into a small pond just to frighten his passenger, editor Maxwell Perkins. Zelda was arrested on another occasion, when she sped across the Queensborough Bridge so fast that police thought she was the "Bobbed-Haired Bandit," Cecilia Cooney, making a getaway.

A fledgling author showed him a story written in an "over-excited" style. "Cut out all those exclamation points," he told him. "An exclamation point is like laughing at your own joke."

During the last terrible years in Tinseltown a Hollywood director put a finger in his face and remarked, "Pay *you*. Why you ought to pay *us*."

In the last two years of his life Fitzgerald was a ghost of his former ebullient self. Drinking Coca-Cola by the case instead of alcohol, he tried to conserve all his energy in order to finish his work. His final novel, *The Last Tycoon*, was written in bed for this reason, though a fatal heart attack prevented him from completing it.

Paying her respects as Fitzgerald lay in a Hollywood funeral parlor, Dorothy Parker remembered the words of the anonymous mourner at Jay Gatsby's funeral in *The Great Gatsby*. "The poor son-of-a-bitch!" was all she said as she filed by the coffin.

∇ ∇ ∇

Horace Fletcher (1849–1919)

The author of *Glutton or Epicure* (1899) advocated cutting out regular meals and eating only when really hungry, consuming only very small amounts of food at any one time, and chewing each tiny mouthful vigorously and thoroughly before swallowing. Horace Fletcher, a Lawrence, Massachusetts, businessman turned nutritionist, believed that this regimen—followed from the time he went on a diet and lost 65 pounds at age 40—would promote better digestion and health as excellent as his own. Fletcherism, described more fully in a later book of that title, swept the country, and thousands attended Fletcher's lectures and followed his instructions to the letter. As a result of the health fad, the word Fletcherize, to masticate food thoroughly—at least 32 chews to the bite—became a common expression that remains in some dictionaries. Fletcher had really borrowed his idea of 32 chews to the bite from British Prime Minister Gladstone, who "made it a rule it give every tooth of mine a chance," and who claimed he owed much of his success in life to this rule. Slogans like "Nature will castigate those who don't masticate" won Fletcher many famous converts, including John D. Rockefeller, Thomas Edison, William James and the West Point cadets. Philosopher James, however, had to give up Fletcherism after only three months. "It nearly killed me," he wrote later.

∇ ∇ ∇

Edwin Forrest (1806–1872)

The eminent American actor was a great rival of the older English tragedian, William Macready, who at 78 played his last role, as Macbeth, and who died in 1873 at the age of 100. In 1849 both actors were appearing in New York, where each had ardent fans, the "common man" favoring Forrest and the elite supporting Macready. The rivalry degenerated into "a struggle between democracy and Anglomania," in one critic's words, and on May 10th a mob led by E.Z.C. Judson (see NED BUNTLINE), possibly encouraged by Forrest, attacked the Astor Place Opera House, where Macready was playing Macbeth. In the Astor Place Riots 22 people were killed and 36 wounded, this probably the worst such theater disaster of all time. Judson went to jail for a year for his part in the affair.

∇ ∇ ∇

Stephen Foster (1826–1864)

Foster composed his first song, "Sadly to Mine Heart Appealing," when he was only 13 and had no musical training. He went on to write some 175 more in his lifetime, including "My Old Kentucky Home," "Camptown Races," "Old Folks at Home" and "Jeanie with the Light Brown Hair." After separating from his wife, Foster left the South for New York, where he lived, drunk half the time, in cellars in the poorest sections of the city, subsisting on raw turnips or whatever else he could scrounge. He wrote his last songs (including "Beautiful Dreamer" and "Old Black Joe") on scraps of wrapping paper or whatever else he could find. He died after an accidental fall in a Bowery flop house.

The first line in Foster's famous song "The Old Folks at Home" should go "Way down upon the Suwannee River," for there is no "Swanee River." Foster, after considering the Pedee and Yazoo rivers, settled on the Suwannee for his song after consulting an atlas. Needing a two-syllable name, he changed Suwannee to Swanee. Had he seen the Suwannee, he might not have immortalized it. Running through swamps for most of its course in Georgia and Florida, the Suwannee's water is coffee-black. Originally it was called the San Juan, which was corrupted into Suwannee by constant mispronunciation.

∇ ∇ ∇

Gene Fowler (1890–1960)

"Writing is easy," the American author and newspaperman advised a beginner. "All you do is sit staring at a blank sheet of paper until the drops of blood form on your forehead." (See also RED SMITH.)

While working as a scriptwriter in Hollywood Fowler eliminated distracting visitors to his office by putting a sign on his door, reading: "Horace Witherspoon, Jr.: Famous Polish Impersonator."

∇ ∇ ∇

Benjamin Franklin (1706–1790)

Even as a small child Franklin is said to have been industrious, starting work when only 10 years old and showing evidence of a thrifty, inventive wit from the beginning. From an early age he found tedious the long graces his father said before and after meals. One morning, while helping his father salt down the winter's provisions, he turned to him and said: "I think, Father, if you were to say grace over the whole cask once for all, it would be a vast saving of time."

Franklin's literary career began with a hoax when he was a boy of 16. At the time he submitted an anonymous letter to his brother's *The New England Courant*, pretending that he was a woman subscriber, Silence Do-Good, the widow of a parson. This resulted in 14 essays, the Do-Good Papers, on a wide variety of topics. Franklin's authorship of the papers wasn't discovered for almost a century and a half. This was his first recorded hoax, but hoaxes were among his favorite literary devices and throughout his life he wrote hundreds of letters under assumed names to domestic and foreign newspapers.

Titan Leeds, publisher of *The American Almanack*, was the victim of another Franklin hoax. Franklin, in his own *Poor Richard's Almanac* of 1733, predicted that Leeds would die "on Oct. 17, 1733, 3 hr. 29 min., P.M." When Leeds vehemently denied this in a letter to *Poor Richard's* dated October 18, Franklin insisted that he *was* dead, declaring that "Mr. Leeds was too well bred" to write such an indecent, scurrilous letter. The hoax was patterned on Swift's similar "Bickerstaff Hoax," but Franklin carried on his version, right up to the day that Leeds actually died five years later.

Few if any famous American authors wrote under as many pseudonyms as Franklin. At one time or another he used: Proteus Echo, Esq., Richard Saunders (Poor Richard), Philomath, Father Abraham, Anthony Afterwit, The Busybody and Mrs. Silence Dogood. As for the last pen name, one is hard put to think of many male writers, excepting William Sharp ("Fiona Macleod"), Prosper Mérimée and William Thackeray, who took a woman's name for a pseudonym. (See HARRIET BEECHER STOWE for some women who took *male* names.)

Franklin, the English ambassador and the French minister were dining together at the end of the Revolutionary War and agreed that each should give a toast.

Said the English ambassador: "To George the Third who, like the sun at noonday, spreads his light and illumines the world."

The French minister proceeded with: "His Majesty, Louis the Sixteenth, who, like the moon, fills the earth with a soft, benevolent glow."

Then Franklin said: "To George Washington, General of the armies of the United States, who, like Joshua of old, commanded both the sun and the moon to stand still, and both obeyed."

Franklin in no way founded *The Saturday Evening Post*, despite the "Founded A.D. 1728 by Benjamin Franklin" that appeared on the magazine's cover. This has been known for years. The only connection between *The Saturday Evening Post* and Franklin is that the magazine was once printed in the same printshop where Franklin's newspaper, the *Pennsylvania Gazette*, was printed.

His many accomplishments during his 21 years in business as a printer included the reprinting of Richardson's *Pamela* (1744), which was the first novel printed in America.

The elders of a nearby church asked Franklin if he really thought that a house of God needed his lightning rod invention to protect it from the elements. "Gentlemen," Franklin replied, "I would not hesitate to put my lightning rod atop your church. Being a religious man, I cannot believe that God is biased when distributing his lightning!"

Franklin's son William, who became a colonial governor of New Jesey, was an illegitimate child born in 1731. No one has established who his mother was—a family servant and a prostitute have been among those suggested—but Ben Franklin was the child's father, bringing the baby home to his wife Deborah shortly after they were married that same year. William was adopted and raised as their own.

Franklin, David Garrick and other notables attended a party given by Lord Shelburne at his Wycombe estate in the spring of 1772. The other guests watched as Franklin approached a turbulent stream, gold-headed bamboo cane in hand, and said that he could calm the water. The doctor walked upstream about 100 yards. Waving his cane over the stream three times in the best abracadabra fashion, he stepped back and soon basked in admiration as the others marvelled at how he had miraculously made the rough surface as smooth as glass. Even Garrick was impressed with his performance. Franklin finally explained that he had simply spread oil on troubled waters—that he had released on the rough surface a few drops of oil concealed in his hollow "magic cane" (an old trick of American whalers).

The good doctor took his chess seriously, was not above cheating at it and was a poor loser. While ambassador in France he would often play by candlelight long into and through the night, and there is one story that he refused to open an important diplomatic dispatch from America until after a game was concluded. Thomas Jefferson related that Dr. Franklin was playing with the old Duchesse du Bourbon, who about equalled him in skill, when he happened to put her king into prize and took it. "No," the duchesse protested, "we do not take kings so!" "We do in America," Franklin replied.

He often wore a beaver cap in Paris and the ladies so loved him that they adopted a curly hairstyle that imitated it.

"What condition of man most deserves pity?" was the question posed to guests at a dinner party in Paris. For his answer Franklin offered: "A lonesome man on a rainy day who does not know how to read."

Dr. Franklin was in Paris in 1783 when the Montgolfier brothers and Jacques Charles were experimenting with the first balloon flights. He enthusiastically watched and reported the results. Most Parisians were thrilled with the flights (women even wore hairdos in the shape of the balloons), but someone asked Franklin why so much fuss was being made about these contraptions, which were, after all, only toys! Franklin's riposte was repeated by all Paris: "What is the use of a new born baby?"

By the time he left France, Franklin's French was fluent and almost perfect, as his letters show, but early in his stay his understanding was minimal. One old story has him attending the theater at this time with Mme. de Bouffleurs, wife of the French man of letters Jean Bouffleurs. Franklin joined in the vigorous appluase all evening. Only later did he learn that much of the applause had been directed at actors on stage who had delivered lines praising himself.

Lousi XVI grew so irritated with all the attention and praise lavished upon "l'ambassadeur électrique," as Dr. Franklin was called, that he ordered a Sèvres porcelain chamber pot made with Franklin's portrait on the bottom and presented it to Countess Diane de Polignac, the doctor's most ardent supporter.

Franklin advocated "fresh-air baths" every morning, and the first thing he did on rising was to strip naked, open wide all the windows in his bedroom and stand there breathing in the invigorating air. He believed that this kept him healthy and when in Paris tried to convert his friends to his belief. Several of his French friends did try, but quit after a few days when they caught colds, the Doctor's regimen never catching on in Paris.

So many hundreds of Europeans approached Ambassador Franklin for references that he composed a mock letter of introduction for applicants:

> Sir, the Bearer of this, who is going to America, presses me to give him a Letter of Recommendation, tho' I know nothing of him, not even his Name. This may seem extraordinary, but I assure you it is not uncommon here. Sometimes indeed one unknown Person brings me another equally unknown, to recommend him; and sometimes they recommend one another! As to this Gentleman, I must refer you to himself for his Character and Merits, with which he is certainly better acquainted than I can possibly be.

He wrote in his *Autobiography*:

> In my first voyage from Boston, being becalm'd off Block Island, our people set about catching cod and hauled up a great many. Hitherto I had stuck to my resolution of not eating animal food, and I consider'd the taking of every fish as a kind of unprovoked murder, since none could do us any injury to justify the slaughter.
> But I had formerly been a great lover of fish, and when these came hot out of the frying pan, they smelt admirably well. I balanc'd some time between principle and inclination, till I recollected that, when the fish were opened, I saw smaller fish taken out of their stomach; then thought I, "If you eat one another, I don't see why we mayn't eat you." So I din'd upon cod very heartily. So convenient a thing it is to be a *reasonable creature*, since it enables one to find or make a reason for every thing one has a mind to do.

The word *stormonter* is obsolete except in a historical sense and never made the dictionaries, but it tells an amusing story about Benjamin Franklin, who numbered among his many gifts a genius for coining words. Lord Stormont, the British ambassador in Paris during the Revolution, was the most assiduous spreader of tales about America's defeats at the hands of Great Britain—his aim, of course, to color the facts and discourage European nations from supporting the American cause. One time a French friend came to Franklin with Stormont's story that six battalions of Americans had laid down their arms. The Frenchman wanted to know if this was true. "Oh, no," Franklin replied gravely, "it is not the truth, it is only a Stormont." Within a day his witticism swept through Paris and *stormonter* became a new French synonym for lying. Franklin is also responsible for the word *harmonica*, the musical instrument he invented in a rude form and named from the Italian *armonica*, "harmonious."

Franklin's life-sized likeness has been exhibited in Madame Tussaud's ever since she opened her wax museum in London. In fact, at the time Madame Tussaud made her model of him wax likenesses were all the rage in Europe, and the doctor was prominently displayed in several collections. One American owned a life-sized model of Franklin that he dressed in fashionable clothes and staged many practical jokes with.

There were those who said that by virtue of his amatory prowess Franklin, not George Washington, should be father of his country. A letter written by Franklin to Mme. Brillon in 1779, when he was over 70 and she about 30, may best summarize his philosophy:

> What a difference, my dear friend, between you and me! You find innumerable faults in me, whereas I see only one fault in you (but perhaps it is the fault of my glasses). I mean this avarice which leads you to seek a monopoly on all my affections, and not to allow me any for the agreeable ladies of your country. Do you imagine that it is impossible for my affection to be divided without being diminished? The sounds brought forth from the pianoforte by your clever hands can be enjoyed by 20 people simultaneously without diminishing at all the pleasure for me, and I could, with as little reason, demand that no other ears but mine be allowed to be charmed by those sweet sounds.

Dr. Franklin wore his hair naturally and objected to the French wasting flour as powder for their coiffures while people went hungry in France. "You [could] have, in France, an excellent way of waging war without spending any money," he once remarked sarcastically to French Controller-General Jacques Turgot. "All you have to do is agree not to get your hair curled...Your hairdressers [he had estimated there were 100,000 of them] will make up the army; their pay will come from your savings, and their food from the grain you usually devote to the making of hair powder."

Franklin could be as stingy as he was witty. One time a relative borrowed $50 from him and then asked for a piece of paper so that he could give him a note for the loan. "What!" Franklin cried. "Do you want to waste my stationery as well as my money!"

He may have popularized the saying "a penny saved is a penny earned," but a historian who examined records of the Bank of North America, where Franklin kept his money, had this to say of him: "The name 'Poor Richard' might easily have derived from his bank account rather than his almanac. He was overdrawn at least three days out of every week."

When Franklin was 23 and a journeyman printer, he composed the following epitaph for himself:

The Body
of
Benjamin Franklin, Printer
(Like the cover of an old book,
Its contents torn out,
And stript of its lettering and gilding,)
Lies food for worms:
Yet the work itself shall not be lost,
for it will (as he believed) appear once more,
In a new
And more beautiful edition,
Corrected and ammended
by
The Author.

A mock epitaph was written for Franklin by a contemporary printer:

Benjamin Franklin, a * in his profession; the type of honesty; and! of all; and although the ☞ of death put a . to his existence, each ¶ of his life is without a / /.

Franklin bequeathed $9,000 to Philadelphia and Boston, directing the cities to use the money to make 5% annual loans to artisans. After almost 200 years this $9,000 has grown to about $4 million—though not the $18 million he figured it would come to—and is still being used to make loans to worthy applicants, including medical students, at low rates of interest.

∇ ∇ ∇

Philip Morin Freneau (1752–1832)

"The poet of the American Revolution," or "that rascal Freneau" as George Washington called him (for his support of Jefferson's anti-Federalist policies), edited *The National Gazette*, which Jefferson said "saved our Constitution, which was fast slipping into monarchy." Freneau also supported himself as a teacher, clerk of foreign languages for the secretary of state, secretary to a prominent planter in Santa Cruz, post office employee and sea captain. But the greatest American poet before Bryant never made anything from his poetry, which sank him in poverty again and again. In a letter to a friend he explained why he thought "two little volumes" of his had "fallen nearly deadborn" from the New York press. "After all," he wrote, "as I take it, the genius of the City of New York is so entirely commercial, that I expect it swallows up all ideas of poetry, or refuses any attention to poetical productions, further than what is calculated for the fly market stalls [ancestors of our ubiquitous flea markets], or to be sung at some Tammany Convivial Meeting or the Bacchanian Sons of the Hotels."

He based his poem "The British Prison Ship" on his own experiences when he was captured by the British during the Revolution and imprisoned on the infamous *Scorpion* in New York Harbor. After being starved and brutally treated he was finally exchanged as a prisoner of war.

His unusual end came as an old man when he was out walking. Caught in a sudden snowstorm and unable to make his way home, he froze to death.

▽ ▽ ▽

Baroness Elsa von Freytag-Loringhoven (d. 1927)

No one seems to know where her title originated, for the Baroness's real name appears to have been Ploetz, her father a German builder. In the last years of World War I she was a familiar figure in New York's Greenwich Village and wrote for the famous *Little Review* before it moved from New York to Paris. Earning her living by working in a cigarette factory, she walked the Village streets dressed in eccentric outfits, including a Mexican blanket and a Scottish quilt, often, in the words of one writer, sporting "a shaven head, with postage stamps stuck on her cheeks and tea balls hanging from her breasts, on her head a coal scuttle or a velvet tam-o-shanter adorned with spoons and feathers." She ended her life a suicide in Paris, turning on the gas in her tenement room and leaving a suicide note that was later printed in *transition*. (See also WILLIAM CARLOS WILLIAMS.)

▽ ▽ ▽

Robert Frost (1874–1963)

Someone asked Frost to explain a poem he had just recited. "What do you want me to do?" he said. "Say it over again in worser English?"

Frost's jealousy of other poets, especially those who rivaled him, could be carried to irresponsibly childish lengths. Once, while Archibald MacLeish recited a poem at a crowded reading, he sat at the rear of the auditorium and set fire to a sheaf of papers he had in his hand, beating out the flames when most of the audience turned. Said critic Bernard De Voto, who worshipped Frost, following the paper-burning incident: "You're a good poet, you're a good poet, Robert, but you're a bad man."

In the process of baiting Carl Sandburg at a U.S. Chamber of Commerce luncheon honoring "Great Living Americans," Frost told his rival poet, "I'd as soon play tennis with the net down as write free verse."

"A true sonnet," Frost once explained, "goes eight lines and then takes a turn for the better or worse and goes six or eight lines more."

"Oh, Mr. Frost, isn't it a lovely sunset!" a young woman exclaimed to the poet while they were standing on the porch one evening. "I never discuss business after dinner," said Frost.

Frost divided his readers into four groups. "Twenty-five percent read me for the right reasons," he explained; "twenty-five percent like me for the wrong reasons; twenty-five percent hate me for the right reasons. It's that last twenty-five percent that worries me."

"Poets are like baseball pitchers," Frost, a lifelong fan, observed. "Both have their moments. The intervals are the tough things."

"How do you go about writing a poem?" a student asked him.
"Well, first," he replied, "something has to happen to you."
When that answer didn't satisfy the student, he added: "Then you put some words on a piece of paper and ride them like a horse until you have a poem."

When Frost was in his late eighties a fellow traveler on a train called out to him, "Congratulations on your longevity!"
"To hell with my longevity," Frost replied. "Read my books."

He lived to a hearty and healthy 89, known as his country's greatest poet and reading a poem at John F. Kennedy's inauguration two years before he died, though he stumbled on the words in the glaring sunlight. For this occasion he altered the last line of the poem he read, "The Gift Outright," from "Such as she was, such as she would become" to the more optimistic "Such as she was, such as she *will* become." But despite his long, healthy years his personal life had been tragic: one son dying in infancy, another son committing suicide, a daughter going insane, another daughter dying in childbirth. "When I am too full of joy," he told poet Robert Lowell, "I think how little good my health did anyone near me."

Margaret Fuller (1810–1850)

It was hard for members of either sex to classify the transcendentalist author, which led Edgar Allan Poe to observe that humanity could be divided into three classes: "Men, women, and Margaret Fuller." As for Margaret Fuller, a child prodigy who read Ovid at eight, she sensed greatness in herself and was quick to convey her premonition, sometimes comparing herself to the Roman goddess of war and handicrafts. Wrote Lowell in his verse satire *A Fable for Critics*:

> She always keeps asking if I don't observe a
> Particular likeness twixt her and Minerva.

Mrs. Horace Greeley happened to shake Mrs. Fuller's hand one day when the American author was wearing kid gloves.

"Ech! skin of a beast!" she cried out.

"What kind of gloves are *you* wearing?" Mrs. Fuller asked.

"Silk," she replied.

"Ech! entrails of a worm!" Mrs. Fuller replied.

In a moment of joy and passion Margaret Fuller announced: "I accept the universe!" On being told of this English author Thomas Carlyle observed, "Egad, she'd better!"

∇ ∇ ∇ ∇ ∇ ∇ ∇ ∇ ∇

Erle Stanley Gardner (1889–1970)

The American mystery novelist, one of the most prolific authors of all time, began his career as a writer for pulp magazines, which paid by the word. An editor noticed that his heroes almost always killed his villains with the last bullet in their gun, after firing five shots, and demanded to know why. "At three cents a word," Gardner explained, "every time I say *bang* in a story I get three cents. If you think I'm going to finish the gun battle while my hero has got fifteen cents worth of unexploded ammunition in his gun, you're nuts."

Gardner attached this note to a manuscript he sent to a picky editor: "It's a damn good story. If you have any comments, write them on the back of a check."

Hamlin Garland (1860–1940)

The Pulitzer Prize-winning author was served a dish of mushrooms at a dinner party, assured by the hostess that they weren't a poisonous variety. But he still hestitated over the dish, staring off into space, pondering.

"Are you still afraid of the mushrooms, Mr. Garland?" his hostess asked.

"No," Garland replied. "I was just thinking of the effect on American letters should you be wrong."

∇ ∇ ∇

Richard Gerard and Henry Armstrong (fl. early 20th century)

The "Sweet Adeline" in the famous song of the same name was originally "Sweet Rosalie." Gerard and Armstrong wrote "You're the Flower of My Heart, Sweet Rosalie" in 1903, tried to sell it and couldn't. When they decided to name the song's heroine in honor of popular prima donna Adeline Patti and shortened the title to "Sweet Adeline," it sold and eventually became the barbershop quartet hit of all time.

∇ ∇ ∇

George Gershwin (1898–1937)

The great composer wasn't known for his modesty. "Tell me, George," Oscar Levant once asked Gershwin, putting on a serious voice, "if you had it all to do over, would you fall in love with yourself again?" Gershwin, however, got the best of Levant when they were traveling on a train to California. "How come I always get the top berth and you get the bottom?" Levant complained. "That's the difference between talent and genius," Gershwin replied.

∇ ∇ ∇

Wolcott Gibbs (1902–1958)

When the landscaping at Moss Hart's lavish new country home was pointed out to Gibbs, the author and critic is reported to have remarked, "It only goes to show what God could do if he had the money."

Gibbs is credited by *Guinness* with the shortest dramatic criticism in theatrical history. Reviewing the Broadway farce *Wham!* he wrote only "Ouch!"

Abraham Lincoln Gillespie (fl. 1920–1932)

A former Philadelphia math teacher who immigrated to Paris after he suffered severe head injuries in a car accident, Gillespie was admired for a time by European avant-garde writers, who emulated his invented language. What he meant is still debatable. Once he was asked why he'd left America for Europe and he replied, "Because in Europe I find Meaning Scurry in their Organise-Self-Divert." Another time he told American poet Robert McAlmon (about whom someone else had said: "I'd rather live in Oregon and pack salmon/Than live in Nice and write like Robert McAlmon") that he was "the only form-packing symbol-realisticator, tuckfunctioning moderncompactly." (See HEMINGWAY.)

∇ ∇ ∇

Charlotte Perkins Stetson Gilman (1860–1935)

The American poet and feminist author, incurably ill, committed suicide on August 17, 1935, leaving this note behind:

> Human life consists in mutual service. No grief, pain, misfortune, or "broken heart," is excuse for cutting off one's life while any power of service remains. But when all usefulness is over, when one is assured of an unavoidable and imminent death, it is the subject of human rights to choose a quick and easy death in place of a slow and horrible one.

∇ ∇ ∇

Ellen Glasgow (1874–1945)

The Southern novelist, who won the 1942 Pulitzer Prize for *In This Our Life*, is buried with her dogs Billy, a French poodle, and Jeremy, a Sealyham terrier, in Richmond, Virginia. The dogs, which died first and were the subject of lengthy obituaries in local papers, were originally buried in her garden, but she left instructions in her will to have them exhumed when she died and their remains placed in her coffin. She also left instructions that she was to be buried nowhere near her father, whom she hated.

While they were alive Miss Glasgow's dogs received even fonder treatment. She fed and clothed them royally and even showed them pictures of other dogs to choose as playmates. When she traveled she sent home picture postcards addressed to Mr. Billy Bennet and Mr. Jeremy Glasgow, as she had named her dogs.

Samuel Goldwyn (1882–1974)

The film pioneer was a modern-day Mr. "Malaprop" unrivaled for his fractured English. Goldwyn, born in Warsaw, Poland, came to America when only 13; immigration officials gave him the name Goldfish as the closest equivalent to his Polish name. Later, he legally changed this to Goldwyn, from the Goldwyn Pictures Corporation, which had been named for himself and his partners, the Selwyn brothers. Of this coinage Judge Learned Hand said years later: "A self-made man may prefer a self-made name." A self-made man Goldwyn was. Even before forming Goldwyn Pictures he had produced Hollywood's first full-length feature, *The Squaw Man*. After Goldwyn Pictures became part of Metro-Goldwyn-Mayer in 1924, he struck out on his own as an independent producer, his 80-odd movies including *Dodsworth, Wuthering Heights, The Little Foxes, Pride of the Yankees, The Best Years of Our Lives, Porgy and Bess, The Secret Life of Walter Mitty* and *Guys and Dolls*. Goldwyn received the Medal of Freedom in 1971 for "proving that clean movies could be good box office." No doubt many of the thousands of Goldwynisms attributed to him—word manglings, mixed metaphors, malapropisms, grammatical blunders and the like—were invented by press agents, writers, friends and enemies. But, genuine or not, they became part of the legend surrounding the man.

One of his first Goldwynisms came when as a young producer facing severe financial problems he declared himself "on the brink of an abscess."

Once he accused Metro-Goldwyn-Mayer director George Cukor of "biting the hand of the goose that laid the golden egg."

Observed F. Scott Fitzgerald of him: "You always knew where you were with Goldwyn—nowhere."

"But Mr. Goldwyn," a colleague asked at a script conference, "what is the *message* of this film?" "I am just planning a movie," he replied. "I am not interested in messages. Messages are for Western Union."

"I want a movie," he instructed one director, "that starts with an earthquake and works up to a climax."

"This is a perfect scenario," he told a new screenwriter. "It is the first time in my life that I've seen a perfect scenario. There's absolutely nothing wrong with it. I want you to have a hundred copies made so I can distribute them to all the other writers so that everybody should see a really perfect script. And hurry," he called as the thrilled writer hastened from his office, "before I start rewriting it."

Someone at a story conference suggested making a movie about Bismarck. "Who the hell wants to see a picture about a herring?" he demanded.

"You're going to call him 'William?'" he demanded of a scriptwriter on one of his films. "What kind of a name is that? Every Tom, Dick and Harry is called William. Why not call him Bill?"

"The most important thing in acting is honesty," he observed. "Once you've learned to fake that, you're in."

Rejecting one novel for a film, he observed, "Take away the essentials and what have you got?"

"At least let me destroy all letters that are ten years old or more," his secretary suggested in an effort to restore some order to his cluttered files. "O.K.," he agreed, "but don't forget to make copies."

Of one film he said, "It's greater than a masterpiece—it's mediocre."

On reading the title of the book *The Making of Yesterday: The Diaries of Raoul de Roussy de Sales, 1938–1942,* he commented: "How do you like that? Four years old and already the kid keeps a diary!"

"Gentlemen, do not underestimate the danger of the atom bomb," he warned associates after Hiroshima. "It's dynamite!"

There must be at least several hundred more Goldwynisms attributed to him. Here's a long selection:

- In a toast to Britain's Field Marshal Montgomery: "Here's to Marshall Field Montgomery Ward."
- "An oral contract isn't worth the paper it's written on."
- "Include me out."
- "In two words: im-possible!" (Goldwyn categorically denied this one.)
- "We have passed a lot of water since this." (For "a lot of water has passed under the bridge.")
- "A man who goes to a psychiatrist should have his head examined." (Also said to have been invented by Lillian Hellman.)
- "We have to get some fresh platitudes."
- "It's dog eat dog in this business and nobody's going to eat me."
- After a director changed a night scene to a daytime shot: "Nobody can change night into day, or vice versa, without asking me first!"

- "I've got a great slogan for the company: 'Goldwyn pictures griddle [for girdle] the earth!'"
- Of an actress he had ballyhooed who didn't pass muster with the public: "Well, she's colossal in a small way."
- On being told that a film script was "too caustic": "Never mind the cost. If it's a good picture, we'll make it."
- "Our comedies are not to be laughed at."
- To rival producer Darryl F. Zanuck: "We're in terrible trouble. You've got an actor and I want him."
- To Garson Kanin: "Sidney Howard tells me you're a real clever genius."
- To a bridge partner who protested that she hadn't overbid and how could she know he had nothing: "Didn't you hear me keeping still?"
- "If you won't give me your word of honor, will you give me your promise?"
- "Where did you get this beautiful new Picasso?" "In Paris. Somewhere over there on the Left Wing."
- "Modern dance is so old fashioned."
- "What's that?" "A sundial. It tells time by the sun." "My God, what'll they think of next?"
- "I've been laid up with intentional flu."
- "He worked his way up from nothing, that kid. In fact, he was born in an orphan asylum."
- "We can get all the Indians we need at the reservoir."
- "Goldwynisms! Don't talk to me about Goldwynisms, f'Chrissake. You want to hear some Goldwynisms go talk to Jesse Lasky!"
- On his deathbed: "I never thought I'd live to see the day." (Invented by Clifton Fadiman.)

∇ ∇ ∇

Emma Goldman (1869–1940)

The expression "If I can't dance, it's not my revolution" actually originated with the American anarchist Emma Goldman in the early 1900s. She supposedly said this when her lover and fellow anarchist Alexander Berkman berated her one night for dancing wildly in a radical hangout. The publisher of the anarchist paper *Mother Earth* was deported to Russia in 1919 but left that country two years later after a disagreement with communist authorities.

∇ ∇ ∇

Mother Goose (Mrs. Elizabeth Goose; 1665–1757)

The famous book of nursery rhymes often called *Mother Goose's Melodies* is said to have been printed at Boston in 1719 by Thomas Fleet, from verses his mother-in-law, Mrs. Elizabeth Goose, created or remembered and repeated.

There is no doubt that Mrs. Goose existed. She was born Elizabeth Foster in Charlestown, Massachusetts, and at the age of 27 married Isaac Goose (formerly Vergoose) of Boston, inheriting 10 stepchildren and bearing six children of her own. One of her daughers married the printer Thomas Fleet, who had a shop on Pudding Lane in Boston. At this point the facts became unclear, yielding, at any rate, to a good story. According to John Fleet Eliot, a great-grandson of Thomas Fleet, Mrs. Goose took care of all her seven grandchildren, and the printer was "almost driven distracted" by her unmelodic singing and constant storytelling— a practice she had no doubt perfected with her own 16 children. By word of the great-grandson we have it that Fleet finally decided to profit from his annoyance and published Elizabeth Goose's songs and stories—among which were the first real limericks—in a book that contained other rhymes, too, but which he called *Songs for the Nursery, or Mother Goose's Melodies for Children.* Yet although the great-grandson wrote in 1860 that Fleet's book had been in the library of the American Antiquarian Society in Worcester, no one has ever been able to find a copy of it.

▽ ▽ ▽

John Bartholomew Gough (1817–1886)

This English-born bookbinder who made his home in New York, "the poet of the d.t.'s," as he was called, became a temperance author and lecturer after he had been saved from alcoholism by a pledge he took. His moral authority was diminished somewhat when in 1845 he was found drunk in a New York brothel after being missing for a week. No one seemed to believe his story that he had been carried to the brothel after accidentally drinking drugged cherry soda.

▽ ▽ ▽

Horace Greeley (1811–1872)

Though born in New Hampshire, Greeley lived in New York from the time he was 23, when he founded the *New Yorker*, a critical review (not to be confused with today's magazine of the same name). Though he cried "Go West, Young Man" in his *New York Tribune*, which he founded in 1841, he himself remained in New York's serene Gramercy Park neighborhood, where he kept goats in his backyard. A forgetful man, Greeley would often stroll through the neighborhood mulling over some problem in his mind, and on one occasion, "his mind intent on great affairs," he walked into the home of his next-door neighbor, poet William Allen Butler (*q.v.*), mistaking it for his own.

Greeley's handwriting was the despair of printers in a typewriterless world. The *New York Tribune* editor wrote so illegibly that an employee he fired used his letter of discharge as a recommendation letter for another job. Another time

Greeley gave written instructions for a sign painter to letter ENTRANCE ON SPRUCE STREET over a door. This the sign painter interpreted and painted as EDITOR ON A SPREE.

His infamous handwriting also caused him trouble when he penned the following letter:

> Dear sir:
>   I am overworked and growing old. I shall be 60 on next February the 3rd. On the whole, it seems I must decline to lecture henceforth except in this immediate vicinity. If I go at all, I cannot promise to visit Illinois on that errand, certainly not now.
> Yours truly,
> Horace Greeley

Soon after he received this reply:

> Dear sir:
>   Your acceptance to lecture before our association next winter came to hand this morning. Your penmanship not being the plainest, it took some time to translate it; but we succeeded and would say your time, February 3rd, and the terms, $60, are entirely satisfactory. As you suggest, we may be able to get you other engagements.
> Respectfully,
> M.B. Castle

In times past the word *news* was treated as a plural, Queen Victoria once writing to the king of Belgium: "The news from Austria are very sad and make me very anxious." Greeley demanded, legend says, that his reporters on the *New York Tribune* always treat *news* as a plural noun. "Are there any news?" he cabled a reporter one time. "Not a new," the reporter wired back.

"Sure I buy the *Tribune*," a fellow train passenger told Greeley. "I use it to wipe my arse with."

"That's why you have more brains in your arse than in your head," the *Tribune* editor replied.

While Greeley was hard at work at the *Tribune* a temperance fanatic burst into his office. "What is it?" Greeley growled and the man made his pitch for a contribution to the cause. "No, I won't give anything," Greeley replied and he went on writing. But the man insisted. "Why, Mr. Greeley, won't you give me $10 to save an immortal soul from hell?" he asked. "No," Greeley repeated, "not half enough people go to hell now."

A politician collared the American editor at a convention and proudly confided to him that he was a "self-made man."

"That sir," Greeley replied, "relieves the Almighty of a terrible responsibility."

He suffered from a dreadful insomnia that got worse during his campaign for president in 1872. After he lost the election to President Grant he went immediately to the bedside of his dying wife and for several weeks hardly slept at all. This resulted in the delirium that led to his death that same year.

∇ ∇ ∇

Zane Grey (1872–1939)
An impoverished dentist who privately printed his first western novel, Grey went on to write over 60 books with a combined sale in his lifetime of 13 million copies. For a period of eight years, from 1917 to 1925, his name never left the best-seller lists, a record that has never been broken. In fact, by the 1960s his total U.S. sales had topped 30 million copies, thanks in part to the large number of manuscripts he left behind that were published after his death.

∇ ∇ ∇

Edgar A. Guest   See DOROTHY PARKER; DU BOSE HEYWARD.

∇ ∇ ∇

Peggy Guggenheim (1898–1979)
Peggy Guggenheim, a patron of the arts in many ways, told the story of the time she was traveling back to Paris with Irish playwright Samuel Beckett and they had to stop in Dijon for a night. Beckett asked for a double room and a delighted Peggy assumed he wanted to sleep with her. But when she climbed naked into his bed that night he said no, he certainly didn't want to make love. "Then why did you take the double room?" she demanded. "It was cheaper," Beckett said.

∇ ∇ ∇

John Gunther (1901–1970)
Two of the best extemporaneous puns in radio history were made on the show *Information Please* by Gunther and emcee Clifton Fadiman. The American author was asked to identify a Middle Eastern ruler, which the brilliant Gunther quickly did. "Are you Shah?" asked the witty Fadiman. "Sultanly," Gunther replied.

Gunther told the story of an American journalist in Japan just before World War II. The man wrote home to a friend: "Don't know if this will ever arrive because the Japanese censor may open it." A few days later he received a note from the Japanese post office reading: "The statement in your letter is not correct. We do not open letters."

Edward Everett Hale (1822–1909)

Hale, his great uncle the martyr/spy Nathan Hale, was a Unitarian clergyman as well as a writer, and his literary efforts, while not regarded as great literature, did much to help "raise the tone of American life." His story "The Man Without a Country" (1863) helped strengthen the Union cause during the Civil War; his novelette *Ten Times One Is Ten* (1871), dealing with the ethical influence of a dead man's ghost on his friends, led to the formation of youthful "Lend-a-Hand Societies" and "Harry Wadsworth Clubs"; and his novel *In His Name* (1873), the romantic story of the 12th-century Waldenses, led to the founding of several benevolent religious organizations such as the "King's Daughters."

Contrary to what many people have believed since grade school, Hale's famous story "The Man Without a Country" (1863) is not a true tale. Only the name of the yarn's main character is real. In the story Lt. Philip Nolan cries out, "Damn the United States! I wish I may never hear of the United States again!" and is of course sentenced to sail the seas all his life on a Navy ship, without ever hearing his country's name again. Nothing like this happened to the real Philip Nolan, an adventurer whose career Hale used as background. Hale later regretted using the man's name and wrote a book called *Philip Nolan's Friends* (1876), "to repair my fault, and to recall to memory a brave man," as he put it. The tale was actually inspired by the remark of Congressman Vallandigham that he did not wish to live in a country that supported Lincoln's administration, and was written to arouse patriotism during the Civil War.

When Hale was chaplain of the U.S. Senate someone asked him, "Dr. Hale, do you pray for the Senate?" "No," he replied. "I look at the Senators and pray for the people." (See also CLEMENT VALLANDIGHAM.)

∇ ∇ ∇

Sarah Josepha Hale (1788–1879)

There seems to be no doubt that the "Mary" and the "little lamb" in the well-known nursery rhyme were real, but there is some uncertainty about who wrote the poem. Sarah Josepha Hale first published the 24-line verse over her initials in the September 1830 issue of *Juvenile Miscellany*. In time it became known that the poem was based on the true experiences of 11-year-old Mary Sawyer, who had a pet lamb that followed her to the schoolhouse at Redstone Hill in Boston one day in 1817. In fact, Mary Sawyer confirmed the story a half-century later, during a campaign to save the famous Old South Church of Boston from being torn down. The prototype for Mary (by then Mrs. Mary Tyler) unraveled a pair of stockings she said had been made from her lamb's wool, cut the wool into short strands, tied these with ribbons and fastened them to cards which she sold at ten cents each to raise money for the church. The cards told the story of her pet following her to school but claimed that a young man named John Roulstone chanced to observe the strange pair trotting toward the schoolhouse and was inspired to write the famous poem. Mrs. Hale flatly denied this, but the restored Redstone Hill schoolhouse that Henry Ford bought to preserve as a landmark in 1926 bears a memorial plaque naming Roulstone as the author of the first three quatrains of the poem and Mrs. Hale as the author of the last 12 lines.

∇ ∇ ∇

Henry Wager Halleck (1815–1872)

Only one person in American or world history had the honor of being called *Old Brains* and he probably didn't deserve it. Union General and author Henry Wager Halleck (1815–72) was a fortifications expert and able organizer, but the prestige he enjoyed for the victories of U.S. Grant and others under his command were unwarranted—he wasn't the "Old Brains" behind them as many believed, contributing little to Union strategy. His books on the science of war, however, were well regarded.

∇ ∇ ∇

Richard Halliburton (1900–1939?)

Another famous literary swimmer, like Byron and Poe, the adventurer and travel writer also swam the Hellespont. However, he nearly drowned doing it. Halliburton then tried to swim from Charybdis to the rock of Scylla, failing because of the treacherous currents. Trying to run from Marathon to Athens as Pheidippides did, he get drunk 12 miles into the race when he could get only wine to drink along the road. His life probably ended, appropriately enough, when he was lost at sea while sailing from Hong Kong to San Francisco in a Chinese junk.

∇ ∇ ∇

Alexander Hamilton (1755–1804)

Either he or James Madison was America's first presidential speechwriter. In any case, George Washington asked Madison to write him a Farewell Address at the end of his first term. When the President decided on another four years, he shelved the speech, but at the end of his second term Washington revised Madison's draft and sent it to Hamilton, who, it is said, developed a different speech from it, most of which President Washington retained.

That the great American statesman and principal author of the *Federalist Papers* died in a duel with Aaron Burr is part of American folklore. But it is seldom mentioned that Hamilton—who explained in a letter that he felt obliged to comply with the duelling custom of the time or be rendered useless in public affairs—fought the duel at the same spot where his eldest son, only 20 years old, had fallen in a duel three years earlier.

∇ ∇ ∇

Oscar Hammerstein (1847–1919)

The American impressario was buttonholed by a desperate wild-eyed man who proposed a bizarre plan. "Mr. Hammerstein, I will perform an act on your stage that will be the talk of the world," he promised. "You can advertise it in advance and you can charge $100 a ticket. Here is my proposition: If you'll put $50,000 in escrow for my wife, I'll go on your stage, and in full view of your audience, commit suicide."

"Marvellous," Hammerstein replied, "but what will you do for an encore?" (This riposte is also attributed to showman Billy Rose.)

∇ ∇ ∇

Dashiell Hammett (1894–1961)

The mystery writer began his working career as a detective at Pinkerton's. He got his first promotion there for catching a man who had stolen a Ferris wheel.

Hammett became a private investigator after answering a Pinkerton newspaper ad. He soon learned that law enforcement was far from an infallible business. In one case the police gave him a detailed description of a fugitive, down to a mole on the man's neck—without mentioning that the man had only one arm.

Lillian Hellman wrote that one night while they were living together they were in the course of a violent, drunken argument when Hammett suddenly fell silent and began "grinding a burning cigarette into his cheek."

"What are you doing?" she cried.

"Keeping myself from doing it to you," he said.

(See also NATHANAEL WEST.)

∇ ∇ ∇

Warren Gamaliel Harding (1865–1923)

Harding was decidedly the most unliterary of American presidents, even though he had been a newspaper editor and thought himself a great writer. "I like to go out into the country and bloviate," he once wrote. H.L. Mencken said that his use, or abuse of English was "so bad that a sort of grandeur creeps into it." After

Harding died, American poet e.e. cummings observed, "The only person who ever committed six errors in one sentence has passed away."

∇ ∇ ∇

John Henry Harper (1797–1875)
Toward the end of the last century the founder of *Harper's* (then *Harper's New Monthly Magazine*), reminisced about literary work whose "subject matter really lies beyond the pale of what is justifiable in literature," making one wonder how much "great literature" has been lost and is still being lost because it is "impossible to print":

> The most notable specimen of this class came in several years ago from a small Massachusetts manufacturing city, a "shoe town," as the natives call it. It was a most remarkable piece of literary workmanship; there was vital power in every line. But the subject! The story purported to be a narrative of the last week in the lives of two human derelicts—an immoral woman and a "black sheep" English younger son, who had met by chance at the edge of the abyss. That man could write! He himself must have been the "black sheep" to have plumbed as he did the utmost depths of despair and degradation. The pictures of terror were too horrible for a normal mind to enter upon; one instinctively revolted at this glimpse into an actual hell. There was but one thing to do—to skim it over rapidly and get the dreadful thing out of the place. But it was literature, and great literature, too. It was the kind of book that the devil himself might have written, and it came in the ordinary way by express from a dull and decorous New England town.

∇ ∇ ∇

Benjamin Harris (fl. 1673–1716)
Harris fled England after writing a seditious pamphlet. While living in Boston the English bookseller and publisher issued the first newspaper published in America. *Publick Occurrences Both Forreign and Domestick*, which appeared on September 25, 1700, was a newsy, three-page, 6-by-9.5-inch paper with the fourth page left blank for private correspondence. It was supposed to appear once a month, "or, if any Glut of Occurrences happen, oftener," but four days later the governor and council suppressed it.

∇ ∇ ∇

Frank Harris (1856–1931)
Author of that by-now-tame piece of pornography *My Life and Loves*, Harris also invented a pornographic card game called "Dirty Banshee," complete with playing cards depicting satyrs and goddesses engaged in sexual acts. He had Lloyd's of London insure his card file of the 2,000 women he claimed he had seduced in his lifetime.

Quipped Oscar Wilde of the American author, long a resident of London: "Frank Harris is invited to all the great houses of England—once."

Another time Wilde said of Harris: "He has no feelings. It is the secret of his success."

Said George Bernard Shaw of Harris: "He is neither first rate, nor second rate, nor tenth rate. He is just his horrible unique self."

Harris liked to tell stories lifted from other authors and claim them as his own. One time he was relating a tale clearly taken from Anatole France and everyone listening knew it. When he finished, Oscar Wilde finally broke the embarrassed silence that fell upon the group. "Frank," he said, very gravely, "Anatole France would have *spoiled* that story."

"Has Harris ever spoken the truth?" a friend asked Max Beerbohm one day. "Sometimes," Beerbohm said. "When his imagination flags."

Harris's preoccupation with sexual intercourse and his constant talk of little else led Rebecca West to remark, "Frank Harris believes he has the sole performing rights in sex."

Harris pursued good wine, food and sex up until his very last days. When asked the secret of his vigorous old age, he attributed it to the nightly enema he invariably took.

$$\nabla \ \nabla \ \nabla$$

Joel Chandler Harris (1848–1908)

Harris's Uncle Remus tales, first collected in *Uncle Remus: His Songs and His Sayings* (1880) and later in many other books, were among the first and remain the greatest of black folk literature. In the books, Uncle Remus, a former slave, entertains the young son of his employer with traditional tales that in St. Augustine's words "spare the lowly and strike down the proud," including the "Tar Baby" stories and other tales of Brer Rabbit (always the hero), Brer Fox and Brer Wolf. Harris, born a "poor white" or "red-neck," a pineywoods "Georgia cracker," collected the authentic tales from numerous former slaves. One who helped him a great deal was an old gardener in Forsyth, Georgia, called Uncle Remus, and Harris named his narrator after him. The tales, however, probably go back to Africa, where they were born among people who spoke the Bantu language. Other versions of the Brer Rabbit tales have been old by Anna Bontemps and Langston Hughes.

As Harris lay dying someone asked him how he felt. His last words, in reply, were: "I am the extent of a tenth of a gnat's eyebrow better."

∇ ∇ ∇

Bret Harte (1836–1902)

Harte, who published a poem in a New York City newspaper when he was only 11, left school in 1849 and was supporting himself by the time he was 16. Journeying to California, he became the assistant editor of the *Northern Californian*. Harte might never have continued his wanderings and found the material for his frontier tales had he not been fired from this job. He was discharged for taking advantage of his editor's absence and writing and publishing a scathing attack on the massacres of Indians by American settlers.

As editor of a California gold town newspaper, Harte wrote the obituary of a prominent local woman, noting that "she was distinguished for charity above all other ladies of this town." On reading the proofs he noticed that the printer had rendered this: "She was distinguished for chastity above all the other ladies of this town." Harte corrected the error, referring the compositor back to the original copy by putting a large query (?) in the margin. The next day he picked up the paper and read to his horror that the lady was "distinguished for chastity (?) above all the ladies of this town."

"My dear Mr. Harte, I am so delighted to meet you. I want to tell you how much I loved reading 'Little Breeches,'" said a young woman, thinking Harte had written the then-popular poem.
"Thank you, madam," Harte replied, "but I have to tell you that you have put the breeches on the wrong man."

When Harte left America and took up residence in London Mark Twain called him "an invertebrate without a country."

∇ ∇ ∇

Julian Hawthorne (1846–1934)

Julian Hawthorne wrote several popular novels, mysteries, fantasies, biographies and a number of short stories, none of which compared in quality with his father Nathaniel's work. He was also a con man on a minor scale. One time he sold Mark Twain and thousands of others shares in a bogus silver mine, and in 1913 he served a one-year term in a federal prison for mail fraud.

Nathaniel Hawthorne (1804–1864)

While a student at Bowdoin College, Hawthorne wrote in a letter home: "What do you think of my becoming an author and relying for support on my pen? Indeed, I think the illegibility of my handwriting is very author-like."

He was fined twenty-five cents while a student at Bowdoin for "walking unnecessarily on the Sabbath."

Hawthorne's wife remembered one of the most striking sights in literary history, three American masters skating together on the Concord River: "Henry Thoreau is an experienced skater, and was skating dithyrambic dances and Bacchic leaps on the ice...Next to him followed Mr. Hawthorne, wrapped in his cloak, moved like a self-impelled Greek statue, stately and grave. Mr. Emerson closed the line, evidently too weary to hold himself erect, pitching headforemost, half lying on the air."

As a preface to his famous story "Rappaccini's Daughter" Hawthorne originally wrote a paragraph claiming that the tale was written by a Frenchman named Aubepine and offering a brief appreciation of the French author. Some readers immediately recognized that Aubepine meant "hawthorn" in French and that Hawthorne was actually discussing his own work.

Finishing the proofs of his short story collection *Mosses from an Old Manse* (1854), he advised his publisher, "Upon my honor, I am not quite sure that I entirely comprehend my own meaning in some of these blasted allegories."

In 1849, with a change in national administrations, Hawthorne lost his political post of surveyor of the port of Salem. It was the lowest point in his life and he went home dejected and desperate. It's said that his wife, learning of his trouble, never mentioned his dismissal or need to get another job. Instead, she lit a fire in the grate, set pen, ink and paper on the table, and put her arms on his shoulders, saying, "Now you will be able to write your book." Hawthorne sat down to begin his masterpiece *The Scarlet Letter* (1850), which Henry James described as the first American fiction "as exquisite in quality as anything that has been received" from Europe.

In a letter to an editor written in 1851 Hawthorne wrote: "I am glad you think my style plain. I never, in any one page or paragraph, aimed at making it anything else, or giving it any other merit—and I wish people would leave off taking about its beauty. If it has any, it is only pardonable as being unintentional. The greatest possible merit of style is, of course, to make the words absolutely disappear into the thought."

Hawthorne's son Julian, also an author, was mistaken for his father by an adoring fan. "Oh, Mr. Hawthorne," she cried, "I've just read *The Scarlet Letter*, and I think it's a real masterpiece!"

"Oh that," Hawthorne replied, dismissing the book with a wave of his hand, "that was written when I was only four years old."

"Ah, well! I don't know that you will ever feel that you have really met him," Oliver Wendell Holmes once said of the brooding author. "He is like a dim room with a little taper of personality burning on the corner of the mantel."

Hawthorne felt all his life that the number 64 had a mystical significance for him and constantly scribbled it on his papers. He died in 1864.

After his death his widow edited, or, rather, bowdlerized his diaries. The word *bosom* was deleted wherever it appeared, as was *strumpet*, and even *bed*. *Scabby* in one entry became *defaced*, *boozy* was changed to *intoxicated*, and *smelt* became *perceived*. Where Hawthorne "vulgarly" wrote that "I got into bed," Mrs. Hawthorne substituted "I composed myself to sleep."

∇ ∇ ∇

Lafcadio Hearn (1850–1904)

"My friends are so much more dangerous than my enemies," the American author (who later became a Japanese citizen under the name Koizumi Yakumo) told his friend Ernest Fenellosa. "These latter help me so much by their unconscious aid that I almost love them. They help me to maintain the isolation indispensable to quiet regularity of work."

"Literary success of any enduring kind," he said, "is made by refusing to do what publishers want, by refusing to write what the public wants, by refusing to accept any popular standard, by refusing to write anything to order."

∇ ∇ ∇

William Randolph Hearst (1863–1951)

No one knows if he was inspired by the similar Richard Twiss affair (see *British Literary Anecdotes*) but the American newspaper publisher and model for "Citizen Kane" was expelled from Harvard in 1885 after he gave a chamber pot to each of his professors—each chamber pot bearing each professor's portrait.

In 1896 Hearst hired artist R.F. Outcault away from the *New York World* to draw his comic character the Yellow Kid for Hearst's *New York Journal*. But the *World* continued the Yellow Kid cartoon, the first color comic, using another artist to draw the antics of the sassy little kid in his bright yellow nightgown. The resulting sensational battle between the two "Yellow Kids," plus the use of "yellow" to describe sensational books since at least 1846, led to the term "Yellow journalism" or "Yellow press" for sensational, unscrupulous reporting, which was coined in 1898 and applied to Hearst's Spanish-American War stories.

In 1898 Hearst sent combat artist Frederick Remington to Cuba. "There is no trouble here," Remington insisted in a telegram, wanting to come home. Hearst, who denied the story, supposedly replied: "You furnish the pictures and I'll furnish the war."

Hearst spent some $7 million before his chain of papers showed a profit and reigned supreme in yellow journalism, but his tactics were as important as his bankroll. In 1932, to cite just one of many examples, his *New York Mirror* illustrated a concocted story about British hunger marchers storming Buckingham Palace with what was really a 1929 photo showing a crowd of well-wishers waiting outside the palace for news of the condition of ailing George V (who recovered).

Someone told Hearst's mother that her son was losing a million dollars a year in the *Journal*'s circulation war with Pulitzer's *World*. "Is he?" Mrs. Hearst shrugged. "Then he will only last about thirty years."

Hearst's *Journal* editors, suspecting that the *New York World* was ransacking its obituary columns, faked an obituary for one Reflipe W. Thanuz. The *World* promptly stole it, only to have their rival point out that Reflipe W. was "we pilfer" spelled backward and that Thanuz was a phonetic spelling of "the news." When enough time had passed, the *World* avenged itself by planting the name Lister A. Raah in a news story. After printing it the *Journal* learned that this was an anagram of "Hearst is a liar."

Novelist Gertrude Atherton was one of the few people on the staff of Hearst's *San Francisco Examiner* who wasn't a heavy drinker; her colleagues included Ambrose "Bitter" Bierce and managing editor Sam Chamberlain, who had earned the sobriquet "Sam the Elegant [for his style of dress], Sam the Drunken," and who once got drunk in San Francisco and turned up at a bar in Antwerp! "Poor man," Atherton once said of Hearst, "he prided himself on having the most brilliant editorial staff in the United States, but he paid high for the privilege: every one of them was a periodical or steady drinker, and there was a memorable occasion when all of them were down at Los Gatos taking—or pretending to take—the Keeley cure, and he had to get out the paper himself with the aid of the printers. He used to say that no one suffered more from the drink habit than he, although he never drank, himself."

∇ ∇ ∇

Ben Hecht (1894–1964)

As a reporter the "Pagliacci of the Fire Escape," as his Bohemian friends called him, regularly faked stories. For one headliner, EARTHQUAKE RIPS CHICAGO, he and another reporter worked two hours digging the "fissure" on the beach that his apocryphal earthquake had supposedly opened and that illustrated the front page story.

Hecht tried his hand at almost every from of writing, from erotic novels to screenplays, and earned good money at most of them. He rarely answered letters. In fact, he customarily didn't bother to open his mail unless he thought there was a check inside, which he could usually determine by holding the envelope up to the light.

Trying to persuade Sherwood Anderson to puff his first novel *Erik Dorn*, Hecht took him out for drinks, the conversation soon turning to the novel. "Ben, boy," Anderson finally said, "we've been friends now for seven years. That's a long time to be friends. It kind of wears off and loses its point, friendship does. My idea is that we become enemies from now on. Real enemies. I'll begin with your book *Erik Dorn*..." Despite Anderson, *Erik Dorn* became a bestseller.

∇ ∇ ∇

Thomas Heggen (1919–1949)

The author's bestselling novel *Mr. Roberts* was based in large part on his experiences as an officer aboard a cargo ship in the Pacific during World War II, where he had his own private war with his commanding officer. Heggen actually threw the Captain's potted palm tree overboard several times, as is depicted in the pivotal scenes of the book.

∇ ∇ ∇

Lillian Hellman (1905–1984)

The British hosts of a 1931 Hollywood party segregated the guests after dinner in the traditional fashion, with the women going upstairs and the men gathering below. Refusing this sexist custom, Hellman, like George Sand and Amy Lowell before her, lit up a cigar and sat down with the men, telling her own dirty stories. (See also AMY LOWELL.)

"They're fancy talkers about themselves, writers," the American author told an interviewer. "If I had to give young writers advice, I would say don't listen to writers talk about writing or themselves."

Harper's Magazine sent a questionnaire to a number of prominent men and women, asking: "During what activity, situation, moment or series of moments do you feel most masculine?"

Hellman replied: "It makes me feel masculine to tell you that I do not answer questions like this without being paid for answering them."

When she was asked in 1952 to cooperate with the U.S. House Un-American Activities Committee by informing on friends and associates, the writer replied, "I cannot and will not cut my conscience to fit this year's fashions."

In her last days a nurse told a friend of Miss Hellman that the playwright was "half-paralyzed and almost totally blind: she couldn't eat, couldn't walk; couldn't find a comfortable spot in her bed, couldn't stand up ... was probably dying." Thanking the nurse for the information, the friend visited the writer's room, asking her how she felt. "Not good," she answered and he asked why. "This is the worst case of writer's block I ever had in my life," she replied. *"The* worst case."

∇ ∇ ∇

Hinton Rowan Helper (1829–1909)

The North Carolinian's *The Impending Crisis of the South: How to Meet It* (1857) was hated as much as *Uncle Tom's Cabin* in the South. In fact, lynch mobs hanged three people just for owning the book. Ironically, Helper, who advocated free labor and the end of slavery, was a white supremacist who despised blacks.

∇ ∇ ∇

Ernest Hemingway (1899–1961)

Hemingway was 19 and in an Italian hospital recuperating from his wounds and reflecting on his mortality when he met a young British officer. Captain E.E. Dorman-Smith, later a general, wrote out these lines from Shakespeare (*Henry IV, Part 2*, act 3, scene 2) that became "a permanent protecting talisman" for the writer, words that he later quoted in "The Short Happy Life of Francis Macomber": "By my troth, I care not: a man can die but once; we owe God a death...and let it go which way it will, he that dies this year is quit for the next."

His first book of short stories, *In Our Time* (1925) sold only 500 copies. The 15 stories included such often-printed classics as "Big Two-Hearted River," "Indian Camp" and "My Old Man."

He told an interviewer for *The Paris Review* that he rewrote the ending of *A Farewell to Arms* 39 times before he was satisfied with it.

In 1947 The House of Books Ltd. catalog offered for $75 a book described as damaged on page 95 by a spot caused by contact "with Mr. Eastman's nose when Mr. Hemingway struck him with it in a gesture of disapproval of the critical essay, 'Bull in the Afternoon.'" The book was Max Eastman's *Art and the Life of Action*, a collection of essays containing the piece Hemingway took exception to. Hemingway had pushed it in Eastman's face to start their famous wrestling match in Max Perkins' office at Schribner's, a match both authors claimed to have won. Later Hemingway gave the book to *Esquire* publisher Arnold Gingrich. The nose smudge on page 95 is witnessed by Maxwell Perkins.

"He is so great an artist," Marjorie Kinnan Rawlings said of him, "that he does not ever need to be on the defensive. Yet he is constantly defending something that he, at least, must consider vulnerable."

Hemingway typically used a typewriter for dialogue and wrote the rest of his fiction in longhand. A back injury forced him to write standing up toward the end of his career. He shared this last habit with a surprisingly large number of writers, including Thomas Jefferson, Benjamin Disraeli, Lewis Carroll, Virginia Woolf, Vladimir Nabokov, William Saroyan and Thomas Wolfe, among others.

"Hemingway," Gertrude Stein once told the writer, "after all you are ninety percent Rotarian."

"Can't you make it eighty percent?" said Hemingway with a smile.

"No I can't," said Gertrude Stein without one.

"The most essential gift for a good writer," he told a young interviewer, "is a built-in shock-proof shit-detector."

Speaking of a Hollywood where Jack Warner of Warner Brothers had defined writers as "schmucks with Underwoods," Hemingway said: "Let me tell you about writing for films. You finish your book. Now, you know where the California state line is? Well, drive to it, take your manuscript and pitch it across. First, let them toss the money over. *Then* you throw it over, pick up the money and get the hell out of there."

Director Howard Hawks bet Hemingway that he could make a film out of what he considered the author's worst book, "That goddamned piece of junk...*To Have and Have Not*."

"You can't make a picture out of that," Hemingway replied.

"O.K.," Hawks said, "I'll get Faulkner to do it. He can write better than you anyway."

Faulkner took the screenplay assignment and the film was completed in 1945.

He explained the "Hemingway style" to an interviewer: "In stating as fully as I could how things really were, it was often very difficult and I wrote awkwardly and the awkwardness is what they called my style. All mistakes and awkwardness are easy to see, and they called it style."

Hemingway found it difficult to bear the expatriate writer Robert McAlmon, who had been his first publisher. One time McAlmon greeted him with: "If it isn't Ernest, the fabulous phoney. How are the bulls?" Replied Hemingway: "And how is North American McAlmon, the unfinished Poem?" (See also GILLESPIE.)

He was once asked the name of his analyst. "Portable Corona Number 3," he replied.

To Hemingway biographers were little better than graverobbers or morticians. The highest praise he had for Arthur Mizener when he published his biography of F. Scott Fitzgerald, *The Far Side of Paradise* (1951), was to call his book "good undertaking," better than most morticians did. "Amost as good as the job they did on my father's face when he shot himself," Hemingway said. "One remembers the face better as it actually was. But the undertaker pleases those who come to the funeral."

Hemingway's famous remark about the rich, the rest of us and money has its roots in a remark critic Mary Colum made to Hemingway at lunch one day. "I am getting to know the rich," he told her. Replied Colum: "The only difference between the rich and other people is that the rich have more money." Hemingway later put the remark to good use in his short story "The Snows of Kilimanjaro"—at the expense of his friend F. Scott Fitzgerald— having the story's central character recall "poor Scott Fitzgerald and his romantic awe [of the rich] and how he had started a story once that began, 'The rich are different from you and me.' And how someone had said to Scott, yes, they have more money." The only truth to this is that Fitzgerald's story "The Rich Boy" begins: "Let me tell you about the very rich. They are different from you and me." Fitzgerald soon complained to Hemingway, advising him that "Riches have never fascinated me, unless combined with the greatest charm or distinction." Later Maxwell Perkins, editor to both Hemingway and Fitzgerald at Scribner's, on Fitzgerald's request changed "poor Scott Fitzgerald" in the story to "poor Julian." But mistakes by biographers have made "the famous Hemingway-Fitzgerald exchange" a part of literary history that will probably be repeated for years. (See also SCOTT FITZGERALD.)

A very generous man, he would often when short of cash borrow 100 francs from barmen in the Ritz. Then he would give the same 100 francs to them as a tip for serving him, along with the promise, "I'll pay you back next week."

"Easy writing," he remarked to a friend in Paris, "makes hard reading."

After publication of *The Sun Also Rises* (1926) he could, in his own words, "no more make love than Jake Barnes," the novel's emasculated hero. His second wife, Pauline, finally suggested that he pray. "There was a small church two blocks from us and I went there and said a short prayer," he later told a friend. "Then I went back to our room. Pauline was in bed waiting. I undressed and got in bed and we made love like we invented it. We never had any trouble again. That's when I became a Catholic."

He admitted long after publishing *The Sun Also Rises* that his heroine Brett was based on Lady Duff Twysden, whi died at 43 of tuberculosis. "Her pallbearers had all been her lovers," he recalled. "On leaving the church, where she had had a proper service, one of the grieving pallbearers slipped on the church steps and the casket dropped and split open."

Reminiscing about his early days in Paris, he told his friend A.E. Hotchner:

> ...every day the rejected manuscripts would come back through the slot in the door of that bare room where I lived over the Montmartre sawmill. They'd fall through the slot onto the wood floor, and clipped to them was that most savage of all reprimands—the printed rejection slip. The rejection slip is very hard to take on an empty stomach and there were times when I'd sit at that old wooden table and read one of those cold slips that had been attached to a story I had loved and worked on very hard and believed in, and I couldn't help crying.

Many of his early stories were written, rejected and returned, and then all but two of them ("Up in Michigan," gathering dust in a desk drawer, and "My Old Man," being considered by *Cosmopolitan*) were lost forever. His wife Hadley had been bringing all the manuscripts and carbons down to Lausanne so that he could work on them during their Christmas holiday in the mountains. During the brief time after she reached the Gare de Lyon and a porter carried the luggage to her train compartment the valise with the manuscripts was stolen. At first Hemingway could not believe that the carbons, too, were gone and he took a train back to Paris to make sure. "It was true all right," he recalled much later, "and I remember what I did in the night after I let myself into the flat and found it was true." He would never tell anyone what he did that night in early December 1922, the secret dying with him.

He was a good boxer but often beaten. Canadian author Morley Callaghan, for example, got the better of him in a boxing match in Paris and Hemingway was incensed with Scott Fitzgerald, the timekeeper, for letting the round go one minute too long. "All right, Scott," he shouted. "If you want to see me getting the shit knocked out of me, just say so. Only don't say you made a mistake." There were other losses as well, including two thrashings at the hands of his friend Gene Tunney. One time Tunney stopped Hemingway's wild swinging with a "liver punch" that turned him gray. On another occasion, after Hemingway delivered a perhaps unintentional low blow, an outraged Tunney threw a vicious punch that he stopped just short of the writer's face. Staring Hemingway in the eye, he warned him, *"Don't you ever do that again!"*

Hemingway was in the vanguard of the troops liberating Paris at the end of World War II, and one of the first people he looked up was his friend Pablo Picasso. Picasso wasn't home, but his concierge, used to people bringing presents of food during the war, asked him if he didn't want to leave a gift. Thinking this a good idea, Hemingway brought back from his jeep a large case on which he wrote "To Picasso from Hemingway." Later, closer inspection revealed it was a case of hand grenades.

He read his own obituary in newspapers throughout the world when, unknown to reporters, he survived a plane crash in Africa in 1960. One obituary even said that he had crashed trying to fly the plane to the level that the leopard reached in his famous story "The Snows of Kilimanjaro."

In his *Misadventures of a Fisherman: My Life With and Without Papa*, Jack Hemingway, the oldest of Ernest Hemingway's three sons, describes going to his father in despair over not being able to decide on a career for himself. "I get down so bad I wonder if it's worth going on living," the young man confessed. At this point Hemingway, remembering his father's suicide, made the boy exchange promises with him that "Neither one of us will ever shoot himself, like Grandfather."

∇ ∇ ∇

George W. Henry (fl. 1859)

This energetic author and revivalist preacher was known throughout America as the "holy shouter," his shouts and screams, it is said, "putting the fear of God into many a sinner." He was perhaps outdone only by Carrie Nation (*q.v.*) in choosing a title for a book. His masterpiece, published in Oneida, New York, in 1859, was called: SHOUTING: GENUINE AND SPURIOUS, IN ALL AGES OF THE CHURCH, FROM THE BIRTH OF CREATION, WHEN THE SONS OF GOD SHOUTED FOR JOY, UNTIL THE SHOUT OF THE ARCHANGEL: WITH

NUMEROUS EXTRACTS FROM THE OLD AND NEW TESTAMENT, AND FROM THE WORKS OF WESLEY, EVANS, EDWARDS, ABBOTT, CARTWRIGHT AND FINLEY. GIVING A HISTORY OF THE OUTWARD DEMONSTRATIONS OF THE SPIRIT SUCH AS LAUGHING, SCREAMING, SHOUTING, LEAPING, JERKING, AN FALLING UNDER THE POWER & C.

∇ ∇ ∇

O. Henry (William Sydney Porter; 1862–1910)

O. Henry was the pen name of American writer William Sydney Porter. Born in North Carolina, Porter went to Texas as a young man to seek his fortune. After trying several occupations, including journalism, he became a bank teller in Houston, where he was indicted for embezzlement in 1896. Only a small sum (a little over $1,200) had been involved, and Porter's crime was more one of mismanagement than theft, but he fled to South America. When he returned to his dying wife several years later, he was imprisoned and served a three-year sentence.

While imprisoned for embezzlement he was employed in the prison pharmacy. There he used the medical reference work *U.S. Dispensatory,* which listed in its pages the name of French pharmacist Étienne-Ossian Henry. From this name he took the pseudonym O. Henry that he used to conceal his true identity when he began writing his first stories.

In prison he met a safecracker named Dick Price who had cut his nails deep into the quick, exposing the nerve endings and making his fingers extra sensitive. O. Henry based his safecracker Jimmy Valentine in "A Retrieved Reformation" on Price. Price himself was later promised a pardon for helping the state open a safe in a criminal case, but was double-crossed and died in prison.

O. Henry was always hard up for money, often because he was being black-mailed by a man who knew that he had been in jail. In fact, he would frequently come into the Doubleday offices and demand $25 or $50 advances, never revealing of course that the money was going to the blackmailer. In any event, he constantly needed money and didn't trust publishers very much. When a publisher named Hampton solicited a story from him for his *Hampton's Magazine,* O. Henry demanded $500, paid in advance. Hampton wanted to pay nothing until he read the story and so they compromised: The author would get $250 for the first half of the story and $250 more on delivery of the second half. O. Henry soon turned in the first half, but Hampton never paid the first $250 or even answered the author's letters. The perfidious Hampton, it turned out, published the first half of the story without paying for it, with an offer of $250 to anybody who could complete it.

Magazine publisher Frank Munsey told O. Henry, who owed him several stories, that he would receive no more advances unless he advised Munsey what he needed the money for. O. Henry immediately mailed him an envelope containing one long blonde hair. The advance was granted.

At the height of his career the *New York World* paid O. Henry the then grand sum of $100 for each of his short stories. But he often failed to deliver his tales to meet deadlines and his editor refused to pay him in advance, making a deal with the author to pay him $50 for delivering the first half of each story and $50 on receipt of the completed tale. Some critics believe that this is why the beginnings of a number of O. Henry stories seem unrelated to the endings. Whenever the author badly needed money, they contend, he would hurriedly write any beginning that came to mind and often ignore it later, when he had more time to finish the story.

He suffered all his life from hypoglycemia, or hyperinsulinism, the opposite of diabetes, his classic summary of the condition being, "I was born eight drinks below par."

It is often said that O. Henry pulled a classic boner when he wrote at the opening of "The Gift of the Magi": "One dollar and eighty-seven cents. That was all. And 60 cents of it was in pennies." But the fault-finders are mistaken, because it would have been possible at the time to make up the remaining $1.27 without using pennies. When O. Henry wrote his celebrated short story in 1906 two- and three-cent pieces were still in circulation.

O. Henry was a confirmed city person. Even in his last year, suffering from hypoglycemia and the effects of his life-long alcoholism, he insisted on returning to Manhattan from North Carolina, where he had been taking a "cure" for a few months. "There was too much scenery and fresh air," he explained to a friend. "What I need is a steam-heated flat with no ventilation or exercise."

During the long period he spent in his beloved Bagdad on the Hudson (New York City), he drank an average daily two quarts of whiskey. This never prevented him from writing his 50 to 65 stories a year (some 600 over his lifetime).

When O. Henry was taken to the New York Polyclinic Hospital during his final illness, he emptied his pockets at the reception desk. "I've heard of people being worth thirty cents," he remarked, "and here I am going to die and only worth thirty-three cents." He died soon after, his famous last words, quoting a popular song, being: "Turn up the lights, I don't want to go home in the dark."

His life ended with an O. Henry twist he would have liked. His funeral, in Manhattan's Little Church Around the Corner, was somehow scheduled at the same time as a wedding.

∇ ∇ ∇

Patrick Henry (1736–1799)
"I know not what course others may take, but as for me, give me liberty or give me death!" cried the American revolutionary, who was mainly responsible for drafting the Bill of Rights, in a speech in the Virginia Convention on March 24, 1775. Even as he spoke his wife was chained, hopelessly insane, in the basement of his house.

∇ ∇ ∇

Josiah Henson (1789–1883)
Harriet Beecher Stowe's model for Uncle Tom in her novel *Uncle Tom's Cabin* was a real-life Maryland-born slave named Josiah Henson, who wrote a widely read autobiographical pamphlet. Henson was far from an Uncle Tom in the term's recent sense. Like many slaves, he served as the overseer, or manager of a plantation before he escaped to Canada and became a methodist preacher. Once free, he started a prosperous sawmill, founded a trade school for blacks, whites and Indians, and helped over 100 slaves escape to Canada. When he journeyed to England on business, the Archbishop of Canterbury was so impressed with his speech and learning that he asked him what university he had studied at. "The University of Adversity," Henson replied.

∇ ∇ ∇

Victor Herbert (1859–1924)
The composer of the widely popular *Babes in Toyland* refused to plug a march that a young man from his home town had written, believing it to be of inferior quality. "I thought you said you were encouraging down home talent," the young man said. "I am," replied Herbert. "I'm encouraging it to stay at home."

∇ ∇ ∇

Oliver Herford (1863–1935)
The humorist, poet and cartoonist was talking to an actor noted for his vanity. "Why I'm a smash hit!" the man declared. "Only yesterday, during the last act, I had the audience glued in their seats!"

"Wonderful! Wonderful!" exclaimed Herford. "Clever of you to think of it."

Herford was approached by the most boring member of the Players Club. "Oliver, I've been grossly insulted," the man told him. "Just as I passed that group over there I overheard someone say that he would give me $50 to resign from the club."
  "Hold out for a hundred," Herford advised, "you'll get it."

He and a noted military man were being jointly honored at a banquet when the hostess suddenly and without any consultation announced that "Mr. Oliver Herford will now improvise a poem in honor of the occasion." "Oh, no," he protested, sliding lower in his chair. "Have the general fire a cannon."

Herford's young nephew was sitting on his lap in a crowded trolley when an attractive woman entered the car and was forced to stand in front of them. "My boy," Herford said to his nephew, "why don't you get up and give the lady your seat?"

∇ ∇ ∇

Joseph Hergesheimer (1880–1954)
In answering a biographical question the novelist remarked, in the third person: "He [Hergesheimer] has no children and, more than willing to forgo both the biological justification and joys of parenthood, he believes that in this particular he has benefited humanity."

Disappointed in the rather shallow hopes and plans of a young woman he knew, Hergesheimer told her, "You have hitched your star to a wagon."

Posters announcing that Hergesheimer and H.L. Mencken would address an audience in New York plainly said that the two men would speak "together." The two decided to take the announcement literally, walking onstage together, standing side by side, and each giving his separate lecture at the same time.

∇ ∇ ∇

Du Bose Heyward (1885–1940)
The Pulitzer Prize-winning author of the novel *Porgy* (1927), made into the opera *Porgy and Bess* by George Gershwin, was lecturing in Detroit, where many considered poet Edgar A. Guest to be local laureate. One woman in the audience asked Heyward what he thought of the immensely popular poet and Heyward was forced to admit that he didn't consider Guest's rockinghorse rhymes to be

real poetry. "Mr. Heyward," an indignant lady asked him, "what kind of a car do you drive?"

Heyward had to admit he didn't own a car.

"Eddie Guest," said the lady, "drives a Cadillac!"

∇ ∇ ∇

Patty Smith Hill (fl. 1893)

Patty Hill and her sister Mildred J. Hill, two kindergarten and Sunday school teachers, wrote a book entitled *Song Stories for the Sunday School.* One of the songs had the lyrics "Good morning to you, good morning to you, good morning dear children, good morning to you." Later the sisters kept the same melody and changed the words to "Happy birthday to you, Happy birthday to you…" Today heirs of the Hill sisters get their share of the over one million dollars in royalties that the song, copyrighted in 1935, brings in every year, and "Happy Birthday To You" is one of the two most popular songs in the English language (the other being Robert Burns' "Auld Lang Syne"). It is sung in scores of foreign languages as well, including the African language Eroe.

∇ ∇ ∇

Walter Hines (1855–1918)

When Walter Hines Page, later ambassador to Great Britain, edited *The World's Work*, he received the following letter from a would-be contributor:

"Sir: You sent back last week a story of mine. I know that you did not read the story, for as a test I had pasted together page 18, 19 and 20, and the story came back with these pages still pasted; and so I know you are a fraud and turn down stories without reading them."

Replied Page:

"Madame: At breakfast when I open an egg I don't have to eat the whole egg to discover it is bad."

∇ ∇ ∇

Alfred Hitchcock (1889–1980)

A customs official asked the British-born American movie director and producer his occupation. "Producer," Hitchcock said. "What do you produce?" the official asked. "Gooseflesh," Hitchcock replied.

Hitchcock, as his famous profile attested, was fond of food. One time he was invited to a dinner where the fare was decidedly unsubstantial. While coffee was being served his hostess said, "I do hope that you will dine here again, Mr. Hitchcock." "By all means," said the director. "Let's start right now."

Hitchcock had telephoned the prolific Belgian novelist Georges Simenon, who wrote his books at incredible speed, sometimes in as little as 10 days. Simenon's wife took the call. "I'm sorry," she said, "but Georges is writing and I can't disturb him."

"Let him finish his book," Hitchcock replied. "I'll hang on."

∇ ∇ ∇

Samuel Gordon Hoffenstein (1890–1947)

This poet and humorist worked for years as a Hollywood scenarist, moving from New York to Los Angeles and doing the screen adaptations of *An American Tragedy* and *Sentimental Journey*, among other novels. One time an interviewer inquired about his lot in Hollywood, expecting a self-pitying reply. "In the movies we writers work our brains to the bone and what do we get for it?" Hoffenstein asked. Then he answered his own question: "A lousy fortune."

∇ ∇ ∇

Oliver Wendell Holmes (1809–1894)

The renowned author and physician was appointed professor of anatomy and physiology at Harvard Medical School in 1847. It is said that his anatomy lectures were so witty and lively that his classes were always scheduled for the end of the afternoon, because only he could keep the students awake after a long, tiring day. Yet he also taught in other departments, having so many duties that he commented that he occupied "not a chair but a settee in the school."

"Good morning, doctor," said a priest leaving the house of one of Holmes' patients. "Your patient is very ill—he is going to die."

"Yes," Holmes said, "and he's going to hell."

"No," the priest insisted. "I have just given extreme unction—and you mustn't say such things!"

"Well," replied Holmes, "you expressed a medical opinion and I have just as much right to a theological opinion."

Holmes' essay *Puerperal Fever as a Private Pestilence*, which in 1855 he printed as a pamphlet to give it wider circulation, dealt with childbed fever and its causes, mainly the transmission of the disease from doctor to patient because of unsanitary practices. "At the time it was delivered this paper was the most important contribution made in America to the advancement of medicine," writes one medical historian. Another historian contends that "No American publication in the nineteeth century saved more lives than this unassuming pamphlet."

Built six months after the *Constellation*, the *Constitution* is America's oldest warship still afloat and in commission. A national historic monument today, she is moored in Boston Harbor, flying the flag of the commandant of the First Naval District. The high point of her illustrious career came on August 19, 1812, when she engaged and defeated the British frigate *Guerriere* off Nova Scotia. During the battle an American sailor, watching British shots fall into the sea, cried: "Huzza! Her sides are of iron!" and *Old Ironsides* she has been since that day. It was in 1830 that Holmes, hearing that she was to be sold by the navy, wrote his famous poem "Old Ironsides" in protest, and she was saved.

The author named and was one of the founders of *The Atlantic Monthly* in 1857. In the words of William Dean Howells, he "not only named but made" the magazine, for public interest in his *Autocrat of the Breakfast Table*, a portion of which appeared in every number of its first volume, kept the *Atlantic* afloat during the Panic of 1857. Holmes' famous opening in the *Autocrat*—"I was just going to say when I was interrupted"—refers to the fact that two earlier *Autocrat* papers had appeared in the *Old New England Magazine* (1831–33) and hadn't been reprinted since then.

Holmes once told a group of clubwomen how he established fees for his lectures. "My fee," he said, "if I select the subject, is $150; if your committee selects the subject, the charge is $250; but in either case the speech is the same."

"A lecturer," he told Herman Melville—who would have liked to earn half the money Holmes did lecturing—"is a literary strumpet, subject for a greater than whore's fee to prostitute himself."

Usually known for his gentle humor, the sagacious poet could be cutting when the occasion demanded it. One afternoon he suffered through a social tea of Boston ladies only to have the hostess ask him as he was leaving, "Well, Doctor, what do you think of afternoon tea?"

Holmes summed up the experience in four words: "Giggle. Gaggle. Gobble. Git!"

Quite an amateur photographer, Holmes once gave a picture to a friend, inscribing the back of it: "Taken by O.W. Holmes and Sun."

Holmes loved to hear compliments, especially in his old age. "I am a trifle deaf," he used to tell those who praised him or his work. "Would you mind repeating that a little louder?"

∇ ∇ ∇

Oliver Wendell Holmes Jr. (1841–1935)
A Civil War hero badly wounded at Balls Bluff, Antietam and Fredericksburg, the son of author Oliver Wendell Holmes survived to become a noted teacher, author and associate justice of the Supreme Court of the United States. In later years he was regarded as reserved, even cold, but there was little hint of these qualities in his youth. On the battlefield one time Holmes noticed a lanky civilian surveying the scene while bullets whizzed by. "Get down, you damn fool, before you get shot!" he shouted. Just as he said it he realized that the "civilian" was President Lincoln.

Not long after his 87th birthday the eminent jurist was taking a stroll with a friend, when an attractive young woman passed by. "Oh, to be seventy again!" Holmes sighed.

On Holmes' 92nd birthday President Franklin Roosevelt visited him and found the jurist alone, reading Plato in his library. "Why do you read Plato, Mr. Justice?" Roosevelt asked. "To improve my mind, Mr. President," replied Holmes.

∇ ∇ ∇

Sidney Hook (1902–1989)
The conservative philosopher and author, a Marxist in his youth, concluded his entry in *Who's Who in America* the year of his deth with these words: "Survival is not the be-all and end-all of a life worthy of man. Those who say that life is worth living at any cost have already written for themselves an epitaph of infamy, for there is no cause and no person they will not betray to stay alive. Man's vocation should be the use of the arts of intelligence in behalf of human freedom."

∇ ∇ ∇

Harry Houdini (Ehrich Weiss; 1875–1926)
The magician and author adopted the stage name Harry Houdini early in his career. Strangely enough, he named himself after another magician he admired—Jean-Eugène-Robert Houdin (1850–1871), a French magician celebrated for the fact that he did *not* attribute his feats to supernatural powers. Houdini, a magician's magician who invented many magic tricks, exposed numerous spiritualists and other fraudulent performers. He also wrote a number of books

and left his extensive magic library to the Library of Congress, where there is now a Houdini Room. The supreme magician has become the object of almost cult-like worship among fellow illusionists. Once he claimed that if anyone could break the shackles of death and contact the living from the grave, he could. Since his death—"He was fifty-two when he died, his life like a deck of cards"—followers have periodically held seances where he is buried in Glendale, New York's Machpelah Cemetery, and where a granite bust of the magician stares down at them. He has inspired a Houdini Hall of Fame at Niagara Falls, New York.

∇ ∇ ∇

Julia Ward Howe (1819–1910)
The poet was widely known in her day as author of "The Battle Hymn of the Republic," but not by everyone. Shortly after her death memorial services were held for her in San Francisco at which the mayor presided. Taking the platform he initiated the ceremonies: "Your attendance here, ladies and gentlemen, shows San Francisco's appreciation of good literature. This meeting is a great testimonial to the immortal author of *Uncle Tom's Cabin*—the late Julia Ward Howard!"

∇ ∇ ∇

William Dean Howells (1837–1920)
The noted author's wife hired a girl to do the housework, and every day she came to clean the girl couldn't fail to notice Howells around the place. Feeling badly about this, the good-hearted young woman approached Mrs. Howells.

"Excuse me, madam," she said, "but I'd like to say something."

"What is it, Kathleen?"

"Well, you pay me five dollars a week now—"

"And I really can't afford any more, Kathleen."

"Oh, I understand that, madam. It's that I am willing to take *four* until Mr. Howells lands a job."

"Does it afflict you to find your books wearing out?" he asked in a 1903 letter to Charles Eliot Norton. "I mean literally…The mortality of all inanimate things is terrible to me, but that of books most of all."

While he served as American consul at Venice, the portly Howells was approached by a friend in the street.

"Howells," the long, lanky man said, "if I were as fat as you are, I would hang myself."

"Well," Howells said in usual good-natured manner, "If I ever decide to take your advice I'll use you for the rope."

"I don't seem to write as well as I used to," an affected author told Howells, expecting to be contradicted. "Oh yes you do," Howells said. "You write as well as you ever did. But your *taste* is improving."

"This is a magnificent poem," Howells told a young poet who had brought him what he said were samples of his work. "Did you write it all yourself."
"Oh yes, sir," said the young poet. "Every word of it!"
Howells rose, leading him to the door. "It's been a pleasure meeting you, Lord Byron," he said. "I was under the impression that you died at Missolonghi a good many years ago."

"What the American public always wants," he told novelist Edith Wharton, "is a tragedy with a happy ending."

He told his landlord in London that he was surprised Prime Minister Balfour patronized the simple shop of a tailor he himself had just visited. "Well, I don't think, sir, Mr. Balfour cares much for his clothes, sir," the landlord replied. "Them distinguished men can't, sir. Their thoughts soar to 'igher things, sir."

∇ ∇ ∇

Elbert Hubbard (1856–1915)

Hubbard's *Essay on Silence* (1898) contained nothing but blank pages. The author, who went down with the *Lusitania*, was not above wordy platitude, however. In fact, Hubbard's inspirational essay, "A Message to Garcia," first published in his magazine *The Philistine* in March 1900, remained required reading in most elementary school English classes until about 30 years ago and, according to one biographer, "so poignantly appealed to industrial magnates that they distributed countless copies to promote greater efficiency among their employees." Sample: "It is not book learning that young men need, nor instruction about this and that, but a a stiffening of the vertebrae which will cause them to be loyal to a trust, to act promptly, concentrate their energies, do a thing—'carry a message to Garcia.'" Hubbard's essay dramatized the true adventure of Lieutenant Andrew Summers Rowan, United States Bureau of Naval Intelligence, who during the Spanish-American War was sent by the American chief of staff to communicate with General Calixto Garcia, leader of the Cuban insurgent forces. No one knew just where the elusive Garcia might be, but Rowan made his way through the Spanish blockade in a small boat, landing near Turquino Peak on April 24, 1898. He contacted local patriots who directed him to Garcia far inland, and returned to Washington with information regarding the insurgent forces. The brave and resourceful Rowan became a hero but Hubbard tranformed him into an almost Arthurian figure in his time.

"This will never be a civilized country," Hubbard once observed, "until we expend more money for books than we do for chewing gum."

∇ ∇ ∇

Langston Hughes (1902–1967)

When working as a delivery boy in Chicago, Hughes was waylaid by a gang of white hooligans. Yelling that "niggers" were not allowed in their neighborhood, they knocked Hughes down and beat him up. That night his jaw began to swell but Langston, ashamed to admit that he had lost a fight, hid it from his family. The next morning, when the swelling was bigger, his mother hauled him to a doctor, who solemnly pronounced that the child was a sure victim of the mumps. Hughes never told his mother what he was really the victim of.

When Vachel Lindsay dined at the Washington, D.C. restaurant where Hughes worked as a busboy the aspiring poet put a batch of his poems beside his plate and slipped away. The flamboyant Lindsay read the poems aloud to an audience that night, recognizing their quality, and Hughes learned about his "discovery" in the local papers the next day. Following Lindsay's advice he began to send his poems to magazines and his career as a poet began.

While recording the plight of homeless vagrants on the outskirts of Reno, Nevada, Hughes took a long walk and came to a small mountain cemetery. On the cemetery gate there seemed to be a mailbox, though there was no house in sight. Upon reaching the gate he realized that what he saw was only an old board that had warped into the shape of a mailbox. The idea of a "mailbox for the dead," however, caught his fancy, and that night he began a story that would fit the title. During his writing he kept recalling his father, whom he had not seen for over 13 years. The next day Langston received a telegram informing him that his father had died the night before at the same time Langston had been writing "Mailbox for the Dead."

Hughes had a good deal of white and Indian blood and in his autobiography tells with amusement of a Southern waiter asking him if he was "a Mexican or Negro"—he could serve a Mexican but not a Negro. Similar incidents plagued Hughes all his life but his sense of humor saw him through. It was a tactic he used even against death. Before he died, for example, Hughes left instructions for his mourners to dress in red, "Cause there ain't no sense/In my being' dead," and requested that at the end of his memorial service a jazz trio play "Do Nothing Till You Hear From Me."

$$\nabla \; \nabla \; \nabla$$

John Huston (1906–1987)
After a preview of his last film, James Joyce's *The Dead* (1987), the director and screenwriter was asked by an interviewer if the picture had done what he wanted it to do. "Yes," he said. "It opens—finally, it opens up another door—and I think that's what Joyce intended. You walk through a series of arches, so to speak, and then, presently, at the end of a corridor, a door opens and you see backward through time, and you feel the flow of time, and realize that you're only part of a great endless procession."

$$\nabla \; \nabla \; \nabla \; \nabla \; \nabla \; \nabla \; \nabla \; \nabla \; \nabla$$

McNair Ilgenfritz (d. 1953)
This aspiring composer thought that by leaving the Metropolitan Opera $150,000 he could accomplish in death what he could not in life—have one of his operas produced by the Met. He failed once again, for the sorely tempted Metropolitan had to refuse his bequest when accused by critics of prostituting the arts.

$$\nabla \; \nabla \; \nabla$$

Robert Ingersoll (1839–1899)
"The Great Agnostic," as Ingersoll was called because of his lectures in defense of freethinking, owned an extensive, celebrated (and much condemned) library of antireligious books. Toward the end of his life an interviewer asked him what the library had cost him. Ingersoll pondered a moment, then replied: "It certainly cost me the Governorship of Illinois, and possibly even the Presidency of the United States."

$$\nabla \; \nabla \; \nabla$$

Prentiss Ingraham (1843–1904)
Ingraham's father, Joseph Holt Ingraham, was also a popular novelist and wrote an infamous fictional history of Aaron Burr, but he did not match the output of his dime-novelist son. Prentiss Ingraham, a solider of fortune, wrote more than

600 novels and a number of plays, including 200 books about his friend Buffalo Bill. He wrote several of his books, 35,000 words each, in one night.

∇ ∇ ∇

Washington Irving (1783–1859)
The first world-famous American writer wrote under at least five pseudonyms at one time or another: Geoffrey Crayon, Gent., Jonathan Oldstyle, Friar Antonio Agrapida, Launcelot Langstaff and Diedrich Knickerbocker.

Irving worked on and finished his comic book, *Diedrich Knickerbocker's A History of New York from the Beginning of the World to the End of the Dutch Dynasty* (1809), while suffering from the intense grief brought by the death of his fiancée, Matilda Hoffman. His next six or seven years were empty and aimless and he remained a bachelor all his life.

"Critics are a kind of freebooters in the republic of letters," he felt, "...like deer, goats and other graminivorous animals [they] gain subsistence by gorging upon buds and leaves of the young shrubs of the forest, thereby robbing them of their verdure and retarding their progress to maturity."

Frequently called "the first American man of letters," Irving nevertheless was dissatisfied with his work, even with his most successful book, *The Sketch Book of Geoffrey Crayon, Gent.* (1819–20), which had made him famous overnight. Late in his life a friend asked Irving which of his books he most valued. "I scarcely look with full satisfaction upon any," he replied; "for they do not seem what they might have been. I often wish that I could have twenty years more, to take them down from the shelf one by one, and write them over."

As far back as 1819 America's first world-famous author was worrying about the great number of books being published in America: "The stream of literature has swollen into a torent—augmented into a river—expanded into a sea...It will soon be the employment of a lifetime merely to learn [books'] names. Many a man of passable information reads scarcely anything but reviews, and before long, a man of erudition will be little better than a mere walking catalogue."

Irving's impatient last words were: "Well, I must arrange my pillows for another weary night! When will this end?"

Helen Hunt Jackson (1831–1885)

The poet, novelist and friend of Emily Dickinson turned to writing after the sudden deaths of her husband and two sons, all within a 10-year period. To make a living she found it necessary to write under the pseudonyms H.H. (Helen Hunt) and Saxe Holm. *Ramona* (1884) and other books on the injustices done to American Indians finally made her famous.

∇ ∇ ∇

Shirley Jackson (1916–1965)

The author and her husband, critic Stanley Edgar Hyman, had about 40,000 books, possibly more than the Bennington Vermont College Library and the Bennington Free Library at the time. It is said that Hyman, calling home to ask her to find a book for him, could invariably tell her exactly where it was, e.g., "On the second floor, to the left of the bathroom door, third row up, sixth book over."

Unsure of the meaning of her famous short story "The Lottery," a *New Yorker* reader wrote to her: "Dear Shirley, I read 'The Lottery.' What does it mean?" She wrote back, on a postcard: "Dear Mr. O'Shaughnessy, I wish I knew."

The success of "The Lottery" inspired her to study witchcraft, and she became convinced that she had supernatural powers. On one occasion she apparently did. After a quarrel with her publisher, Alfred Knopf, she learned that he was going skiing that weekend. Making a wax image of him, she stuck a pin in one leg of the image. Knopf broke that leg skiing.

∇ ∇ ∇

Henry James (1843–1916)

James, who was born in America but later became a British subject, is covered at length in *The Facts On File Book of British Literary Anecdotes*, yet he deserves at least one anecdote here. This one shows that he wasn't a complete Anglophile. "If it is good to have one foot in England," he once observed, "it is still better, or at least as good, to have the other out of it."

∇ ∇ ∇

William James (1842–1910)

Learning that G.K. Chesterton was staying at a house in Sandgate, protected by a high brick wall that flanked his host's garden, the soon-to-be-distinguished American philosopher propped a gardener's ladder up against the wall and scaled it, determined to catch a glimpse of the distinguished English author.

William might have, too, if his far more proper brother Henry hadn't come upon him peeping into Chesterton's garden and made him climb down.

James is one of the few philosophers, if not the only one, ever to experience and record firsthand the effects of an earthquake. His reactions to the great California quake of 1906 are hardly what one would expect, even from a James:

> I was thrown down on my face as it went *fortior*, shaking the room exactly as a terrier shakes a rat. Then everything that was on anything else slid off to the floor, over went bureau and chiffonier with a crash, as the *fortissimo* was reached, plaster cracked, an awful roaring noise seemed to fill the outer air…The thing was over, as I understand the Lick Observatory to have declared, in forty-eight seconds…In any case, sensation and emotion were so strong that little thought, and no reflection or volition, were possible in the short time consumed by the phenomenon. The emotion consisted wholly of glee and admiration; glee at the vividness which such an abstract idea or verbal term as "earthquake" could put on when translated into sensible reality and verified concretely; and admiration at the way in which the frail little wooden house could hold itself together in spite of such a shaking. I felt no trace whatever of fear; it was pure delight and welcome…

A childhood accident caused James' father to lose a leg and may have helped develop the philosophic interests that he passed on to his eldest son. One biographer claims that "the habits acquired with the father's views at dinner and at tea, carried over into the extraordinary sympathetic yet critical manner [William James had] of dealing with anybody's views on any occasion." In any case, the James family arguing at table was often boisterously contentious enough to frighten visitors, notably Ralph Waldo Emerson's son Edward. "Don't be disturbed, Edward," Mrs. James had to tell him one time; "they won't stab each other."

"Never dictate any of your creative work," James instructed a student. "Now let me tell you, I have a brother who used to be a pretty good novelist. But of late he has taken to dictating his stuff, and it has ruined his style. I can't read him any more!"

"I have always said," the esteemed Henry Adams told him, "that you were far away the superior to your brother Henry, and that you could have cut him quite out, if you had turned your pen that way."

An old woman approached him after he gave a lecture on the solar system. "We don't live on a ball rotating around the sun," she said. "We live on a crust of earth on the back of a giant turtle."

"If your theory is correct, madam, what does the turtle stand on?" James asked gently.

"You're a clever man, Mr. James, and that is a good question, but I can answer it. The first turtle stands on the back of a second, far-larger turtle."

"But what does this second turtle stand on?" asked James.

"It's no use, Mr. James!" the old woman crowed. "It's turtles all the way down."

James was shown the six-month-old baby of a friend. Studying and admiring it for a time, he finally said, "It seems a very competent baby." (See also HORACE FLETCHER.)

$$\nabla \ \nabla \ \nabla$$

Robinson Jeffers (1887–1962)
The poet and his wife, Una, lived in a secluded granite house on a cliff overlooking the sea at Carmel, California, and he rarely ventured from home, content to live apart from civilization and write his poems about insignificant man and the ultimate triumph of nature. He told a story of someone below watching him roll a stone into place for the tower he was building on his cliff. Three years later, in 1924, that someone, just returned from China, passed by at twilight again to see Jeffers in the exact same place, rolling another rock into place on top of his slowly emerging tower.

$$\nabla \ \nabla \ \nabla$$

Thomas Jefferson (1743–1826)
The author of the Declaration of Independence liked to tell a story about the document being signed as quickly as it was because the Continental Congress met near a livery stable. It seems that the stable bred huge horseflies that incessantly attacked the members in their short breeches and silk hose. Unable to repel the flies with their hands and handkerchiefs, the delegates quickly affixed their signatures to the momentous document and fled the building.

He was a man who knew no social distinctions. Hating even the honorific "Mr.," he wore the plainest clothes, walked instead of rode to his inauguration as president, received a dandy swordbearing minister dressed in a bathrobe and down-at- the-heel slippers. "If it is possible," he once said of his correspondence, "to be certainly conscious of anything, I am conscious of feeling no different between writing to the highest and lowest being on earth."

Though he practiced seven years as a lawyer and made good money at it, he had a low opinion of lawyers, "whose trade it is," he once said, "to question everything, yield nothing, and talk by the hour."

Jefferson was never truly happy unless in the country, and he was happiest when gardening. He once wrote to a friend that he would rather have been a gardener than president:

> I have often thought that if heaven had given me a choice of my position and calling, it should have been on a rich spot of earth, well watered, and near a good market for the productions of the garden. No occupation is so delightful to me as the culture of the earth, and no culture comparable to that of the garden. Such a variety of subjects, some one always coming to perfection, the failure of one thing repaired by the success of another, and instead of one harvest a continued one through the year. Under a total want of demand except for our family table, I am still devoted to the garden. But though an old man, I am but a young gardener!

While he was traveling as a young man Jefferson's house burned down, almost everything in it destroyed. "Not one of my books saved?" Jefferson asked the slave who brought him the news. "No, master," the slave replied, "but we saved your fiddle." (Jefferson patiently rebuilt his library.)

After the British burned down the Library of Congress in 1814, Jefferson sold to the nation for $23,950 some 13,000 volumes of his own book collection to form the basis of the new national library. Sixteen wagonloads of books—3,000 pounds in each wagon—were shipped from Monticello to the capital over the period of a few days, the carters getting four dollars a load.

In an 1818 letter to a friend he took a stand against the novel, then coming into fashion in America as a fictional form: "When this poison infects the mind, it destroys its tone and revolts it against wholesome reading."

A true horseman, Jefferson always rode two to three hours a day. He was so fastidious about the grooming of his horses that he customarily brushed his white handkerchief across his horse's back when it was brought to him, sending the mount back to the stable if he detected any dust.

Today Jefferson might be regarded as a unitarian or member of an ethical culture society. A sincere deist interested in the ethical teachings of Christianity, he compiled a selection of Jesus' teachings from the New Testament that is still known as Jefferson's Bible.

"Are you to replace Monsieur Franklin?" the French minister for foreign affairs asked Jefferson when he arrived in France to represent the United States in 1785. "I succeed him," Jefferson replied. "No one can replace him."

Writing to John Adams late in his life, Jefferson bemoaned the number of letters he had to answer every year. These came to 2,267, or over six letters a day, many of his answers "requiring...elaborate research" and his prompt attention. "Is this life?" he asked Adams.

Generosity bankrupted Jefferson in his last years. After leaving the presidency, with a personal debt of some $20,000, contracted in maintaining his position properly, he went deeper into debt because people took advantage of him. "Relatives, invited guests, and strangers filled Monticello [frequently beds were made for a score and more, sometimes for fifty]," one writer noted. "They stayed for days, weeks, even months, drank his choice French wines, kept their horses in his stables. For solitude he had to retire to a second home, constructed as a refuge." In his last year, only a national subscription of $16,500 saved him from bankruptcy and enabled him to die in peace. He died on July 4, 1826, the 50th anniversary of the Declaration of Independence, on the same day as John Adams. His last words, on awakening from a coma, were: "Is it the Fourth?" A few months after his death, however, all his silver, furniture, pictures and Monticello itself had to be sold to pay his debts.

∇ ∇ ∇

Nunnally Johnson (1897–1977)
The Hollywood screenwriter, whose films include the classic *The Three Faces of Eve* (1957), was asked how he'd manage writing for the new wide screen. "Very simple," he replied. "I'll just put the paper in sideways."

∇ ∇ ∇

James Jones (1922–1977)
The American novelist was famous among the Parisian literati for his practical jokes. One time his friend, bar-owner Jean Castel, complained to him that business was bad because a crazy old Romanian woman constantly bothered his customers, playing a loud, squeaky mandolin and shouting curses through the doorway. Castel finally announced that he was going to get away from it all in Tahiti for a few weeks. Jones collected money from his friends and sent the Romanian woman there several days before Castel left Paris. When Castel got off the plane, there she was, playing her squeaky mandolin and shouting, "God damn it, welcome to Tahiti, Monsieur Castel!"

The highest word rate ever paid to a professional author is the $15,000 Darryl Zanuck gave Jones for correcting a line of dialogue in the film *The Longest Day*. Jones and his wife Gloria were sitting on the beach when they changed the line "I can't eat that bloody old box of tunny fish" to "I can't stand this damned old tuna fish." The chore of deleting two words and changing four came to $2,500 a word, far higher than the record amount *The Guinness Book of World Records* credits to Ernest Hemingway. Hemingway received $15 a word for a 2,000-word article on bullfighting that he wrote for *Sports Illustrated* in 1960. His payment came to $30,000, 30 times the going rate at that time for an article of that length.

"I do think that the quality which makes a man want to write and be read is essentially a desire for self-exposure and is masochistic," Jones told an interviewer. "Like one of those guys who has a compulsion to take his thing out and show it on the street."

Though he labored against time and pain, working up to 14 hours a day to complete *Whistle*, the final novel in his World War II trilogy, Jones died before he could finish the final chapter. His book was completed by author William Morris, based on Jones' notes and conversations the novelist had had with his good friend.

∇ ∇ ∇

David Jung (fl. early 20th century)
The cookie with a fortune inside was invented in 1918 by David Jung, a contemporary Chinese immigrant who had established Los Angeles's Hong Kong Noodle Company. Jung got the idea after noting how bored customers got while waiting for their orders in Chinese restaurants. He employed a Presbyterian minister (the first fortune cookie author!) to write condensations of Biblical messages and later hired as a writer Marie Raine, the wife of one of his salesmen, who became the Shakespeare of fortune cookies, writing thousands of classic fortunes such as "Your feet shall walk upon a plush carpet of contentment." The Hong Kong Noodle Company is still in business, as are hundreds of other fortune cookie "publishers."

∇ ∇ ∇ ∇ ∇ ∇ ∇ ∇ ∇

George S. Kaufman (1889–1961)
One of the wits at the Algonquin Round Table made an anti-Semitic remark to Kaufman "in the spirit of fun." The playwright retaliated with mock indignation. "For my part, I've heard enough slurs," he cried. "I am now leaving this table, this dining room, this hotel—never ever to return!" Pausing, he glanced at

Dorothy Parker, whose mother was Jewish and father was Christian. "And I trust Miss Parker will walk out with me," he added. "Halfway."

One afternoon at the Algonquin's Round Table Kaufman was asked to supply a definition of satire. "Satire," he replied, "is what closes on Saturday night."

Some of Kaufman's best ripostes were made during sessions of the Thanatopsis poker club, which took its name from the club in Sinclair Lewis' *Main Street* and had as its members such bright literary lights as Ring Lardner, Alexander Woollcott, Harold Ross and Marc Connelly. Kaufman, an expert player, once dropped out of a hand with a pair of tens showing, punning, "I will now fold my tens and silently steal away."

Kaufman worried about the lyrics of Irving Berlin's "Always." "'Always' seems like such a long time," he told the composer. "Why don't you make it, 'I'll be loving you on Thursday.'"

Alexander Woollcott had created the eponymous cocktail the Alexander, made with cream, creme de cacao and other dreadful ingredients. The "lethal mixture...tasted like ice cream," Helen Hayes said. "I drank one down and took another and drank it down, and I was blind." Searching for something to say, fearing everyone would think her drunk if she didn't, Miss Hayes remembered that she would be moving soon to a smaller apartment and wanted to get rid of her large piano. But her words came out: "Anyone who wants my piano, is willing to it." After a long, terrible silence, Kaufman said: "That's very seldom of you, Helen."

Kaufman had a precocious wit and vocabulary. When he was four, his mother told him his aunt would be visiting soon. "It wouldn't hurt to be nice to her, would it?" she asked. "That depends," Kaufman replied, "on your threshold of pain."

"What's my motivation for doing it?" a young method actor asked when Kaufman told him to make a certain stage movement. "Your job," Kaufman replied.

"There's no scenery at all," said an actress describing a new play she was rehearsing. "In the first scene, I'm on the left side of the stage and the audience has to imagine I'm eating dinner in a restaurant. Then in scene two, I move over to the right side of the stage, and the audience has to imagine I'm in my drawing room."

"And the second night," Kaufman said, "*you* have to imagine there's an audience out front."

Kaufman's bridge partner, who played terribly all afternoon, asked to be excused to go to the men's room. "Gladly," Kaufman replied. "For the first time today I'll know what you have in your hand."

The author of a panned Broadway show had the misfortune to run into Kaufman shortly afterward. "I understand," Kaufman said, "that your play is full of single entendre."

Popular singer Eddie Fisher, appearing on a television show, told Kaufman that women refused to date him because he looked so young. He asked Kaufman's advice and the author replied:

> Mr. Fisher, on Mount Wilson there is a telescope that can magnify the most distant stars up to twenty-four times the magnification of any previous telescope. This remarkable instrument was unsurpassed until the construction of the Mount Palomar telescope, an even more remarkable instrument of magnification. Owing to advances and improvements in optical technology, it is capable of magnifying the stars to four times the magnification and resolution of the Mount Wilson telescope— Mr. Fisher, if you could somehow put the Mount Wilson telescope *inside* the Mount Palomar telescope, you *still* wouldn't be able to detect my interest in your problem.

Charlie Chaplin was said to be richer than he was famous. One day he remarked to Kaufman that his blood pressure was down to 108. "Common or preferred," Kaufman inquired.

Kaufman was outraged at Paramount Pictures' offer of $30,000 for the film rights to one of his plays. He countered by offering $40,000 for Paramount.

The playwright met with Broadway producer Jed Harris at Harris's Waldorf Astoria suite and for some reason known only to himself Harris squatted naked on the floor for the whole meeting. If he meant to shock Kaufman it didn't work, for the great wit didn't say a word about his nakedness until he was leaving. Then, with hand on the doorknob, Kaufman stared at Harris and advised, "Jed, your fly is open."

After the flop of his adaptation of the French farce *Someone in the House*, Kaufman suggested the following advertising slogan to the producer: "Avoid crowds, see *Someone in the House* at the Knickerbocker Theatre."

Between acts the writer-director sent a telegram to actor William Gaxton, who was playing the president in Kaufman's 1932 Pulitzer Prize-winning play *Of Thee I Sing*: AM WATCHING YOUR PERFORMANCE FROM THE REAR OF THE HOUSE. WISH YOU WERE HERE.

After reading a manuscript filled with spelling errors, Kaufman told the author: "I'm not very good at it myself, but the first rule about spelling is that there is only one z in *is*."

Waiters were Kaufman's pet hate; he believed they were actually trained to exasperate him and other customers. His many remarks about the breed culminated with his mock epitaph for a dead waiter: "God finally caught his eye."

"After all, it's only a small, insignificant theater," explained a summer stock producer who had used a Kaufman play without paying royalties.
"Then you'll go to a small, insignificant jail," Kaufman replied.

"How do I get our leading lady's name in the *Times*?" the press agent for a musical asked Kaufman when he was drama critic at that newspaper. "Shoot her," Kaufman advised.

"Guido Nazzo is nazzo guido," Kaufman wrote in a review of a young operatic tenor. The wisecrack was so widely repeated that it nearly ruined the singer's career. Kaufman was so truly sorry that he apologized to Nazzo and offered him a part in one of his plays.

All through dinner the woman at his side didn't shut up, giving him her opinions on a wide variety of subjects and never letting him get a word in edgewise. When dessert was served, Kaufman finally turned to her and said, "Madam, don't you have any unexpressed thoughts?"

When Kaufman was scriptwriter for the Marx Brothers' *Coconuts*, Groucho tried to slip one of his jokes into a scene. Kaufman thought it was terrible. "They laughed at Fulton and his steamboat, too," Groucho groused. "Not at matinees," Kaufman said.

S.N. Behrman had been given a farewell party on the eve of his planned departure from Hollywood to New York. He didn't leave the next day because the studio asked him to do some emergency rewriting. When Kaufman ran into him on the lot, he quipped, "Ah, forgotten but not gone."

After Clifford Odets had written a rather anemic play Kaufman asked him, "Odets, where is thy sting?"

Clarence Budington Kelland (1881–1964)

The popular novelist, noted for his wit, was in great demand as a toastmaster. "Gentlemen," he once said, as he began his introductory remarks, "the obvious duty of a toastmaster is to be so infernally dull that the succeeding speakers will appear brilliant by contrast. However ..." and here Kelland glanced at the listing of speakers he would introduce, "I've looked over this list and I don't believe I can do it."

∇ ∇ ∇

Rockwell Kent (1882–1971)

The colophon—trademark or emblem—of Viking Press was in fact responsible for the American book publisher's name, rather than the other way round. When the company was founded in 1925, the founders wanted to call it Half-Moon Press, after Henry Hudson's ship, and they commissioned Rockwell Kent to design a suitable colophon. However, the artist did not care for the old English vessel and, using artistic license, elected to draw a *drakkar*, a type of ship used by the Vikings. The design was so effective that the company changed its name.

∇ ∇ ∇

Jerome Kern (1885–1945)

An affected actress annoyed the composer and playwright throughout rehearsals with her rolled *r's*. "Tell me, Mr. Kern," she finally said, "you want me to c-rr-ross the stage, but I'm behind a table. How shall I get acr-rr-ross?"

  "Why, my dear," Kern replied, "just r-r-oll over on your *r's*."

∇ ∇ ∇

Jack Kerouac (1922–1969)

Kerouac is said to have typed out his famous novel *On the Road* on one continuous role of teletype paper. "Beat generation" seems certainly to have been coined by the novelist as a name for the fifties' "lost generation," though it was first used in John Clellon Holmes's novel *Go!* (1957). Kerouac once recalled that he borrowed the term from a drug addict named Herbert Huncke and used it in a wider application: "John Clellon Holmes and I were sitting around trying to think up the meaning of the Lost Generation and the subsequent existentialism and I said, 'You know, this is really a beat generation,' and he leapt up and said, 'that's it, that's right.'" Later Kerouac claimed "beat" meant "beatific, blissfully happy." That "you got the beat." (See also TRUMAN CAPOTE.)

Frances Parkinson Keyes (1885–1970)

The popular American romance novelist was the inventor of the little blue flag with the gold star in it that since World War II has been the American symbol of remembrance for loved ones lost in war and was the inspiration for the term "gold star mother."

▽ ▽ ▽

George Lyman Kittredge (1860–1941)

This Harvard educator and author was asked by a colleague why as brilliant a scholar as himself didn't have a Ph.D. "My dear sir," Kittredge replied, "who could *examine* me?"

▽ ▽ ▽

Charles Klein (1867–1915)

The popular playwright, who went down with the *Lusitania*, had great successes with *The Music Master* (1904) and *The Auctioneer* (1901), but his *The Ne'er Do Well* did terribly. Sitting dejectedly in the audience as the final curtain went down on opening night he felt a finger tap him on the shoulder. "Mr. Klein," the young lady behind him said, "before the curtain rose I took the liberty of cutting off a lock of your hair. Now I would like to give it back."

▽ ▽ ▽

James J. Kilroy (1902–1962)

No catchphrase has rivaled "Kilroy was here" ever since it appeared on walls and every other available surface during World War II. It was first presumed that Kilroy was fictional; one graffiti expert even insisted that *Kilroy* represented an Oedipal fantasy, combining "kill" with "roi" (the French word for "king"). But word sleuths found that James J. Kilroy, a politician and an inspector in a Quincy, Massachusetts, shipyard, had coined the slogan. Kilroy chalked the words on ships and crates of equipment to indicate that he had inspected them. From Quincy the phrase traveled on ships and crates all over the world, copied by GIs wherever it went, and Kilroy, who died in Boston in 1962 at the age of 60, became the most widely "published" man since Shakespeare.

▽ ▽ ▽

Alfred Kinsey (1894–1956)

Shortly after the scientist's monumental *Kinsey Report On Sexual Behavior* was published, his wife told a reporter, "I don't see so much of Alfred any more since he got so interested in sex."

Marc Klaw (1858–1936)

The Broadway producer remarked that all first-night audiences were composed of two types of people: "Theatre habitués and sons of habitués."

∇ ∇ ∇

Alfred Knopf (1892–1984)

The esteemed publisher was talking about book returns from bookstores when he observed, "Gone today, here tomorrow."

∇ ∇ ∇ ∇ ∇ ∇ ∇ ∇ ∇

Louis L'Amour (1908–1988)

Probably the most prolific western author of all time, with 101 books and hundreds of millions of dollars in sales, the writer once observed, "I'm like a big old hen. I can't cluck too much about the egg I've just laid because five more are pushing to come out."

∇ ∇ ∇

Sidney Lanier (1842–1881)

His four-year imprisonment during the Civil War broke the Southern poet's health and he suffered from consumption the rest of his short days, often abandoning his work because of feebleness and poverty. "Pretty much the whole of life has been merely not dying," he once told a friend.

∇ ∇ ∇

Ring Lardner (1885–1933)

The humorist once told the gullible Harold Ross of *The New Yorker* that he wrote his stories by jotting down "a few widely separated words or phrases on a piece of paper" before he "went back and filled in the spaces." Ross always believed him.

Lardner claimed that an ex-coroner he knew once wrote an ode to his mother with the line: "If perchance the inevitable should come…"

He was by nature aloof and detached. At a Dorothy Parker party he told everyone who didn't know him that he was a recent emigrant from Poland so that they wouldn't expect him to speak.

Until Lardner wrote *You Know Me, Al* (1916), one critic observed, "no one had ever considered *of* to be an auxiliary verb. Who would of thought of it but the man with the phonographic ear for American speech."

At a Friar's Club dinner a fellow member asked Lardner to read a syruppy poem by the man's late brother, who had passed away 20 years ago. On finishing, Lardner turned to the man and inquired, "Did your brother write this before or after he died?"

Asked to contribute to a symposium on how the wives of prominent men had helped them, Lardner did not give any of the usual hackneyed answers to the trite question. He replied:

> In 1914 or 1915, I think it was July, she cleaned my white shoes. She dusted my typewriter in 1922. Late one night in 1924, we got home from somewhere and I said I was hungry and she gave me a verbal picture of the location of the pantry. Another time I quit cigarettes and she felt sorry for me. Once on a trip just as I was nearly crazy trying to guess whether I should take the lower or upper berth she solved the problem by crawling into the lower berth.

Though he wrote some of the funniest stories in the English language, Lardner was a quiet, solemn man who rarely smiled or laughed. "A noble dignity flowed from him," F. Scott Fitzgerald once said. And his friend, sportswriter Hugh Fullerton, said he "looked like Rameses II with his wrappings off." He so disliked jokes that whenever anyone warned him "Stop me if you've heard this one," he invariably cried "Stop!"

Of his friends the Fitzgeralds he said: "Mr. Fitzgerald is a novelist. Mrs. Fitzgerald is a novelty."

Lardner was well into his cups at the Lambs Club when a wild-haired, wild-eyed actor passed the bar. The writer looked up and said nothing, but when the actor passed by a second time, he stopped him and inquired, "How do you look when I'm sober?"

Perhaps the most famous of Lardner's quips was inspired by the writer's move with his family from Chicago to New York, where he began his syndicated column. Somehow the Lardners went astray in the Bronx. The famous exchange came when the author's son asked him if they were lost, Lardner later recreating the scene in his short story "The Young Immigrants," told from a child's viewpoint:

"Are you lost, Daddy?" I asked tenderly.

"Shut up," he explained.

"Don't make the mistake of enclosing a self-addressed envelope big enough for the manuscript to come back in," Lardner told a young writer. "This is too much of a temptation for the editor."

After visiting "Silent Cal" Coolidge at the White House, Lardner confided to friends, "I told him my funniest story, and he laughed so hard you could hear a pin drop."

He was "six foot three inches of kindness," said Scott Fitzgerald, one of his favorite drinking companions out in Great Neck, New York. One time the two of them performed a drunken dance on the lawn of the Nelson Doubleday estate in nearby Oyster Bay. They were honoring Joseph Conrad, who was staying there as Doubleday's guest, but Conrad never got to see the three-o'clock-in-the-morning ballet, which was interrupted by an unliterary caretaker.

∇ ∇ ∇

Berthold Laufer (1873–1934)

The Chicago-born writer has been nominated by Russel Ash and Brian Lake in their *Bizarre Books* (1986) as the author of the most unusual scholarly works. These include *Ostrich Egg-shell Cups of Mesopotamia, Was Oderic of Pordenone Ever in Tibet?* and *The Eskimo Screw as a Culture-Historical Problem*. However, his work is not nearly so unusual as several popular books cited by Ash and Lake, including *The Romance of the Holes in Bread* (1924), *The Romance of Leprosy* (1949), and *The Romance of Lust* (1873–76, four volumes).

∇ ∇ ∇

Gypsy Rose Lee (Rose Louise Hovick; 1892–1984)

A writer of mysteries as well as a stripper, the esteemed ecdysiast had a low opinion of writing as a profitable profession. "Royalties are nice and all that," she observed, "but shaking the beads brings in money quicker."

A pretentious chorus girl tried to snub the stripteaser. Said Ms. Lee of the lady: "She is descended from a long line that her mother fell for."

∇ ∇ ∇

William Ellery Leonard (1876–1944)
This prolific poet taught at the University of Wisconsin. Though New Jersey born, Professor Leonard remained within the city limits of Madison for decades out of his fear of trains and travel, or the "locomotive god," which is the title of his psychoanalytic autobiography.

∇ ∇ ∇

Frank Leslie (1821–1880)
Engraver and publisher Henry Carter used the pseudonym Frank Leslie in England before immigrating to New York, where he founded the immensely popular *Frank Leslie's Popular Monthly* in 1876. His magazine proved so successful because Carter hit upon the idea of dividing his drawings into blocks which several engravers worked upon and later reassembled, this enabling him to publish illustrated current events long before his competitors. On his death his widow legally adopted his pseudonym as her name in seeking to protect his interests.

∇ ∇ ∇

(Harry) Sinclair Lewis (1885–1951)
A young woman wrote to the author asking for a position as his secretary. She promised to do anything for him, emphasizing that "When I say anything, I mean *anything*." Mrs. Lewis happened to come upon the letter and answered it, advising the young woman that Lewis already had a secretary and that she, his wife, did everything else herself. "And when I say everything," she added, "I mean *everything*."

Even while at Yale Lewis was noted for his nonstop talking, which could literally go on for hours. So much noted, in fact, that he was nicknamed "God Forbid"—meaning God forbid that one be cornered by him.

At Yale he kept a diary in which one entry read: "*the village virus*—I shall have to write a book of how it getteth into the veins of a man good and true." This was the germ of the idea of *Main Street*, written 15 years later.

A possibly apocryphal story has it that at a class reunion long after his Yale days, "Red" Lewis was hailed by speaker after speaker as a giant among authors whose genius they had all recognized and nurtured even in his undergraduate days. But when it came his turn to speak, the novelist remembered it this way: "When I came to Yale I was a freckle-faced, red-haired, gangling, gawky green-horn from a small town in Minnesota, and all of you either ignored me or high-hatted me. Now that I've been lucky enough to achieve a little notoriety, you've changed your tune and are trying horn in on the act. You were not my friends then, and you're not my friends now. And as far as I'm concerned, you can all go to hell." With that he walked out of the room.

As with Kipling, Lewis's first editorial employer thought little of his literary ability. Declared publisher Frederick A. Stokes in 1910 when Lewis worked for him as a manuscript reader; "You are not cut out to be a writer, that's all there is to it."

His first novel, *Our Mr. Wrenn* (1914), would be accepted only if he would agree to extensive changes, no easy condition for such a monumental ego. For over an hour a kind but firm editor explained just what these changes would be. Lewis listened, squirming in his seat, and when she finally finished, he said: "Now *praise* me!"

When Lewis was first introduced to critics Henry Mencken and George Jean Nathan, he draped his arms around their necks and began one of the long, immodest monologues he was so famous for:

> So you guys are writers, are you? Well let me tell you something. I'm the best writer in this here gottdamn country and if you, Georgie, and you, Hank, don't know it now, you'll know it gottdamn soon. Say, I've just finished a book that'll be published in a week or two and its the gottdamn best book of its kind that this here gottdamn country has had and don't you guys forget it! I worked a year on the gottdamn thing and it's the goods, I'm a-telling you! Listen, when it comes to writing a novel, I'm so far ahead of most of the men you two think are good that I'll be gottdamned if it doesn't make me sick to think of it! Just wait till you read the gottdamn thing. You've got a treat coming, Georgie and Hank, and don't you boys make no mistake about that!

When Lewis finally left, Mencken observed, "Of all the idiots I've ever laid eyes on, that fellow is the worst."

"A numbskull," his fellow *Smart Set* editor agreed.

But later, after *Main Street* appeared in 1920, Mencken found himself writing to Nathan:

Dear George:

Grab hold of the bar-rail, steady yourself, and prepare yourself for a terrible shock! I've just read the book of that *Lump* we met at Schmidt's and, by God, he has done the job! It's a genuinely excellent piece of work. Get it as soon as you can and take a look. I begin to believe that perhaps there isn't a God after all. There is no justice in the world. Yours in Xt.,

M

In a 1926 letter he declined the Pulitzer Prize for his novel *Arrowsmith*: "Every compulsion is put upon writers to become safe, polite, obedient, and sterile. In protest, I declined election to the National Institute of Arts and Letters some years ago, and now I must decline the Pulitzer Prize." He never received a Pulitzer but he did consent to become a member of the National Institute of Arts and Letters in 1935.

He enraged people throughout the country when, shortly after he published *Elmer Gantry* in 1927, he accepted an invitation to speak in a Kansas City church. Once in the pulpit, he took out his watch. Then he advised the congregation that he was going to give God 15 minutes to prove His existence by striking him dead.

Walking down Madison Avenue one morning in May 1928, Lewis suddenly stopped and exclaimed to his wife Dorothy Thompson: "Within a year this country will have a terrible financial panic. I know! Can't you see it? Can't you smell it? I can see people jumping out of windows on this very street!" His amazing prophecy of course came true a year later with the stock market crash of 1929 that ushered in the Great Depression.

It is said that his animated "ceaseless volubility" was unmatched in literary annals. Recalled Rebecca West of a visit with him: "After five solid hours I ceased to look upon him as a human being; I could think of him only as a great natural force, like the aurora borealis."

He became almost persona non grata is England, saying things like "England is the nicest part of America." English historian Philip Guedalla told a friend, "You are an American and I have a message for you. If your country does not recall Sinclair Lewis at once, there will be war between England and the United States."

"How many of you are serious about being writers?" Lewis asked a group of students attending his lecture at Columbia University on the writer's craft. All of the students raised their hands. "Well, why the hell aren't you all home writing?" Lewis said, ending his lecture.

Queen Liliuokalani (1838–1917)

The Hawaiian queen is the only ruler known to have written her or his national anthem. A prolific songwriter, she wrote the words and music to "Aloha Oe" ("Farewell to Thee"), today Hawaii's unofficial state song.

∇ ∇ ∇

Abraham Lincoln (1807–1865)

Whether the stories are true or not it has long been part of American legend that he learned to read by the light of a fireplace and learned to write with charcoal on the back of a shovel. Another story has him borrowing David Ramsay's *Life of Washington* from a farmer, losing the book, and working for him three days to pay for it.

"It may be doubted whether any man of our generation has plunged more deeply into the sacred fount of learning," Lincoln was advised of a prominent historian.

"Yes, or come up drier," he replied.

Immediately after delivering the Gettysberg Address he commented: "Lamon, that speech won't scour [a word he used to express the conviction that something lacked merit], and the people are disappointed." This wasn't true of most of the audience, who were simply too deeply stirred to react.

Reported the *Chicago Times* on the Gettysburg Address: "The cheek of every American must tingle with shame as he reads the silly, flat, and dishwatery utterances of the man who has to be pointed out to intelligent foreigners as the President of the United States."

One story has it that when Barnum brought his circus to Washington early in the Civil War, he presented his midgets General Tom Thumb and Admiral Nutt to President Lincoln. After shaking hands Lincoln remarked, "You have some pretty small generals, Barnum, but I think I can beat you."

Lincoln, furious about McClellan's failure to attack despite his numerical superiority over the Confederates, channeled his anger by writing the general a one-line masterpiece of sarcasm: "If you don't want to use the army, I should like to borrow it for a while. Yours respectfully, A. Lincoln."

Discussing a book with the British correspondent G.W.E. Russell, he remarked: "People who like this sort of thing will find this the sort of thing they like."

Lincoln lost his temper with a woman who wrote him requesting his autograph and a "sentiment" at a time when thousands were dying every day. "Dear Madam," he replied. "When you ask from a stranger that which is of interest only to yourself, always enclose a stamp. There's your sentiment, and here's my autograph. A. Lincoln."

Frantic with grief after the president's funeral, Lincoln's 12-year-old son Tad asked a caller at the White House, "Do you think my father has gone to heaven?"
"I have no doubt of it," the man replied.
"Then I am glad," Tad said, "for he never was happy after he came here. This was not a good place for him."

Traveling in a wild region of the Caucasus, Tolstoy was befriended by a devout Circassian chief who wanted to hear about the world outside his mountains. After Tolstoy went on at length about the outside world, the chief insisted: "But you have not told us about the greatest general and ruler of the world. We want to know something about him. He was a hero. He spoke with a voice of thunder, he laughed like the sunrise, his deeds were strong as the rock and as sweet as the fragrance of roses. He was so great that he even forgave the crimes of his greatest enemies and shook brotherly hands with those who had plotted against his life. His name was Lincoln and the country in which he lived is called America...Tell us of that man."
Word of Abraham Lincoln had reached even this remote area.

∇ ∇ ∇

Vachel Lindsay (1879–1931)

Lindsay's poetry readings by no means appealed only to the "untutored democratic masses." After he appeared at Oxford University it was reported: "By two minutes he had the respectable and intellectual and cynical audience listening. By ten, intensely excited; by twenty, elated and losing self-control; by half an hour completely under his influence; by forty minutes roaring like a bonfire. At the end of the hour they lifted off the roof and refused to disperse ..."

No American poet read his poems as well, in tones ranging from whisper to bellow, his body all the while speaking as subtly and emphatically as his voice. It was a natural gift, with him from the beginning, and he rather prosaically attributed it to his forefathers who had for centuries called hogs.

He recited or performed his poem "General William Booth Enters into Heaven" all over the United States. But he insisted that whenever possible he be backed up by music of "kettle drums, piccolo, flute, and birchbark moosecall."

The poet chose a horrible way to kill himself—he drank disinfectant. He may have been influenced in his choice of method by British poet Charlotte Mew, who committed suicide the same way three years earlier. (See LANGSTON HUGHES.)

∇ ∇ ∇

George Lippard (1822–1854)

The eccentric author's *Quaker City* (1844), the best-selling novel of its time, had as its premise that a kind of devil-worship congress governed America. But today he is remembered mainly for his creation of the legend that the Liberty Bell in Philadelphia proclaimed freedom throughout all the land on July 4, 1776.

∇ ∇ ∇

Horace Liveright (1886–1933)

The noted publisher, who published the early work of Ernest Hemingway and other great writers, made a deal with Theodore Dreiser to sell the movie rights to *An American Tragedy* (1925), his commission being 50 percent of anything over $50,000. When he made the difficult sale Dreiser cursed him for taking his commission, threw a cup of coffee in his face and stalked out of the restaurant where he had been invited by Liveright to celebrate the sale. Liveright turned to his associate, Bennett Cerf, wiping the coffee off his face. "Bennett," he said, "let this be a lesson to you. Every author is a son of a bitch."

The publisher of Sherwood Anderson, Dreiser, Hemingway, T.S. Eliot, Ezra Pound, Dorothy Parker, Edgar Lee Masters, Robinson Jeffers, Bertrand Russell and so many other greats was a serious and generous man when it came to literature, but his editorial offices were called "the asylum" by people who worked there. To set the tone, Liveright—who lived up to his name—had in his office a hidden bedroom where he conducted his daily affairs; when he pushed a button on the wall, a section of bookcase swung out to reveal a bed all done up in lace. He found this necessary to keep his affairs secret from both his wife and his mistress.

∇ ∇ ∇

Richard Adams Locke (1800–1871)

Twelve Ameicans have walked on the moon by now and none has seen any evidence of life there, but in 1835, according to *New York Sun* reporter Richard

Adams Locke, the eminent British astronomer Sir John Herschel trained a powerful new telescope on the moon and observed some 15 species of animals residing on the satellite, including what seemed to be a race of winged men. Locke's article, supposedly reprinted from the actually defunct *Edinburgh Journal of Science*, raised the circulation of James Gordon Bennett's newspaper from 2,500 to 20,000 and inspired one ladies' club to raise money to send missionaries to the moon. A book that the *Sun* reporter made from the article sold over 60,000 copies, and was studied assiduously by a scientific delegation from Yale. Locke finally admitted his hoax the following year, calling it a satire on absurd scientific speculations that had gotten out of hand. His friend Poe, who never believed a word of the story, nevertheless admitted that it had anticipated most of his own "Hans Pfaall," and was the reason he left that story unfinished.

▽ ▽ ▽

John Griffith "Jack" London (1876–1916)

A foolhardy magazine editor sent a note to London's hotel demanding a story the American author was late in delivering. "Dear Jack London," it read. "If I don't receive the story within 24 hours, I'll come up to your room and kick you downstairs, and I always keep my promises."

For once London did not retaliate with his fists.

"Dear Dick," he wrote back. "If I did all my work with my feet, I'd keep my promises, too."

Near the end of the 19th century, Frank Norris wrote: "The Great American Novel is not extinct like the Dodo, but mythical like the Hippogriff ... the thing to be looked for is not the Great American Novelist, but the Great Novelist who shall also be American." Observed Jack London a little later: "I'd rather win a water-fight in a swimming pool, or remain astride a horse that is trying to get out from under me, than write the great American novel."

His appetites were odd, to say the least. Often he would sit down to a meal of raw duck.

Toward the end of his life he told a friend: "I write for no other purpose than to add to the beauty that now belongs to me. I write a book for no other reason than to add three or four hundred acres to my magnificent estate."

He would have liked knowing that he is the most widely read American author in the world (according to a recent survey). He loved to be idolized. When his Korean houseboy Manyoungis took to calling him "Mr. God," he thoroughly enjoyed the designation and deification.

Ray Long (d. 1954)

Soon after he was dismissed from his post as the longtime editor of *Cosmopolitan* magazine, Ray Long committed suicide. Thus began the most violent period in American magazine history. Next, Long's successor Harry Payne Burton was fired and then took his own life with an overdose of sleeping pills. Then, an assistant editor who had hoped for the job of *Cosmopolitan* editor hanged herself when she didn't get the post. Finally, the woman in charge of the magazine's editorial production jumped or fell off a ship in the Atlantic and drowned.

∇ ∇ ∇

Henry Wadsworth Longfellow (1807–1882)

Longfellow's first published poem, "The Battle of Lowell's Pond," appeared in the *Portland* (Me.) *Gazette* when he was only 13 years old.

It was just after he had witnessed his little daughter Edith strongly protesting her mother's attempts to curl her hair that he wrote the famous "There Was a Little Girl":

> There was a little girl
> Who had a little curl
> Right in the middle of her forehead;
> And when she was good
> She was very, very good.
> But when she was bad she was horrid.

A huge submerged rock off the coast of Gloucester, Massachusetts, caused so many shipwrecks in the 18th century that it was called Norman's Woe. Wrote Longfellow in his diary for December 17, 1837: "News of shipwrecks horrible on the coast. 20 bodies washed ashore near Gloucester, one lashed to a piece of wreck. There is a reef called Norman's Woe where many of these took place; among others the schooner *Hesperus*...I must write a ballad upon this." The ballad proved to be "The Wreck of the Hesperus" (1842), which Longfellow wrote in bed while suffering nights from severe insomnia.

While he was a professor at Harvard Longfellow decided to shed his work and devote himself entirely to poetry, to "rise and right [himself] like a ship that throws out some of its cargo." Soon after, in 1854, he resigned his post.

Longfellow became the first (and one of the few) American poets to earn a living solely by writing poems. He was also the first American to be honored with a bust in the Poet's Corner in Westminster Abbey.

"Some critics," he observed, "are like the chimney-sweepers; they scrape a long time in the chimney, cover themselves with soot, and bring nothing away but a bag of cinders, and then sing out from the top of the house as if they had built it." Another time he compared critics to "woodpeckers, who, instead of enjoying the fruit and shadow of a tree, hop incessantly around the trunk pecking holes in the bark to discover some little worm or another." Youthful critics especially annoyed him. "A young critic," he said, "is like a boy with a gun; he fires at every living thing he sees. He thinks only of his own skill, not the pain he is giving."

Late in Longfellow's life an English tourist who made a call on him explained that he usually visited the historic ruins in countries where he traveled. "But you have no ruins in your [young] country," he told the poet, "and I thought I would call and see *you*."

There was more true tragedy in Longfellow's life than in his poems. In the summer of 1861 his wife of 18 years was sitting by an open window when she dropped a lighted match on her long dress. Longfellow, awaking from a nap, managed to smother her flaming body with a rug, but was too late to save her life. The poet was so badly burned on the face that he later adopted the beard he became noted for. And, although great fame came to him (*The Courtship of Miles Standish* sold 15,000 copies the first day it was published in 1858), the tragic domestic accident halted the poet's creative work for many years. His grief is still clearly seen in "The Cross of Snow," written 17 years after his wife's death.

Longfellow was asked how, when an old man, he could write so many happy, childlike things, full of joy and wonder. He replied that Governor Endicott's pear tree, 200 years old, "still bears fruit not to be distinguished from a young tree in flavor."

∇ ∇ ∇

Augustus Baldwin Longstreet (1790–1870)

He is little known today but the Georgia jurist and author was famous in his time for his humorous sketches of life in the American Southwest. It is said that English novelist Thomas Hardy borrowed an entire chapter, almost word for word, from Longstreet's *Georgia Scenes, Chronicles and Incidents* (1835) for his *Trumpet Major*.

∇ ∇ ∇

Anita Loos (1893–1981)

Her famous *Gentlemen Prefer Blondes* (1925), which had such diverse admirers as James Joyce, George Santayana, Mussolini and Churchill, was written as a spoof of her good friend H.L. Mencken's taste for "dumb blondes." It is little noted that Loos, who wrote that Wilson Mizner (*q.v.*) was "the love of my life," wrote over 100 silent movie scripts for D.W. Griffith's Biograph Company and wrote the titles for Griffith's masterpiece, *Intolerance* (1916). She got her start as a screenwriter by mailing an unsolicited script to Griffith.

On returning to Hollywood and scriptwriting from New York she quipped, "Well, back to the mink-lined rut."

∇ ∇ ∇

George Horace Lorimer (1867–1937)
The longtime editor of *The Saturday Evening Post* had an ironclad rule never to allow evern a hint of impropriety to appear in his magazine. Readers were thus shocked when the first installment of Katherine Brush's serial *Red-headed Woman* ended with the heroine having a drink at her boss's house while his wife was away and the second installment began with them having breakfast together. To answer the flood of indignant mail from readers Lorimer prepared a form letter: "The *Post* cannot be responsible for what the characters in its serials do between nstallments."

∇ ∇ ∇

H.P. (Howard Phiillips) Lovecraft (1890–1937)
This popular fantasy and science fiction author suffered from a rare ailment called *poikilothermia*, which made him unable to maintain a constant body temperature. Lovecraft had to wear many layers of warm clothing on the hottest days and even on moving to Florida wore a heavy overcoat during the summer.

∇ ∇ ∇

Amy Lowell (1874–1925)
Amy Lowell wrote her first poem when she was 28, after returning from an Eleonora Duse dance recital in Boston. "I knew nothing whatever about the technique of poetry," she later wrote. "I was as ignorant as any one could be. I sat down and wrote this poem. It had, I think, every cliché and every technical error which a poem can have, but it loosed a bolt in my brain and I found out where my true function lay…"

On learning that England was going to war in 1914, while she visited there, Miss Lowell was heard to say: "And it was this month that my book of poems was coming out here! What attention will it get with this going on? What has happened to England? Why don't they stop the war?"

She enjoyed a good cigar, just as George Sand did before her and Lillian Hellman did after her. Indeed, when the prospect of a wartime shortage loomed in 1914 with the beginning of World War One, she contacted her dealer and ordered *10,000* of her favorite Manila brand.

Many marvelled at Amy Lowell's girth and some poked fun at it. At one 12-course dinner that the wealthy poet gave for her literary friends in Paris, Ezra Pound and Allen Upward conspired against her. In an after-dinner speech Upward used as his text an imagist poem she had published depicting herself bathing in a moonlit garden. Pound entered on cue with a huge, round tub that he placed before the poet, quipping that Les Imagistes were now succeeded by Les Nagistes.

Her great girth was the subject of many malicious comments by literary folk. Ezra Pound, for one, called her the only "hippopoetess" in the Modernist Zoo.

A garage owner refused to believe that the poet was a Lowell when her car broke down outside Boston and she wanted him to charge the repairs to her. If you don't believe me call my brother, he's the president of Harvard University, she told the man and he did so. "Some big fat dame whose engine broke down wants to charge her bill—claims she's your sister," he explained to Abbott Lawrence Lowell.
"What is she doing now?" Lowell asked.
"She's across the road…sittin' on a stone wall smoking a cigar!"
"That's my sister, all right!" said Lowell.

When her baggage was being unloaded at Piraeus during a European trip, one of the poet's suitcases slide into the water through a broken landing net and sank. The suitcase happened to contain all her underwear. "My drawers, oh, my drawers," Amy Lowell cried, standing on the edge of the pier, wringing her hands. She finally paid to have the area dredged, recovering her suitcase.

∇ ∇ ∇

James Russell Lowell (1819–1891)
In later years Lowell could be as manic as he had been morose before his future wife Maria rescued him from depression early in his career. While usually a charming gentleman, he often startled staid Boston with his actions. Once he "ate with knife and fork" the flower centerpiece at a literary dinner (which brings to mind Ezra Pound, who once ate a bunch of tulips at lunch); another time he shimmied up a lamppost, sat there and crowed like a rooster; he would frequently scale tall stone walls and walk along the top. In fact, friends feared to see Lowell

coming along the street, never knowing if he would seize them and swing them about in the air.

When American ambassador to England, Lowell wrote verses welcoming his "Dear Little God-Daughter," Sir Leslie Stephen's daughter Virginia, hoping that she would prove "a sample of heredity." She became better known to the world as Virginia Woolf after her marriage to author Leonard Woolf in 1912.

$$\triangledown \ \triangledown \ \triangledown$$

Robert Lowell (1917–1977)

A conscientious objector during World War II, the poet was sentenced to five months in prison for refusing to serve in the army. At one jail where he was incarcerated his cell was next to Louis Lepke's. "I'm in for killing," the Murder Incorporated gangster told him. "What are you in for?" Replied Lowell, "I'm in for refusing to kill."

The poet got his nickname "Cal" in prep school, where his "scruffy habits and rebellious pronouncements" inspired his St. Mark's classmates to name him after the infamous Roman emperor Caligula.

Jean Stafford told of how early in their marriage he reproved her for setting traps to catch the mice behind the walls in their bedroom. She insisted that their gnawing kept her awake nights, but Lowell replied, "Why not let them live? There's enough food for all of us."

Manic depression plagued him all his adult years, an illness that often brought great delusions with it. During one hosptialization he read an "improved" version of the great elegy "Lycidas" to a fellow poet, assuring him that it was all right—he was Milton.

Lowell took fellow poet Allen Tate literally when told that there was no room at his house, that he'd have "to pitch a tent on the lawn" if he wanted to stay there. Lowell bought a tent at Sears and lived on Tate's lawn for the next two months.

He revised his work so much before its completion, according to his first wife, Jean Stafford, that a poem he began with the title "To Jean: On Her Confirmation" wound up being called "To a Whore at the Brooklyn Navy Yard."

Clare Boothe Luce (1903–1987)

The author's first play, *Abide With Me,* failed, but this did not discourage Miss Boothe. According to drama critic Richard Watts: "One almost forgave *Abide With Me* its faults when its lovely playwright, who must have been crouched in the wings for a sprinter's start as the final curtain mercifully descended, heard a cry of 'Author,' which was not audible in my vicinity, and arrived to accept the audience's applause just as the actors, who had a head start on her, were properly lined up and smoothed out to receive their customary adulation."

George Bernard Shaw was the inspiration for her work in the theater. One time she met him in a theater lobby and gushed, "Except for you, I wouldn't be here." Replied Shaw: "And now, let me see, dear child, what *was* your mother's name?" (See also DOROTHY PARKER.)

∇ ∇ ∇

Nancy Luce (fl. mid-19th century)

The 19th-century New England poet loved her chickens so much that they were the only things she wrote poems about. She kept busy in her Martha's Vineyard farm by writing poems and inscribing them on eggs, along with the name of the chicken that laid each particular egg.

∇ ∇ ∇ ∇ ∇ ∇ ∇ ∇

Bernarr Macfadden (1868–1955)

Confession magazines, which have been with us now for over 65 years, are an American invention that was an outgrowth of long, soul-searching letters sent to physical culture crusader Bernarr Macfadden's *Physical Culture* magazine in 1919. Macfadden's first confession book was *True Story,* the great-grandmother of the genre, which currently has a circulation of five million, but there are scores of other confessions on the newsstands today. The first stories dealt with sweet young things who were so wicked that they dared to elope against their parents' wishes etc., while contemporary tales have virtually no taboo theme and range from well-written confessions about incest to stories such as "My Bride Is a Man" (where Julie was Jules before her sex-change operation). The yarns, which earn five to 10 cents a word, aren't all written by readers. Professional writers turn out a large number, perhaps the majority of them, though some magazines do require an author to sign a release saying his or her story is based on a true experience.

▽ ▽ ▽

Alfred T. Mahan (1840–1914)

Mahan's *The Influence of Sea Power Upon History, 1660–1783* (1890) had an enormous influence on modern naval warfare. The full extent of this influence can best be seen not in the success of the American naval officer's theories in America or Great Britain, but in the fact that both the German and Japanese navies required that every warship carry a copy of Mahan's work and that every naval officer read it.

▽ ▽ ▽

Bernard Malamud (1914–1986)

Malamud confided that he had actually been in a happy mood when he began work on his fourth book, *A New Life* (1961). But one day while he was writing the book at Yaddo, the writers' colony, a visitor happened to knock at his door. "I had just written something that moved me," Malamud later recalled. "He saw my wet eyes. I told him I was enjoying writing my book. Later the legend grew that I had wept my way through it."

▽ ▽ ▽

Herman J. Mankiewicz (1897–1953)

Mankiewicz's drinking problem and sharp, irreverent tongue—which cost him several Hollywood jobs—caused his wife much trouble. One time a friend who hadn't seen the couple in several months asked the screenwriter, "How's Sara?"

"Sara who?" Mankiewicz replied, acting puzzled.

"Sara. Your wife, Sara."

"Ah, you mean Poor Sara."

▽ ▽ ▽

Don Marquis (1878–1937)

The American humorist and poet was much less successful with his serious works, including his poems, than with the antic adventures of archy the literary cockroach and his friend mehitabel the cat. "Publishing a volume of poetry today," he once said, "is like dropping a rose-petal down the Grand Canyon and waiting for the echo."

It was Marquis who also observed: "If you want to get rich from writing, write the sort of thing that's read by persons who move their lips when they're reading to themselves."

Marquis, an accomplished drinker, entered his favorite bar after a month on the wagon. "I've conquered that God-damned will power of mine," he said to te bartender. "Gimme a double scotch."

∇ ∇ ∇

J.P. (John Phillips) Marquand (1893–1960)

Marquand satirized Brahmin Boston, yet he himself came from an old New England family; Margaret Fuller was his great aunt. One of the first things he did when his novels began making money was to join an exclusive Boston club. On an early visit there, he informed an elderly member that old Mr. Sears— whose mansion now housed the club—had made his daughters back away when they left his presence so that they would never turn their backs disrespectfully on him. "Times have changed since then," the elderly member rather ruefully admitted.

∇ ∇ ∇

Groucho Marx (1895–1977)

On receiving a copy of S.J. Perelman's first book, Groucho wrote to him: "From the moment I picked your book up until I laid it down I was convulsed with laughter. Someday I intend reading it." Perelman's publishers later used the comedian's remark as an endorsement.

Groucho received word that Warner Brothers would sue the Marx Brothers if they used *A Night in Casablanca* as the title for their next film, because it was too much like the Warner's title *Casablanca*. "We'll sue *you* for using the word *Brothers*," he wrote in reply.

∇ ∇ ∇

William "Bat" Masterson (1853–1921)

The legendary western gunslinger, gambler and sheriff worked as a sports reporter and editor on the *New York Morning Telgraph* in the early 1900s and was considered a great boxing and horse racing authority. One day a Texas editor named Dinklesheets burst into the bar at the old Waldorf Astoria, shouting that he was going to settle an old score with Bat. "Bat's going for his cannon!" someone cried and the bar cleared out, Dinklesheets first. Masterson later confided in his quiet, unruffled way that he had only been reaching for a pack of cigarettes.

Brander Matthews (1852–1929)

His students at Columbia asked the author and critic, called "the last of the gentlemanly school of critics in America," his opinion of a play he'd attended the night before.

"Well, gentleman," he said, "the play was in four acts, and I was there as guest of the author. After the first act the audience sat silent and I applauded. After the second act I sat quiet while the audience hissed."

"And after the third act?"

"Well, gentlemen, after the third act I went out and bought standing room and came back and hissed too."

∇ ∇ ∇

John Milo Maxwell (1866–1960?)

Maxwell was copy editor of the *Chicago Globe* when Theodore Dreiser came to Chicago. He gave the future novelist the following practical advise: "Life is a god-damned stinking, treacherous game, and nine hundred and ninety-nine men out of every thousand are bastards."

∇ ∇ ∇

Robert McAlmon (1895–1956)

The poet Winifred Bryher (Winifred Ellerman) proposed marriage to the avant-garde writer after reading and becoming "enthralled and enchanted" with a poem he had published in a Greenwich Village literary magazine. Though neither poet had ever seen the other before, McAlmon quickly accepted and the story was reported in the *New York Times* in 1921 under the head "Heiress Writer Weds Village Poet." The marriage, however, was one of convenience, for McAlmon was a homosexual and Bryher a lesbian, her family forbidding her to travel widely unless she got married. The two sailed for Europe where McAlmon, put on a generous allowance, rarely lived with his wife, though they stayed legally married for six years, until 1927. (See also ERNEST HEMINGWAY.)

∇ ∇ ∇

Mary McCarthy (1907-1989)

After her parents died in the great flu epidemic of 1918 the novelist and critic was raised for a time by a great-aunt, under what she called "circumstances of almost Dickensonian cruelty and squalor," which included beatings with a razor strap and being forced as a punishment to stand outside for three hours at a time in the snow. One time she won a school prize and was then beaten lest she become "stuck up."

Josephine Clifford McCrackin (1838–1920)

The journalist, short story writer and early conservationist, who crusaded for the California redwoods, married a U.S. cavalry officer who became insane and held her prisoner in the desert outpost where they were stationed. Finally, she managed to escape through the desert and make her way to California, where she began her romantic writing career and wrote her first-hand accounts of western life.

∇ ∇ ∇

Carson McCullers (1917–1967)

Taking a bus from Georgia to meet her daughter in New York, the Southern novelist's mother struck up a conversation with a rather reserved woman. The ebullient Mrs. McCullers went on and on about her daughter's great literary talent and accomplishments, proudly monopolizing the conversation. Finally, the other woman managed to mention that her father had also been an author. "What is your name?" Mrs. McCullers asked. "Countess Tolstoy," she replied.

As a young writer the novelist idolized Katherine Anne Porter, but even from the beginning she was intensely competitive. One time she pointed out Miss Porter to a friend, remarking, "There is the greatest female writer in America—but just wait until next year."

McCullers claimed that when she first came to New York she somehow took a room in a whorehouse. She only became aware of her mistake when the madam, whom she thought her landlady, sent a client to her room.

∇ ∇ ∇

Dwight Macdonald (1906–1982)

In his anthology *Parodies* (1960) the author and critic parodied book dedications with this dedication:

To my dear sons
Michael and Nicholas
without whose school bills
this anthology would not have been made.

Claude McKay (1890–1948)

McKay, a Jamaican who immigrated to the United States, worked as a waiter for many years while writing his poems, stories and novels. His poem "If We Must Die" was written in reaction to the 1919 Harlem race riots, but its stirring words of resistance were chosen 20 years later as a World War II rallying cry by both Senator Henry Cabot Lodge Jr., who read the poem into the *Congressional Record*, and Prime Minister Winston Churchill, who read it to the British people.

∇ ∇ ∇

Cotton Mather (1663–1728)

The youngest student ever admitted to Harvard, at the age of 12, the American religious leader wrote 450 different works over his lifetime (not all of them were full-length books), making him one of America's most prolific authors. This output does not include his enormous diary, which has been published in seven volumes. Mather spoke seven languages and was the best-read American of his time with a library of more than 2,000 volumes.

∇ ∇ ∇

Louis B. Mayer (1885–1957)

To critics who complained that his movies were written by committee, the Hollywood producer replied: "The number one book of the ages was written by a committee, and it was called the *Bible*."

∇ ∇ ∇

Tom Meany (1903–1964)

Probably there are a few ghostwriters who have themselves hired ghostwriters, but I know of only one: sportswriter Tom Meany. When he was a ghostwriter for Christy Walsh, Babe Ruth's business manager, during the 1936 World Series, Meany was so busy with other assignments that he had to hire a ghost to ghost for him. "The only ghost writer I ever employed," Walsh later wrote (or had still another ghostwriter write), "had a ghost writer of his own."

∇ ∇ ∇

Herman Melville (1819–1891)

Perhaps more than any other major American author, Melville fashioned his work on easily recognized prototypes. *Moby Dick* was based on a real-life white whale, Mocha Dick; *Billy Budd* was based on the *Somers'* Mutiny court-martial; *Benito Cereno* was taken in places word for word from a true account of slaves seizing a ship. The list could go on and on. Even Bartleby, the clerk in the Dead Letter Office in Melville's famous short story "Bartleby, the Scrivener, A Story of Wall Street" (1853), was based upon a real person: Melville's friend George Adler, a German philologist sent to an asylum for his agoraphobia.

His novel *Typee* was based upon his own "life among the cannibals" after he deserted the whaling ship *Acushnet* in the South Seas. All of his experiences, however, apparently didn't get into the book. His editors, for example, forced him to delete the last sentence in this passage about the boarding of the *Dolly* by native women: "Our ship was now given up to every specie of riot and debauchery. Not the feebelest barrier was interposed between the unholy passions of the crew and their unlimited gratification."

Moby Dick was indebted to myriad sources, many of which Melville used word for word, including an account of the sinking of the whaleship *Essex* by a whale in 1820. Captain Pollard and other sailors aboard the *Essex* survived their long ordeal at sea by resorting to cannibalism. Years later a relative of one of the *Essex* crewmembers approached Captain Pollard and asked if he did not remember the man. "Remember him!" laughed the old salt. "Hell, son, I et him!"

Ralph Waldo Emerson's optimistic views of life and mankind were hardly shared by all his contemporaries, either in America or in England, where Carlyle found him rather naive. "Trust men," Emerson wrote in one of his essays, "and they will be true to you; treat them greatly and they will show themselves great." The more worldly Melville, who learned of life in the holds of whalers and on cannibal isles, came upon these words in a volume of Emerson's work. Next to them in the margin, he wrote: "God help the poor fellow who squares his life according to this."

Readers of his day knew Melville for his South Seas books *Mardi* and *Oomoo*, not for his masterpieces. Melville never thought much of his prospects for immortality. "What reputation Herman Melville has is horrible," he wrote to a friend late in his career. "Think of it. To go down to posterity as 'the man who lived among the cannibals.'"

Moby Dick behind him and working on *Billy Budd*, which would be found in manuscript among his papers, Melville spent the last 29 years of his life in New York, forgotten by almost everyone. Working "a most inglorious" job as a customs officer, like Hawthorne before him and Edwin Arlington Robinson after him, he described his vocation as "worse than driving geese to water" and lived for the evenings when he could write in his bleak Gramercy Park room.

In the days before their friendship broke Melville wrote to his great friend:

If ever my dear Hawthorne, in the eternal times that are to come, you and I shall sit down in Paradise, in some little shady corner by ourselves; and if we shall by any means be able to smuggle a basket of champagne there (I won't believe in a temperance heaven), and if we shall cross our celestial legs in the celestial grass that is forever tropical, and strike our glasses and our heads together, till both musically ring in concert, then, O my dear fellow mortal, how shall we pleasantly discourse of all the things manifold which now so distress us...Yes, let us look forward to such things.

When Melville was at his desk writing, his absorption in his work was amazing to behold. According to Nathaniel Hawthorne's son Julian, a novelist himself, "he looked like all the things he was describing—savages, sea-captains, the lovely Fayaway in her canoe, or the terrible Moby Dick himself."

Moby Dick, despite some good reviews, was a commercial failure. Altogether only 3,797 copies were sold in Melville's lifetime. After the first year an average of 23 books were sold annually.

His last words were the same as those of his character Billy Budd: "God bless Captain Vere!"

So little known was Melville at his death that the *New York Times* at first failed to print his obituary. Belatedly the *Times* printed a brief item reporting the death of "Hiram" Melville.

Nine years after Melville's death Harvard professor Barrett Wendell evaluated Melville in his *Literary History of America*: "Herman Melville with his books about the South Seas...and with his novels on maritime adventure, began a career of literary promise, which never came to fruition." As amazing as it seems, this was standard critical opinion at the time, sometimes accompanied by the warning that Melville had a "wild imagination"—when, as noted, each and every one of his plots and subplots can be traced to a real-life occurence.

Elizabeth Shaw Melville, the novelist's wife, tidied up his desk after his death, putting whatever she decided to save in a breadbox. When the breadbox was opened 28 years later by Professor Raymond Weaver of Columbia it was found to contain one of the greatest literary discoveries of all time, the original manuscript of *Billy Budd, Foretopman*, which the author had finished five months before his death.

∇ ∇ ∇

H.L. (Henry Louis) Mencken (1880–1956)

Stripteaser Georgia Sothern, or her press agent, wrote to H.L. Mencken in 1940 asking him to coin a "more palatable word" to describe her profession. The Sage of Baltimore, who had hatched other neologisms (*e.g.*, "bootician" for a bootleg-ger), gallantly responded, suggesting that "strip-teasing be related in some way or other to the zoological phenomenon of molting." Among his specific recom-mendations were a family of lizards called the Geckonidae (not very appetising, either) and ecdysiast, which comes from *ecdysis*, the scientific term for "molting." Miss Sothern adopted the last and it was publicized universally; born to the world was a new word and a new union called the Society of Ecdysiasts, Parade, and Specialty Dancers. But not every artfully unclad body was happy with Mencken's invention. Said the Queen of Strippers and whodunit author Gypsy Rose Lee, whose *G-String Murders* was actually ghost-written by Craig Rice: "'Ecdysiast,' he called me! Why the man is an intellectual slob. He had been reading books. Dictionaries. We don't wear feathers and molt them off…What does he know about stripping?" Most would agree with her that "stripteaser" is far more revealing.

Though it seems hard to imagine the vigorous, iconoclastic Sage of Baltimore as a cautious man, Mencken was an extreme hypochondriac who took few chances with his health. When he was editing an article, for example, he'd often wash his hands five or six times, so much did he fear contacting strange germs.

Mencken wrote an editorial for the *Baltimore Sun* entitled "Object Lesson" that consisted of a million dots and a single footnote. The footnote explained that each dot stood for a federal government jobholder.

He once suggested a novel way to improve higher education: Burn down the universities and hang all the professors. But that was before he married a Goucher College professor of English.

When Joseph Conrad's agent asked $600 for letting Mencken's *The Smart Set* run the author's latest story, Mencken took a look at the magazine's books and budget and wired back: "For $600 you can have *The Smart Set*."

Alexander Woollcott recalled that Mencken had a "Happy Formula" for answering controversial letters. He simply replied: "Dear sir [or Madame]: You may be right."

Mencken wasn't asked this question, he invented it: "If you find so much that is unworthy of reverence in the United States, why do you live here?" Then he answered his own question with another question. "Why do men go to zoos?"

He liked to tell the story of "Ruth Dunbar, education editor of the *Chicago Sun Times*, who was known as Viola before she had to initial her pieces."

Mencken published an article on the bathtub called "A Neglected Anniversary" in the *New York Evening Mail* on December 28, 1917. In this piece he gave a spurious history of the bathtub, stating that it was first introduced to Americans in 1842, that three years later Boston made bathing in bathtubs illegal, and that President Fillmore installed the first tub in the White House, among other deliberate lies. Mencken planned his dirty work as "A piece of spoofing to relieve the strains of the war years," but almost everyone took it seriously and as a result to this day many of Mencken's inventions are presented as fact in books and magazine articles.

Despite the fact that his *Smart Set* offices were in New York City he continued to live in Baltimore and rarely visited New York. "Trying to be a philosopher in New York is like trying to sing in a boiler factory," he complained.

When editing the *Smart Set* Mencken would answer the telephone with the greeting (containing perhaps a germ of sincerity): "The great critic Henry Mencken speaking."

Someone wrote him: "Fifteen years ago you said just the reverse in an article—you are now saying exactly the opposite! how do you explain such a change?"
Replied Mencken: "Formerly I was not as wise as I am now."

The Anti-Saloon League of Virginia seriously contended in its *Bulletin*: "His initials are H.L., meaning the first and last letters of the word Hell." Said a religious paper in Texas: "If a buzzard laid an egg in a dung hill and the sun hatched a thing like Mencken, the buzzard would be justly ashamed of its offspring." Far from ignoring the myriad insults like these he collected and published them in a book entitled *Menckeniana: A Simplexicon*.

"H.L. Mencken," said avant-garde writer Maxwell Bodenheim, "suffers from the hallucination that he is H.L. Mencken—there is no cure for a disease of that magnitude."

He claimed he was the world's champion mixologist and once hired a mathematician to figure out that 17,864,392,788 different cocktails could be mixed from the stock of a first-class bar. When he sold the Canadian film rights to his famous hoax on the origins of the bathtub, "A Neglected Anniversary," he demanded and received as payment two cases of Labatt's Ale a month for as long as he lived.

To a reporter who questioned him about his celebrated drinking he replied: "I've made it a rule never to drink by daylight and never to refuse a drink after dark."

Not long before Mencken died in 1956, eight years after a stroke had made him incapable of reading or writing, depriving him of his life's blood, a friend mentioned a writer who had died in 1948. "Ah, yes," Mencken said, "he died the same year I did."

Mencken wrote his own epitaph: "If after I depart this vale, you ever remember me and have thought to please my ghost, forgive some sinner and wink your eye at some homely girl."

∇ ∇ ∇

Grace Metalious (1925–1964)
"I'm a lousy writer," the best-selling author of *Peyton Place* confessed to an interviewer. "A helluva a lot of people have got lousy taste."

∇ ∇ ∇

Edna St. Vincent Millay (1892–1950)
There has been some controversy over whether the poet's middle name came from New York's St. Vincent Hospital. The matter was conclusively settled recently in a letter to the *New York Times Book Review* from the poet's daughter Norma:

> ...On the docks in New Orleans on a chilly February day 91 years ago Charles Buzzell, my grandmother's younger brother, wasn't feeling well. He had a fever. The ship *El Monte* of the Grace Line was loading cotton for New York and he went on board to watch. He fell asleep unnoticed on a bale of hay; cotton was stacked about him. When he awoke the ship was under way, the hatches battened down. The noise of the ship prevented him from making his plight known. In New York, nine days later, when the hold was opened, Charles was found at the foot of the hatchway where he somehow had managed to crawl. Some sailors thought him a ghost, others wept. The captain got him to St. Vincent's Hospital where doctors said he couldn't live. He did live!
>
> He was a strong young man and the doctors miraculously brought him through. It was said at that time that he had survived longer than anyone had without food or water. A New York paper carried the story with his name slightly changed; he could hardly speak, of course.
>
> Mrs. Henry Tokman Millay (Cora Buzzell), in joyful gratitude at her adored brother's recovery, gave her child, born around that time, a middle name after the saint for whom the hospital had been named. Had it been Doctor's Hospital or Lenox Hill, she doubtless would have reconsidered—they wouldn't scan.

While attending Vassar Edna Millay liked to play the role of the young rebellious poet and she enjoyed baiting school authorities. One time she dared Vassar's president to expel her. "I don't want a banished Shelley on my doorstep," he explained in refusing her.

"A person who publishes a book," she explained to a friend, "willfully appears before the public with his pants down."

In her libretto of Deems Taylor's opera *The King's Henchman* (1927), which is set in the palace of King Edgar in 10th-century England, Millay tried to use no word that came into English after the Norman Conquest. Her "Anglo-Saxon" libretto began "Wild as the white waves/Rushing and roaring..."

∇ ∇ ∇

Henry Miller (1891–1980)
When Miller quit his job as a branch employment manager for Western Union (the Cosmodemonic Telegraph Company of *Tropic of Capricorn*) to devote all his time to writing he vowed never to work for anyone again. Of his four-and-one-half year emnployment he said, "It was a period comparable, for me, to Dostoyevsky's stay in Siberia."

In *Tropic of Cancer* Miller noted that while trying to make a living in Paris during the 1920s he "wrote pamphlets introducing the big new whorehouse...on the Boulevard Edgar-Quinet." For this "pseudonymous writing," he got a bottle of champagne and some free love (he put it differently) "in one of the Egyptian rooms."

∇ ∇ ∇

Joaquin Miller (Cincinnatus Heine Miller; 1837–1913)
Called Joaquin Miller because of an early article he wrote defending Mexican bandit Joaquin Murietta, the author adopted the nickname as his pseudonym. A charismatic literary charlatan who would do anything to attract attention to himself—he wore a huge knife in his belt and often swallowed fish whole—Miller was the toast of America and England as "the frontier poet" and "the Byron of Oregon," though his poems were little more than energetic and he clothed his personal history in romantic exaggeration. When he deserted his wife he left her the following note, which about sums him up for all time: "A man never becomes famous until he leaves his wife, or does something atrocious to bring himself into notice; and besides, literary men never get along well with their wives. Lord Byron separated from his wife, and some of my friends think I am a second Lord Byron. Farewell!"

∇ ∇ ∇

Margaret Mitchell (1900–1949)
The Georgia-born author and journalist claimed that when she finally submitted her famous novel to the publisher's editor who visited her in Atlanta it was only

because an acquaintance had angered her by saying that she was wasting her time writing. The huge manuscript had many unmemorable, even ridiculous titles before *Gone With the Wind* was chosen. These included *Ba! Ba! Black Sheep; Tote the Weary Load; Tomorrow Is Another Day; Jettison* and *Milestones.*

H.S. Latham, the editor to whom she delivered what was to become *Gone With the Wind,* said that it was "the biggest manuscript I have ever seen, towering in two stacks almost up to her shoulders."

The respected editor of the *Pictorial Review,* Herbert R. Mayes, turned down a prepublication offer to serialize *Gone With the Wind.* "A period novel!" he cried. "About the Civil War! Who needs the Civil War now—who cares?"

Mitchell's *Gone With the Wind* set the still-standing record for the most copies of a book sold in a day—50,000 copies, on October 30, 1936.

While crossing the street to an Atlanta movie theater on the evening of August 16th, she was killed by a drunken off-duty cab driver driving at over twice the speed limit. Her husband, walking beside her, was unharmed. The driver had been cited for traffice offenses 28 times in 10 years and caused yet another accident before his involuntary manslaughter conviction for Mitchell's death.

▽ ▽ ▽

Wilson Mizner (1876–1933)

Wilson Mizner wasn't as well known as Dorothy Parker, F.P.A., George S. Kaufman, Heywood Broun, Robert Benchley, Ring Lardner or any of the Algonquin Wits (who met for lunch regularly at New York's Algonquin Hotel), but the Hollywood screenwriter was one of America's greatest wits. One time a friend was extolling former champion boxer Tom Sharkey when Mizner interrupted. "He was dumb," Mizner said, "very dumb. Once he owned a saloon with swinging doors and he was so dumb that he crawled under them for two years before he figured out that they swung both ways."

When Mizner was night manager of the sleazy Hotel Rand in Manhattan he had a sign posted reading: "Carry out your own dead."

He was with promoter Tex Rickard in Alaska when Rickard pulled a gun and shot a man's hat off. "Why did you do that?" he asked. "You know my gal Goldie?" Rickard said. "Well that rat insulted her!" "For God's sake," Mizner said, "*how?*"

Friends of Mizner were discussing the dishonesty of a mutual acquaintance. Said Mizner: "He's the only man I know who has rubber pockets so he can steal soup."

One time he explained his first attempt at writing: "I wrote a short story because I wanted to see something of mine in print other than fingers."

"This game is too big for you," he told a self-styled "big shot" who wanted to sit in a poker game he was banking. "What do you mean?" the man protested, pulling out his wallet. "Cut me in for ten thousand dollars." Mizner calmly took the 10 thousand-dollar bills. "Joe," he snapped, "give the gentleman a blue chip."

Mizner summed up his view of Hollywood romances: "Some of the greatest love affairs I've known have involved one actor—unassisted."

Millionaire Harry K. Thaw had in 1906 shot and killed architect Stanford White, who had once had a relationship with Thaw's wife (the former showgirl Evelyn Nesbit). Years after this celebrated murder, Mizner looked with disdain on a huge and garish Palm Beach house designed by Joseph Urban. Remarked Mizner, "Harry Thaw shot the wrong architect."

Mizner tried to teach boxer Stanley Ketchel the theory of evolution, explaining it very patiently one evening when Ketchel was staying at his house. He then went out with friends for the night, returning at five in the morning to find Ketchel setting by a small bowl of goldfish and obviously enraged. "Your evolution is all bunk!" the boxer shouted. "I've been watching these fish nine hours and they haven't changed one bit!"

He was told that boxer Ketchel had been shot to death by a jealous husband. "Tell them to start counting ten over him and he'll get up," he advised.

Mizner's brother, Addison, on his deathbed in Palm Beach, received a telegram from Wilson in Hollywood. "Stop dying," it read. "Am trying to write a comedy."

Mizner came out of a coma on his own deathbed only to be irritated by a priest trying to comfort him. "Why should I talk to you?" he snapped, in his last words. "I've just been talking to your boss."

A sampler of other Mizner bon mots:

- "A drama critic is a person who surprises the playwright by informing him of what he meant."
- "You're a mouse studying to be a rat."

- "Hollywood is a trip through a sewer in a glass-bottomed boat."
- "The first hundred years are the hardest" (sometimes attributed to T.A. Dorgan).
- "Be nice to people on your way up because you'll meet 'em on your way down."
- "All the movie heroes in Hollywood are in the audience."

∇ ∇ ∇

Arthur R. Momand (1887–1987)

According to his own account, cartoonist "Pop" Momand lived in a community where many people tried to keep up with the Joneses. Momand and his wife resided in Cedarhurst, New York, one of the Long Island's Five Towns, where the average income is still among America's highest. Living "far beyond our means in our endeavor to keep up with the well-to-do class," the Momands were wise enought to quit the scene and move to Manhattan, where they rented a cheap apartment and "Pop" Momand used his Cedarhurst experience to create his once immensely popular *Keeping Up With the Joneses* comic strip, launched in 1913. Momand first thought of calling the strip "Keeping Up With the Smiths," but "finally decided on *Keeping Up With the Joneses* as being more euphonious." His creation ran in American newspapers for over 28 years and appeared in book, movie and musical-comedy form, giving the expression "keeping up with the Joneses" the wide currency that made it a part of everyday language. He recently died at age 100.

∇ ∇ ∇

Marianne Moore (1887–1972)

The esteemed poet was in 1955 commissioned by Henry Ford to create a name for a new Ford car. Moore came up with the "Utopian Turtletop," which, of course, Ford didn't use, though he thoughtfully sent the poet a dozen roses. It soon became apparent that Moore was lucky not to have become linked with the car, which as the Edsel is remembered as the most laughable car in automotive history.

After being introduced to Muhammad Ali as "the world's most famous poetess," she and the world heavyweight champion began to collaborate on a poem about his upcoming title fight with Ernie Terrell. Ali, however, wound up writing all but a few words of the epic:

After we defeat Ernie Terrell
He will get nothing, nothing but hell,
Terrell was big and ugly and tall
But when he fights me he is sure to fall.
If he criticize this poem by me and Miss Moore

to prove he is not the champ she will stop him in four,
He is claiming to be the real heavyweight champ
But when the fight starts he will look like a tramp
He has been talking too much about me and making me sore
After I am through with him he will not be able to challenge
   Miss Moore.

(The amusing encounter between Moore and Ali is recounted at length in George Plimpton's *Shadow Box* [1977].)

∇ ∇ ∇

Zero Mostel (1915–1977)

At Dorothy Parker's funeral service Mostel delivered a line worthy of the great wit herself. Noting that Mrs. Parker had requested that there be no formal ceremony, the actor added, "In fact, if she had had her way, I suspect she would not be here at all."

∇ ∇ ∇

Frank A. Munsey (1854–1925)

The newspaper magnate and founder and editor of *Munsey's* weekly magazine sent a green reporter to cover the season's opening of the Metropolitan Opera House. Not knowing any of the personalities occupying the lavish boxes the cub copied the names for his story from the brass plates on the doors. The next day Munsey called the young reporter into his office. "I've just had a call from Mrs. Stuyvesant Fish," he said. "She read your account of the Metropolitan premiere and thought you might be interested to know that you have succeeded in resurrecting half the dead in Woodlawn Cemetery." The reporter soon learned that the names of the original box owners at the Metropolitan were usually left on the doors permanently.

When the founder of *Munsey's* purchased the *New York Daily News* in 1901, he bought it in cash from the widow of its founder, Benjamin Wood. Munsey paid Mrs. Wood with 340 thousand-dollar bills.

∇ ∇ ∇ ∇ ∇ ∇ ∇ ∇ ∇

Ogden Nash (1902–1971)

Nash created a scandal in the Bronx when he put down that New York City borough with the couplet: *The Bronx?/No thonx*! Nash never apologized, as Bronx politicians demanded he do at the time, but many years later, in 1964, he did make a kind of apology by writing the following poem in response to a request from Bronx Community College:

> I can't seem to escape the sins of
>   my smart-alec youth.
> Here are my amends.
> I wrote those lines, "The Bronx? No thonx!"
> I shudder to confess them.
> Now I'm an older, wiser man
> I cry, "The Bronx, God bless them!"

∇ ∇ ∇

George Jean Nathan (1882–1958)

As handsome as any of the matinee idols he wrote about, Nathan was a highly sophisticated man who dressed in the grand style. "He has," Mencken volunteered, "seventy-five winter overcoats, twenty-five spring coats, six hundred suits, a thousand neckties, and eleven jock straps for both fast or feast days."

Nathan's fame as a maker of epigrams reached those who didn't even know what the word meant. One time he asked a cabby to take him to "Forty-four West Forty-fourth Street." "What's that?" asked the driver. "Some kind of epigram?"

∇ ∇ ∇

Carry (Amelia Moore) Nation (1846–1911)

Carry Nation, convinced that she was divinely appointed to bring about the downfall of the saloon, embarked upon her career in Kansas in 1899, chopping her way through the United States and Europe with her "hatchetings" or "hatchetations." Her temperance lectures were not as interesting as her spectacular destruction of saloon interiors with her trusty axe, but the title of her autobiography, *The Use and Need of the Life of Carry A. Nation* (1904), is a little-known classic.

∇ ∇ ∇

John Neal (1793–1876)

The flamboyant American author was challenged to a duel by statesman William Pinckney's son after he attacked the elder Pinckney in an article. Sailing to England, perhaps to avoid the challenge, he wrote the first study of American authors (long afterward published as *American Writers*). Back in America he devoted himself to developing in his novels an American style emphasizing "coarseness" and natural speech, many of his stylistic innovations becoming the tools of later writers. Neal thought highly of himself. As his preface to *Logan* (1822) he wrote: "I hate Prefaces. I hate Dedications." And went on to dedicate the novel to "anybody; for I know nobody worth dedicating it to…[especially my countrymen, who are] unworthy of me."

∇ ∇ ∇

Frank (Benjamin Franklin) Norris (1870–1902)

Norris never lived to finish his famous wheat trilogy, of which *The Octopus* (1901), first in the series, is considered his finest work. Before he could even begin the last volume, *The Wolf*, the novelist died suddenly after an appendix operation when only 32. He was a vain man who on one occasion persuaded his friends to point at him in a restaurant to draw attention to him. But he had great integrity about his work. "I never truckled," he once said. "I never took off the hat to ashion and held it out for pennies. By God, I told them the truth."

∇ ∇ ∇

Bill Nye (Edgar Wilson; 1850–1896)

Bill Nye, as the Western humorist Edgar Wilson was known, maintained that literature was essential. "There should be a book in every home," he once said. "To the ignorant, the pictures will be pleasing. The wise will revel in its wisdom, and the housekeeper will find that with it she may easily emphasize a statement or kill a cockroach."

When he was editor of the *Laramie Boomerang* the humorist feuded with the editor of the *Sweetwater Gazette*. "Aside from the fact that he is a squinteyed, consumptive liar, with a breath like a buzzard and a record like a convict, I don't have anything against him," Nye said. "He means well enough, and if he can evade the penitentiary and the vigilance committee for a few more years, there is a chance he'll end his life in a natural way. If he doesn't tell the truth a little more plentifully, however, the Green River people will rise as one man and churn him up till there won't be anything left of him but a pair of suspenders and a wart."

Nye may have made the famous quip (also attributed to lawyer William Evarts and Oliver Wendell Holmes): "The pious ones of Plymouth, who, reaching the Rock, first fell upon their knees and then upon the aborigines."

Adolph S. Ochs (1858–1935)

Ochs purchased *The New York Times* in 1896 and raised it to the eminent position it enjoys today. Instead of getting into the "yellow journalism" competition of the day he chose the high road, adopting the two slogans to make his intentions clear. One, still used, was the famous "All the news that's fit to print." The other was: "It does not soil the breakfast cloth."

∇ ∇ ∇

Flannery O'Connor (1925–1964)

"Some people, if they learn to write badly enough, can make a lot of money," said the Southern novelist and short story writer. "Many a bestseller could have been prevented by a good teacher."

She never regretted working in her study four hours every morning, even when she didn't get a word on paper. "I go in every day," she explained, "because if any idea comes between eight and noon, I'm there all set for it."

∇ ∇ ∇

John O'Hara (1905–1970)

The novelist's sensitivity, which bordered on paranoia, was legendary. Once a friend told him, "John, I've just seen *Pal Joey* again, and, you know, I like it even better than I did the first time."
"What was the matter with it the first time?" O'Hara demanded.

A few hundred copies of O'Hara's *Butterfield 8*, published in 1935 and considered a bit wicked in its day, were mistakenly bound in the covers of a biography of the founder of methodism, John Wesley.

Ernest Hemingway and O'Hara didn't get along. Once during the Spanish Civil War Hemingway and two writer friends had pooled their funds and didn't know what to do with the money left over after their expenses. Suggested Hemingway: "Let's take the bloody money and start a bloody fund to send John O'Hara to Yale."

∇ ∇ ∇

Old Sleuth (Harlan Page Halsey; fl. mid 19th century)

Poe (*q.v.*) may have written the first detective story, but Halsey was the first author to use the word "sleuth" as a synonym for a detective. He created the fictional character Old Sleuth, which later became his nickname, and for a time held a copyright on the name. He was so possessive of "sleuth" that he once went to court to prevent another writer from using the word.

Charles Olson (1910–1970)

A huge, broad man six-and-a-half feet tall, the avant-garde poet taught at Black Mountain College in North Carolina. His gentleness inspired one of the local townspeople to see just how strong he was by picking a fight with him. Olson's one punch broke the man's jaw.

∇ ∇ ∇

Eugene O'Neill (1888–1953)

According to Bennett Cerf, the American playwright's first marriage in 1909 resulted from one of his lifelong drinking blackouts, begun after he returned—with a case of malaria—from a gold prospecting adventure in Honduras. He is said to have awoken one morning in a flophouse, a girl beside him. "Who the hell are you?" he demanded. "You married me last night," she said.

Just before he suffered a physical breakdown and was sent to a sanitarium for six months in 1912, O'Neill worked as a reporter for the *New London* (Conn.) *Telegraph*. His early journalistic efforts, like Kipling's, weren't appreciated. His editor attached the following note to one piece: "This is a lovely story, but would you mind finding out the name of the gentleman who carved the lady and whether the dame is his wife or daughter or who? And phone the hospital for a hint as to whether she is dead or discharged or what? Then put the facts into a hundred and fifty words and send this literary batik to the picture framers."

O'Neill's father, James, gave up a promising career as an actor for the financial security of playing the leading role in the *Count of Monte Cristo*, which he played over 5,000 times. "A chip off the old block, eh?" Eugene said to him soon after he too had chosen the theater as a career. "Say, rather, a slice off the old ham," James O'Neill replied.

After he saw his son's *Beyond the Horizon* O'Neill's father told him: "It's all right, Gene, if that's what you want to do, but people come to the theatre to forget their troubles, not to be reminded of them. What are you trying to do—send the audience home to commit suicide?"

O'Neill tried acting, among other occupations, before he turned to writing in 1916. In that year he made his only appearance in an O'Neill play, appearing in his one-act drama *Before Breakfast* as the offstage husband whose only "speech" is a death cry when he cuts his throat with a razor.

O'Neill's stage directions hardly matched the brilliance of his dialogue. In his play *Where the Cross Is Made*, for example, the playwright gives stage directions describing a man with one arm who must sit at a table "resting his elbows, his chin in his hands."

Russel Crouse asked O'Neill if he would shorten the script of *Ah, Wilderness!* so that the curtain could fall earlier. Finally, O'Neill, always adamant about not cutting a word from his plays, reluctantly agreed. The next day he called Crouse and told him, "You'll be happy to learn I cut fifteen minutes." "How?" Crouse replied ecstatically. "Where did you do it? I'll be right over to get the changes!" "Oh, there aren't any changes in the text," O'Neill explained, "but you know we've been playing this thing in four acts. I've decided to cut out the third intermission."

His long play *Strange Interlude*, in two parts with nine acts, opened in Quincy, Massachusetts, in 1932. Its long dinnertime intermission saved a struggling restaurant across the street from going out of business that Depression year. The owner was Howard Johnson.

He once explained in a letter his contempt for drama critics: "Me that was born on Times Square ... and have heard dramatic critics called sons of bitches ... ever since I was old enough to recognize the Count of Monte Cristo's voice [played on the stage for years by his father]."

When asked by the New York Drama Critics Circle to provide a welcoming statement on its founding in 1939, he wrote: "It is a terrible, harrowing experience for a playwright to be forced by his conscience to praise critics for anything ... There is something morbid and abnormal about it, something destructive to the noble traditions of what is correct conduct for dramatists."

After a rehearsal of *The Iceman Cometh* (1946), the playwright and the cast walked along Eighth Avenue in New York toward Gilhuly's, where they were to lunch. The actors in their costumes and makeup looked like the bums they were playing and soon a half a dozen or so real bums began following them. Once everybody got inside Gilhuly's the bouncer began throwing the bums out, but O'Neill spoke to the owner and asked him to let them stay. The real bums and the actors ate side by side as O'Neill's guests.

On the days when he worked on *Long Day's Journey into Night*, the family tragedy that is the most personal of his plays, O'Neill was tortured by his own words. "He would come out of his studio at the end of a day gaunt and sometimes weeping," recalled his wife, Carlotta. "His eyes would be all red, and he looked ten years older than when he went in in the morning."

When O'Neill's plays were first banned in Boston, newspaper reporters there dug up the qualifications of the city censor. He turned out to be the mayor's cousin, who had lost an arm and been fired from his job as a drummer in a burlesque show band.

Unlike many famous writers of his generation, O'Neill would have nothing to do with Hollywood. His response to a request for him to write a screen play as a vehicle for Jean Harlow is perhaps the most unequivocal turndown in the history of the movies. A cable had been sent to him requesting his services and asking for a collect reply in no more than 20 words. The playwright cabled back:

> No No No No No No No
> No No No No No No No
> No No No No No O'Neill.

He had no patience with any kind of personal publicity. In a New York nightclub he was introduced and forced to take a bow as a celebrity playwright. On leaving he was given his bill for $60. Before walking out, he crossed out the total and scrawled across the bill: "One bow—sixty dollars."

Irving Berlin recalled meeting him: "I was worried about what I was going to say to him. I figured on saying how much I respected him, but I didn't have a chance. Soon as we got there, I found he was interested in my old songs; he knew them all, even some I'd forgotten."

When George Bernard Shaw heard that O'Neill had given up drinking he predicted, "He'll probably never write a good play again."

"He swam as no one else that I have ever seen," writer Mary Heaton Vorse said of him, "as though he belonged to the water, as if it were not a separate element." While staying in Rockaway Beach, New York, he often swam in the winter when snow was on the ground. One time in Maine he donned the only suit available in his host's bathhouse—a large woman's suit—so that he could take a swim.

He gave up hope of ever writing again in 1949, and two years later he and his wife Carlotta moved into the Boston residential hotel where he met his end. "I knew, I knew it," he said one day to Carlotta. "Born in a goddam hotel room and dying in a hotel room."

Knowing his life was drawing to a close, O'Neill asked his wife Carlotta to help him destroy his nine-play cycle, *A Tale of Possessors Self-Dispossessed*, which he had been working on for over 20 years. "Go and get the unfinished manuscripts and let's sit in front of the fireplace and burn them," he told her. Later she recalled: "And so we sat, feeding the flames, through the long dusk. When the darkness came, O'Neill had passed into unequivocal silence. You don't know how horrible it was. It was like tearing up children." Somehow a draft of one play in the series, *More Stately Mansions*, survived and was later produced.

Carlotta O'Neill told of the night at Marblehead, Massachusetts, in 1951 when she and her husband, very ill with a disease resembling Parkinson's, argued violently and she "almost pushed him out of the house," only to save him later when she called the doctor. O'Neill stumbled in the snow without his cane. "He left without his coat and hat," she recalled. "I stood by the window, where I could see him trying to make his way out of the driveway. Suddenly, before he reached the road, he slipped and fell heavily into a ditch. It had begun to snow again. I don't know how long I stood by that window, watching the tiny white flakes hide his entire body from view."

In the early 1920s a depressed O'Neill had written the following mock epitaph for himself:

EUGENE O'NEILL
There is something
  To be said
For being dead.

∇ ∇ ∇

Rose Cecil O'Neill (1874–1944)
In 1909 the American author and magazine illustrator published a poem in the *Ladies Home Journal* that she illustrated with Cupid-like imps. The imps proved so popular that she invented a doll called the Kewpie (the name is a form of "cupid"), which she patented and made a fortune with, in the process adding the term *Kewpie doll* to the language.

∇ ∇ ∇

James Otis (1725–1783)
The American revolutionary and political pamphleteer was forced to retire from public life in 1769 when a pro-British commissioner of customs, infuriated at one of Otis' newspaper columns, attacked and severely injured him. Otis always said that he wished he could die by a bolt of lightning. His wish came true one afternoon when he visited a friend's farmhouse. While he stood talking inside, lightning streaked down the chimney and leaped to Otis, killing him immediately but leaving everyone else untouched.

Thomas Paine (1737–1809)

Paine, the author of *Common Sense*, a popular tract that attracted many to the side of the American Revolution in 1776, coined the name United States of America for his adopted country. The name was first used in the subtitle fo the Declaration of Independence: "The Unanimous Declaration of the Thirteen United States of America." It should be added that from as early as 1617 to as late as 1769 the kingdom or republic of Holland was called the United States.

Paine's *Common Sense* sold 120,000 copies within three months, and total sales probably reached over a half-million. His book remains the all-time best-seller in relation to sales versus population (then some two-and-half million): An average one out of every five people in the new republic bought it.

"Where liberty is, there is my country," said Benjamin Franklin.
"Where liberty is not," replied the great revolutionary, "there is mine."

A Swedenborgian approached Paine in his travels across the United States in 1802. "I am a minister of the New Jerusalem Church here," he declared proudly. "We, sir, explain the Scripture in its true meaning. The key has been lost above four thousand years, and we have found it."
"Then it must have been very rusty," Paine replied.

Paine died in poverty in America, six or so people attending his burial. In 1819 Paine's body was stolen from its grave in New Rochelle by William Cobbett, an Englishman who wanted to bury it in England, the author's homeland, for reasons known only to himself. The body was lost, however, soon after British judges ruled that Paine was a traitor who could not be buried on native soil. It has never been recovered.

∇ ∇ ∇

Dorothy Parker (1893–1967)

After reviewing a quintillion quips over these last five or six years I'd say that Dorothy Parker ranks with Oscar Wilde, George Bernard Shaw, Richard Brinsley Sheridan and several others as one of the 10 greatest literary wits in history. Born Dorothy Rothschild in what is now Long Branch, New Jersey, she married Eddie Parker in 1917, kept her married name after their divorce and was commonly called Miss Parker. She certainly had the sharpest tongue at New York's celebrated Algonquin Round Table. Her famous quips include "brevity is the soul of lingerie" and the mock epitaphs "This is on me" and "Pardon my dust." It should be noted that Miss Parker is *not* responsible for the three bon mots most often attributed to her: "Let's slip out of these clothes and into a dry martini"

(Robert Benchley); "Everything worthwhile doing is either immoral, illegal, or fattening" (Alexander Woollcott); and "I'd rather flunk my Wasserman test/than read the poems of Edgar Guest" (Anonymous). Following is one of the largest collections of her bon mots.

Her friend Franklin Pierce Adams' "The Conning Tower" column was the first to publish Parker's celebrated couplet "News Item":

Men seldom make passes
At girls who wear glasses...

Later S. Omar Barker qualified the couplet: "whether men will make passes at girls who wear glasses/depends quite a bit on the shape of the chassis."

She was born two to three months premature on August 22, 1893. But all the rest of her life she never got anywhere on time, a fact that all her friends and she herself recognized. "My premature birth," she once said, "was the last time I was early for anything."

The author told her companions at the Algonquin Round Table that she had been early on one other occasion in her life. Her first husband, Eddie Parker, had lied to her so that they arrived at a funeral a half hour early. She claimed that Eddie began fooling with a knob under the casket and suddenly machinery was heard cranking and humming. The casket and corpse began moving and finally slid through a little door that opened into the fires of the crematorium. She and her husband fled out a side door before anyone else arrived.

Her first writing job was as a caption writer for *Vogue*, the fashion magazine. Her wit was evident in the very first caption she wrote, which appeared under several photos of women's underwear and read: "Brevity is the Soul of Lingerie, as the Petticoat said to the Chemise."

One time the publisher Condé Nast told her that he was going on a cruise. "And Dorothy, I wish you would come with me," he said. "Oh, I wish I could!" she replied, but as soon as he walked out of earshot, she added, "Oh, God, make that ship sink!"

Clare Boothe Brokaw, who later became Clare Boothe Luce, had joined the staff of *Vanity Fair* and encountered Miss Parker in the lobby one morning. "Age before beauty," said the sharp-tongued Clare, holding the door open. "Pearls before swine," Dorothy Parker said, entering first. Clare Boothe Luce later denied this story, and a similar quip was used in one of Alexander Woollcott's pieces, but it has nevertheless become part of the Parker legend. Recalled Mrs. Robert Benchley when she was 80 years old: "I was right there, the time in the Algonquin, when *some little chorus girl* and Dottie were going into the dining room and the girl stepped back and said, 'Age before beauty' and Dottie said very quickly, 'Pearls before swine.' I was right there when she said it."

Another time a mutual friend was extolling the virtues of Clare Boothe Luce to her. "Actually, she's awfully kind to her inferiors," the friend said. "Where does she find them?" Miss Parker asked.

When Dorothy Parker was a young and struggling writer working in a small New York office she was so lonely that she had a sign lettered on the door reading MEN.

For a time Miss Parker worked as a writer for Metro-Goldwyn-Mayer, a Hollywood studio not noted then for its kind treatment of writers. One afternoon she threw open a window in the little cottage Metro provided her and screamed to passersby: "Let me out of here! Let me out of here! I'm as sane as you are!"

She was advised that a young playwright had lifted some bright lines from her short stories for his latest play. On meeting him, she asked what the play was about. "Well, it's very hard to describe," he said, "except that it's a play against all 'isms.'"
"Except plagiarism?" Miss Parker asked.

"Looking at a list of our authors who have made themselves most beloved and therefore most comfortable financially," Miss Parker once said, "it shows that it is our national joy to mistake for the first rate, the fecund rate."

Miss Parker had no idea that A.A. Milne's *Winnie the Pooh* (1926) would become a children's classic. She dismissed it in a review with a succinct "Tonstant weader fwowed up."

"He's a writer for the ages," she said of one overrated author. "For the ages of four to eight."

Parker described her years as a drama critic for *The New Yorker* as a "Reign of Terror."

"His ignorance," she said of *New Yorker* editor Harold Ross, "was an Empire State Building of ignorance. You had to admire it for its size."

Miss Parker's play *Close Harmony*, which she wrote with Elmer Rice, was a failure at the box office. Sometime during the fourth week of its short run she wired Robert Benchley: CLOSE HARMONY DID A COOL $90 AT THE MATINEE STOP ASK THE BOYS IN THE BACK ROOM WHAT THEY WILL HAVE.

"Don't you think she ought to wear a brassiere in this scene?" a producer asked her, pointing at his leading lady. "God no," she replied. "You've got to have something in this show that moves."

Ruth Gordon and George Oppenheimer used thinly disguised characters based on Dorothy Parker in their plays *Over 21* and *Here Today*, which both appeared on Broadway. At the time, a publisher offered Miss Parker a large advance to write her autobiography. "No chance," she replied. "Gordon and Oppenheimer would sue me for plagiarism!"

"Most good women," she remarked, "are hidden treasures who are only safe because nobody looks for them."

She found most of the many guests at Alexander Woollcott's country place particularly tedious one weekend and couldn't think of a good thing to say about them. "Where do you suppose all of these people go when they leave Alec's?" somebody asked her.
"Back into the woodwork," she replied.

Another guest at a party told her that she thought their host was outspoken. "By whom?" she replied.

Miss Parker was asked why she hadn't seen Kaufman and Hart's *Merrily We Roll Along* (1934), in which the character Julia Glenn is modeled on her. She replied, "I've been too fucking busy and vice versa." Another version of the story has her saying the same to a telephoner who called to chat at the wrong time.

Despite her joy of sex, she found that men weren't worth it. Completely disillusioned with the opposite sex by her last years, she quipped, "The fucking you get isn't worth the fucking you get."

"The best way to keep children home," she explained, "is to make the home atmosphere pleasant—and let the air out of the tires."

As a lark she and Robert Benchley subscribed to undertaking trade journals. From them she learned that morticians sprayed tuberose perfume on corpses and began ordering a tuberose scent from London to use as her own perfume.

"Excuse me, everybody, I have to go to the bathroom," she said one afternoon, rising from her chair at the Round Table. She then bent down to Robert Benchley, confiding, "I really have to make a phone call, but I'm too embarassed to say so."

"Every year," she once complained, "back spring comes, with nasty little birds, yapping their fool heads off, and the ground all mucked up with arbutus."

British actor Herbert Marshall was entertaining a circle of admirers at a party and kept advising them of how busy he was, continually referring to his crowded schedule, which he pronounced "shedshoole" in the British manner. "If you don't mind my saying so," an annoyed Miss Parker finally said, "I think you are full of skit."

"I can't talk about Hollywood," she once told a journalist. "When I got away from it I couldn't even refer to the place by name. 'Out there,' I called it. You want to know what 'out there' means to me? Once I was coming down a street in Beverly Hills, and I saw a Cadillac about a block long, and out of the side window was a wonderfully slinky mink, and an arm, and at the end of the arm a hand in a white suede glove wrinkled around the wrist, and in the hand was a bagel with a bite out of it."

"This must be a gift book," she said of Lucius Beebe's *Shoot If You Must*. "That is to say, a book which you wouldn't take on any other terms."

The eminent black writer W.E.B. Du Bois was given a 92nd birthday party featuring entertainment by African spear dancers. During the performance a few spears came dangerously close to Du Bois' head. "Watch it, mate," said Dorothy Parker, seated next to him, "or you'll never see 93."

"Kate's wonderful, isn't she?" a friend said of Katharine Hepburn's Broadway performance in *The Lake*, between acts at the Martin Beck Theater. "Oh, yes," Miss Parker agreed. "She runs the gamut of emotion all the way from A to B." These words became as celebrated as any of her ripostes, but years later she told Garson Kanin that she didn't think there was a finer actress anywhere than Katharine Hepburn; she had made the remark for the same reason she said many things—because it was funny, a joke. Miss Hepburn, however, agreed with her assessment of *The Lake*.

An acquaintance cornered Dorothy Parker at a party and raved on for what seemed hours about her husband. "Why, he's marvellous," she concluded, "and do you know, I've kept him for eight whole years!"

"Don't worry," Miss Parker said, "if you keep him long enough he'll come back in style."

Miss Parker and Stockton Rush were staying at a friend's house where they had drunk to excess at a party the night before. Staggering down to breakfast the next morning, a hungover Rush remarked, "Would it be all right if I cut my throat?" "Move over on the blade and make room for me," Miss Parker told him.

Assured by a loud drunk that he was a good person and a man of real talent, she replied: "Look at him, a rhinestone in the rough."

A priggish matron called Miss Parker, telling her, "I really can't come to your party. So many foolish people will be there and I really can't bear fools."

"That's strange," she replied. "Your mother could."

One bright afternoon as a notoriously stupid Hollywood producer swaggered by them on the street, she commented to a companion, "He hasn't got enough sense to bore assholes in wooden hobbyhorses."

After being shown an apartment on Riverside Drive by a highpowered real estate agent, she turned to him and said: "Oh, dear, this is much too big. All I need is room to lay a hat and a few friends."

Returning from London, a noted actress complained to the press that she'd somehow gotten splinters in her derriere over there. "I suppose she got them sliding down a barrister," Miss Parker remarked.

Parker excelled at the Round Table word game in which players had 10 seconds in which to make a pun from a multisyllabic, assigned word. Given *horticulture* one day, she quickly responded, "You can lead a horticulture, but you can't make her think."

Wyatt Cooper remarked to her that Christine Jorgensen, who had had a much publicized sex change operation in Denmark, was soon to visit her mother in America. "And what sex, may I ask, is the mother?" Miss Parker inquired.

When someone made a remark about all the pretty girls at a Yale prom, Dorothy Parker observed, "If all these sweet young things were laid end to end, I wouldn't be the slightest bit surprised."

The author and her friends were discussing a promiscuous acquaintance. "You know she speaks 27 languages," Miss Parker said, "and she can't say *no* in any of them."

The marriage of two friends who had long lived together inspired the Parker congratulatory telegram reading: WHAT'S NEW?

Mrs. Robert Sherwood had had a difficult pregnancy. When she finally gave birth, Dorothy Parker telegraphed her: GOOD WORK, MARY. WE ALL KNEW YOU HAD IT IN YOU.

Early in 1920 she had an illegal medically controlled abortion in a New York hospital, to which she was admitted with "stomach trouble." The next day Robert Benchley visited and found her in pain and despondent, but she tried to make a joke of her condition. "Serves me right," she told Benchley, "for putting all my eggs in one bastard."

Miss Parker was asked to leave William Randolph Hearst's palatial San Simeon, either for drinking or for sleeping with another guest. Thinking this hypocritical, since Hearst drank and loved there with his mistress, actress Marion Davies, she wrote the following in the visitors' book on leaving:

Upon my honor,
I saw a Madonna
Standing in a niche,
Above the door
Of the famous whore
Of a prominent son of a bitch.

It wasn't in conversation but in her short story "The Little Hours" that Dorothy Parker made her much quoted remark: "And I'll say of Verlaine too, he was always chasing Rimbauds!"

Invited to a party attended mostly by homosexuals, Miss Parker got drunk, covered herself with drapery and climbed out on to the balcony waving a bottle of champagne. "Come and get me boys," she cried. "I'm a man."

She loved animals, over the years keeping an assortment of dogs, cats, a baby alligator and a messy canary that she named Onan because it "spread its seed all over the place." She named one of her dogs Woodrow Wilson, a president who had disappointed her, explaining that he too "was full of shit."

Alexander Woollcott's cat was old and suffering and he wanted to have it put to sleep. "But I don't know how to go about it," he told Dorothy Parker one afternoon at the Algonquin. "Try curiosity," she advised.

She took one of her dogs to a Hollywood party that she found "dreadfully boring." When the dog vomited on the carpet, she turned to her hostess and explained: "It's the company."

Actress Ruth Gordon told of Dorothy Parker being invited to the home of a California wildlife lover who attracted animals to his yard evenings by putting out a large platter of meats far from the house. The animals, however, didn't show up the first time Mrs. Parker visited. "Please come again," her host insisted. "I can't account for tonight. It won't happen again." Miss Parker made a second visit and was again handed a pair of binoculars, but again the animals didn't appear, though she waited until nearly midnight. "Oh, I don't understand it," the host cried. "How could it happen?" Miss Parker shook her head in commiseration. "I thought," she said sadly, "we'd at least get the after theater crowd!"

Alexander Woollcott claimed that when her dog had "a distressing malady" she "issued bulletins about his health. Confidential bulletins, tinged with scepticism: 'He said he got it from a lamp post.'"

Asked by Vincent Sheean what her husband, Alan Campbell, would do without her now that they had broke up, Miss Parker summed up her analysis of him in a sentence. "Don't worry about Alan," she said. "When Alan falls he always lands up on somebody's feet."

Said the author of her mother-in-law Hortense Campbell, a woman she considered something of a poseur: "Hortense is the only woman I know who pronounces the word 'egg' with three syllables."

When she remarried actor and screenwriter Alan Campbell in 1950, someone observed that most of the guests at the wedding hadn't spoken to each other for years. "Including the bride and groom," said Miss Parker.

On the morning of June 14, 1963, she awoke to find her husband, Alan Campbell, dead beside her, the victim of an apparent heart attack. A neighbor who accompanied her to the mortuary asked if there was anything she could do to help. "Get me a new husband," Miss Parker replied. "Dottie, I think that is the most callous and disgusting remark I ever heard in my whole life," said the neighbor after a long silence. "So sorry," said Miss Parker with a sigh. "Then run down to the corner and get me a ham and cheese on rye and tell them to hold the mayo."

Summoned to appear before the House of Representatives Un-American Activities Committee in 1952, she spent the evening before the dread day in a Washington, D.C. bar. There a loudmouth annoyed her, voicing his approval of Hollywood producers who worked "against the Reds." Miss Parker rose and stared at him icily. "With the crown of thorns I'm wearing," she said as she turned and left, "why should I be bothered with a prick like you."

Toward the end she thought little of her celebrated wit. "Damn it, it was the twenties," she once recalled, "we had to be smarty. I wanted to be cute—that's the terrible thing. I should have had more sense. A smartcracker, they called me. I was the toast of two continents—Greenland and Australia.

"There's a hell of a distance between wisecracking and wit," she told an inteviewer. "Wit has truth to it, wisecracking is simply calisthenics with words."

"These were no giants," she said of the Round Table late in her life. "Think who was writing in those days—Lardner, Fitzgerald, Faulkner, and Hemingway. Those were the real giants. The Round Table was just a lot of people telling jokes and telling each other how good they were."

When her doctor told a despondent Dorothy Parker that if she didn't stop drinking she'd be dead in a month. "Promises, promises," she replied.

Confined in an oxygen tent after a suicide attempt, she still had presence of mind enought to ask, "May I have a flag for my tent?"

"If I had any decency, I'd be dead," she said a few years before she died, "most of my friends are."

Somerset Maugham summed her up with: "It is as difficult to say anything about Dorothy Parker that has not been said as it is about the Venus of Milo. Helen could make a scholar famous with a kiss; she can make a fool immortal with a jibe."

∇ ∇ ∇

Francis Parkman (1823–1893)

Poor health made writing difficult for Parkman all his life. His weak eyes made it necessary for him to write in a dark room, like William Prescott (*q.v.*), and he invented a machine that supported his hand so that he could write legibly with closed eyes. While documents and books were read to him he made notes in the dark, turning these notes into his books after he had mastered them. Even with such aid he could only work 15 minutes at a time and for many years composed only six handwritten lines a day.

∇ ∇ ∇

Thomas William Parsons (1819–1892)
This once celebrated author, who is "the Poet" in Longfellow's *Tales of a Wayside Inn*, was famous for his translations of Dante. Parsons met among the most unusual of deaths when he slipped and tumbled down a well.

∇ ∇ ∇

James Gates Percival (1795–1856)
As well as a prolific poet, the remarkably versatile Percival was a practicing physician, a surgeon, an editor, a journalist, a linguist and philologist who spoke 10 languages, a chemistry teacher at West Point, a botanist, and the state geologist of both Connecticut and of Wisconsin. Percival for a time enjoyed a great vogue as a romantic poet noted for his metrical experiments. But he never felt that he mastered any field and lived a miserable existence, his eccentricities and paranoia causing him for some time to reside by his own choice in the New Haven State Hospital.

∇ ∇ ∇

S.J. Perelman (1904–1979)
The Brooklyn-born humorist and screenwriter looked forward to the publication of his magazine pieces, *Dawn Ginsbergh's Revenge* (1929), with the excitement every author has about his first book. Only one little thing ruined publication day. When he opened the book he found that his publisher, Horace Liveright, had unintentionally left his name off the title page.

Perelman once dated a young lady who wrote an advice-to-the-lovelorn column for the *Brooklyn Eagle*. She suggested that he turn the letters into a humor piece for the *New Yorker*, but Perelman thought them too pathetic for his purposes. He did show them to his friend and future brother-in-law Nathanael West, who ultimately used them as the basis for his bitter, satiric novel *Miss Lonelyhearts* (1933).

"How many drafts of a story do you do?" an interviewer asked Perelman. "Thirty-seven," he replied. "I once tried doing thirty-three, but something was lacking, a certain—how shall I say?—*je ne sais quoi*. On another occasion, I tried forty-two versions, but the final effect was too lapidary—you know what I mean, Jack? What the hell are you trying to extort—my trade secrets?"

The humorist finally escaped a horde of Taipei whores who had been following him through the streets, propositioning him. Looking back at them, he punned, "A case of the tail dogging the wag."

For the back cover blurb for his *Road to Miltown* he wrote, "Of the author it has been observed: Before they made him, they broke the mold."

Pointing at his National Book Award, Perelman observed, "This medal, together with my American Express card, will identify me worldwide—except at Bloomingdale's."

∇ ∇ ∇

Maxwell Perkins (1884–1947)
The great editor's absentmindedness was legendary. One story has a distinguished-looking man entering his office while he sat talking to a young writer he had just ushered in. Perkins looked up and began snapping his fingers trying to remember the older man's name, which the man finally volunteered. "Charles Scribner," snapped his employer.

Perkins' wife was housecleaning in the spring of 1935 when she came upon several boxes and barrels of old books that she paid a bookdealer five dollars to cart away. The books turned out to be signed first editions of works by Scribners authors, including F. Scott Fitzgerald, that were worth thousands of dollars. Luckily a friend of Perkins spotted the books on a stand outside a Second Avenue bookstore and, figuring that they were the editor's, bought them back from the bookdealer for $25 and presented them to Perkins.

While at a literary cocktail party Perkins argued that no one attending such affairs ever really listened to what anyone else had to say. To prove his point he said on shaking his hostess' hand in the midst of the crowded room, "I'm sorry I'm late, but it took me longer to strangle my aunt than I expected." "Yes, indeed," his hostess replied. "I'm so happy you have come."

∇ ∇ ∇

William Lyon Phelps (1865–1943)
The distinguished Yale English professor and author was interrupted in the course of a Robert Browning lecture with the question:

"Professor, which gives you the greatest thrill—a student who knows and appreciates Browning as thoroughly as you do, or that same student weaving through an entire Harvard team for a touchdown?"

"I thrill to either performance, young man," Phelps said. "The only difference is that when a student understands Browning, I do not smash my hat."

∇ ∇ ∇

David Graham Phillips (1867–1911)

The promising literary career of this muckraking journalist was cut short when he was murdered by a lunatic who believed that his family had been defamed in one of Phillips' earlier novels. His greatest novel, *Susan Lenox: Her Fall and Rise*, dealing with the success of a country girl who became a prostitute, wasn't published until six years after his death. Neither was the novel published the way the author had written it. His sister and literary executor removed passages that offended her sense of morality.

∇ ∇ ∇

Wendell Phillips (1811–1884)

The abolitionist and author was addressing a hostile audience, which drowned out his voice. Phillips showed no irritation, simply leaning over and delivering his speech to reporters seated in the front row. When the rest of the audience quieted down, out of curiosity for what he was doing, Phillips turned to them and coldly explained, pointing at the press: "Do what you will, ladies and gentlemen. I do not need your ears. Through these pencils I speak to thirty *million* of people."

He first won national fame at a December 8, 1837, meeting in Boston's Faneuil Hall at which people expressed their feelings about abolitionist editor Elijah Lovejoy, whose Alton *Observer* had been attacked four times by a pro-slavery mob, Lovejoy finally being killed while defending it. When Massachusetts Attorney General James T. Austin made a speech declaring that Lovejoy had died "as the fool dieth," comparing his murderers to those American heroes who attended the Boston Tea Party, he seemed to have divided the audience. Until Phillips took the platform. "When I heard," he cried, "the gentleman lay down principles which placed the murderers of Alton side by side with Otis and Hancock, with Quincy and Adams, I thought these pictured lips [pointing toward their portraits in Faneuil Hall] would have broken into voice to rebuke the recreant American, the slanderer of the dead."

John Pickering (1777–1846)

Pickering was a lawyer who as a hobby learned 20 languages, including Arabic. Refusing the chairs of Greek and Hebrew at Harvard, he began his study of American Indian languages that inspired the study of primitive languages throughout the world. In his spare time he wrote one of the first books on Americanisms.

∇ ∇ ∇

Mrs. Amos Pinchot (f. mid 19th century)

This lady penned perhaps the least celebrated of poems written in a dream. Mrs. Pinchot woke up in the middle of the night and scribbled what she thought were immortal lines on her bedside pad. What she read the next morning was:

> Hogamus Higamus
> Men are Polygamous
> Higamus Hogamus
> Women Monogamous.

∇ ∇ ∇

Edgar Allan Poe (1809–1849)

Poe is one of the few American writers whose life has become folklore. In any case, his story is well-known to many people who have never read a book: how this son of itinerant actors quarreled with his foster father, joined the army and was expelled from West Point; his marriage to his 13-year-old cousin Virginia Clemm and her death years later in their Fordham cottage, where they were so poor that she stroked their tortoiseshell cat to keep warm; his love affairs; and his alcoholism. Poe published his first book of poems, *Tamerlane and Other Poems*, anonymously at his own expense. His genius was never tangibly rewarded in his lifetime. "To coin one's brain into silver," he once wrote, "is to my thinking, the hardest job in the world." He had his best year when he edited the *Southern Literary Messenger*— for $800. His *"The Raven" was one of the few poems recognized as a work of genius when it appeared, but this apparently did him no good, for legend has it that it was a year and a half before he pried loose his $10 from the New York Mirror.* After his wife's death, Poe claimed that he lived with only "intervals of horrible sanity." He died at 40, perhaps addicted to drugs, and spent his last days stumbling into Baltimore polling places and casting ballots for drinks.

In 1827 the 18-year-old Poe published anonymously his first collection, *Tamerlane and Other Poems*, which consisted of poems written when he was 12 or 13. Brought out by Boston printer Calvin S.F. Thomas, the number of copies unknown, the 40-page paperbound book in tea-colored wrappers described its author only as "a Bostonian." For some unknown reason the book was suppressed and just a dozen copies have survived. The book is known as "the black tulip and Holy Grail of American book collecting." In 1988 a collector found a stained, frayed copy in a New Hampshire antiques store; he bought it for $15 and it was expected to sell at auction for $300,000.

Though good fortune never caught up with him Poe won some fame when he published "The Raven" in the *New York Mirror*. Once he attended the theater as a dramatic critic and an actor recognized him in the audience. All night long, perhaps hoping to extract a good review, the actor inserted the words "Nevermore, nevermore" into his speeches.

A literary and military tradition has it that Poe was expelled from West Point in 1831 for "gross neglect of duty" because he appeared at a public parade naked. Parade dress instructions called for "white belts and gloves, under arms" and Poe took them literally. He appeared on the parade ground, rifle balanced on his bare shoulder, wearing nothing but white belt and gloves. (James Whistler, *q.v.*, was another American literary figure who failed to make it at West Point.)

Poe's "The Bells" (1849), though much ridiculed as a jingle, is actually a complex poem and at least a technical tour de force that is the foremost example of onomatopoeia in poetry. The poem was suggested by his friend Marie Louise Shaw, who even provided him with the title. Visiting Mrs. Shaw in New York City in 1848, at a time when he was mentally exhausted, Poe was annoyed by the several church bells ringing nearby. He told Mrs. Shaw that he had to write a poem for a deadline and after tea she handed him a piece of paper with "The Bells, by Edgar Allan Poe" written on it, soon adding the words "the little silver bells." Poe began the poem then and there, writing 17 lines, though he took it home and reworked it twice before it was published.

On May 1, 1841, he published in the *Saturday Evening Post* a solution to the murder in Dickens' *Barnaby Rudge*, which was appearing serially in British and American periodicals. An amazed Dickens later confirmed that Poe had figured out the ending before he, Dickens, had even written it.

Poe's poem "A Valentine" is an example of the rare "cross-acrostic": The first letter of the first line, the second of the second, and so on, add up to the name of the woman to whom he sent the poem.

Poe probably had the most elegant handwriting of any noted writer over the ages. Early in his career he won a prize for his story "Ms. Found in a Bottle," the judges influenced in part "by the beauty of his handwriting."

Poe's C. Auguste Dupin, hero of "The Murders in the Rue Morgue" and "The Purloined Letter," is the first detective created by an Americn author, though he was a decidedly intellectual amateur detective. In fact, these two stories and Poe's "The Mystery of Marie Roget" are considered the first modern detective stories.

Although he debunked the famous Moon Hoax (see RICHARD ADAMS LOCKE), Poe created a hoax of his own in 1844 when he wrote an article for the *New York Sun* telling of the 75-hour crossing of the Atlantic in a balloon by eight people who traveled from England to South Carolina. The story, complete with interviews with the participants, was based only on his great imagination.

He was not overly fond of "popular" authors. "The most 'popular,' the most 'successful' writers among us…" he once confided, "are ninety-nine times out of a hundred, persons of mere address, perserverance, effrontery—in a word, busy-bodies, toadies, and quacks."

Poe wrote a number of his poems and stories, possibly even his famous horror tale "The Black Cat," with one of his pet cats perched upon his shoulder. His cat Catarina faithfully lay by his wife Virginia during his wife's fatal illness, providing Mrs. Poe warmth in her cold room.

One of the cruelest cuts of all came from Ralph Waldo Emerson, who remarked when someone mentioned Poe, "Ah, you mean the jingleman!"

Poe's "disastrous battle of life" was best expressed by Baudelaire, who learned English in order to translate Poe's works and made him beloved of French poets like Mallarmé and Valery, despite the later objections of critics like Henry James and T.S. Eliot. Wrote Baudelaire in his famous 1852 essay on Poe: "There are such things as ineluctable destinies; in the literature of every country one reads of certain men who bear the word misfortune written in mysterious characters in the sinuous lines of their brows. Some time ago, a wretch hauled before the courts was observed to have tattooed on his forehead the strange device: *No luck*. Thus he bore with him everywhere the motto of his life, as a book its title, and the cross-examination proved that his story was in conformity with the sign that advertised it. In literary history there are analogous fates. It is as though the blind Angel of Expiation had seized hold of certain men and was beating them with rods for the edification of the others."

He would hardly suggest an athlete to anyone today, but he was an excellent runner and long-jumped 21 feet while at West Point. Another time he swam 7 1/2 miles from Richmond to Warwick, Virginia, "against a tide…running 2-3 miles an hour." Far from a weak man he once horsewhipped a scurrilous critic.

Later in his life Poe seemed to disdain his athletic accomplishments. In the mid-1840s he wrote in his journal: "The foot-race, yesterday...attracted a wonderful share of the public attention. Eleven thousand persons are said to have been present...I myself did not see the contest; feeling little interest in feats of merely physical strength or agility, when performed by rational beings. The speed of a horse is sublime—that of a man absurd. I always find myself fancying how very readily he could be broken by an ass."

So desperate was Poe in the cold December of 1846 that he had to resort to placing the following notice in *The Express*:

> We regret to learn that Edgar A. Poe and his wife are both dangerously ill with the consumption, and that the hand of misfortune lies heavily upon their temporal affairs. We are sorry to mention the fact that they are so far reduced as to be hardly able to obtain the necessities of life. This is indeed a hard lot, and we hope the friends and admirers of Mr. Poe will come promptly to his assistance in his bitterest hour of need.

The highest priced photograph of a literary figure is a daguerrotype of Poe that was auctioned off for $9,000 in 1973.

The eponymous Helen of Poe's famous poem ("Thy hyacinth hair, thy classic face") was poet Sara Helen Whitman, with whom he tried to find solace in 1848 after his wife Virginia died of tuberculosis. At the same time Poe courted a Mrs. Richmond, for whom he wrote "For Annie" ("A dream of the truth/And the beauty of Annie—/Drowned in a bath/Of the tresses of Annie"); his inability to choose between the two led him to attempt suicide. But Poe actually did propose to his Helen—in a Providence, Rhode Island, graveyard. She accepted him on the condition that he quit drinking and when he didn't her mother made her break the engagement.

"Lord help my poor soul!" are said to be his last words. According to another story, he said: "My best friend would be the man who would blow out my brains with a pistol."

∇ ∇ ∇

Katherine Anne Porter (1890–1980)
The short story writer and novelist never began a story at the beginning. "I always write my last line, my last paragraphs, my last page first," she once confided. (See also ELINOR WYLIE.)

Undoubtedly in retaliation for the puritanism of her Aunt Cat, who raised her and thought it sinful for even children to be naked at any time, Katherine Anne in her middle years had her husbands and lovers take nude photographs of her that she promptly sent home to her family.

∇ ∇ ∇

Ezra Pound (1885–1972)

While Pound was teaching at Wabash College as a young man of 22, he became friendly with an English actress of unknown name who specialized as a male impersonator. One January night Pound found her out in the snow, cold and hungry with nowhere to go, and invited her to spend the night in his room. His spying spinster landladies discovered the girl, however, and reported Pound to the college. Although the poet insisted that he had given the lady his bed and had himself slept on the floor, he was promptly dismissed from the Indiana college. The affair is the basis for the canard that Pound was bisexual. Wrote the prophetic poet to a friend: "I'm so natural and trusting and innocent that I create scandal about my ways continually."

Pound self-published his first book of poems, having 100 copies of his 72-page *A Lume Spento* (1908) printed for $8 in Venice. He also reviewed his own book anonymously, highly praising it in the *London Evening Standard*: "Wild and haunting stuff, absolutely poetic, original, imaginative, passionate and spiritual…Coming after the trite and decorous verse of most of our decorous poets, this poet seems like a minstrel of Provence at a suburban musical evening…The unseizable magic of poetry is in the queer paper volume, and words are no good describing it." (See WALT WHITMAN.)

One of the many artists and writers the generous Pound helped over the years was French sculptor Henri Gaudier-Brzeska. Among several benefactions, Pound bought Gaudier a piece of marble from which the sculptor carved a portrait of the poet meant only to represent Pound's emotions. At least one other artist, Horace Brodsky, said that Gaudier had as a joke made a giant phallus of Pound, apparently relating his emotions to a poem entitled "Coitus," which Pound had just published, and the poet's unflagging interest in women. At any rate, Pound liked the work, called "Hieratic Head of Ezra Pound," and later displayed it in his garden, often scrubbing it clean with soap and water.

Early in his career his mother wrote him from America, suggesting that he write a verse epic of the American West. Pound replied, "My Gawd!! What has the West done to deserve it."

He remarked in a letter written to Milton Bronner in 1915, after he had begun the famous *Cantos*: "I am at work on a cryselephantine poem of immeasurable length which will occupy one for the next four decades unless it becomes a bore."

Actually his work on the *Cantos* would occupy him over half a century, almost until his death in 1972.

"A village explainer," Gertrude Stein said in describing him, "excellent if you were a village, but if you were not, not."

Writing to Robert Graves, D.H. Lawrence quipped: "Pound has spent his life trying to live down a family scandal—he's Longfellow's grand-nephew."

Commercial theater was to Pound hardly worthy of the designation "art." After reading James Joyce's recently completed play *Exiles* in 1913, the poet advised him that the commercial stage was "a gross, coarse form of art" playing "to a thousand fools huddled together."

When James Joyce sent Pound the Shawn chapters of *Finnegan's Wake* for possible use in a literary magazine he was planning, Pound wrote back: "Nothing, so far as I can make out, nothing short of divine vision or a new cure for the clap can possibly be worth all the circumambient peripherization."

Pound highly praised Joyce's *Ulysses* in the backwoods vernacular he often affected. "Wall, Mr. Joice," he wrote to him, "I recon' your a damn fine writer, that's what I recon'. An' I recon' this here work o' yourn is some concarn'd litershure. You can take it from me, an' I'm a jedge." But he could be insentitive and condescending to his friend, as when he received a manuscript of poems from Joyce five years later, in 1927, and urged him to file the new poems in the family Bible or photograph album and forget about them. Joyce published the poems anyway, but Pound's opinion probably influence him to choose their title, *Pomes Penyeach*.

His son was christened Omar Shakespear Pound, the proud father remarking of the name: "Just note the crescendo."

He and Ford Maddox Ford often played tennis, or some strange game similar to tennis. "[It seemed to] matter little how often they served fault after fault," an observer noted. "They just went on till the ball was where they wanted, then one or the other cried 'Game,' or 'Hard luck'...It was beyond anyone to umpire or score."

A master of jujitsu he once demonstrated a hold to Robert Frost in a restaurant, throwing the poet over his shoulder.

Referring to his friend T.S. Eliot's success as a critic in England, he observed in 1930 that "[Eliot] arrived at the supreme eminence among English critics largely through disguising himself as a corpse."

"That's not your style at all," he advised T.S. Eliot, irritated about some caustic criticism Eliot had written. "You let *me* throw the bricks through the front window. You go in at the back door and take out the swag."

He grew so paranoid about his crackpot economic theories that he believed he was being followed and watched wherever he went. A visitor playing tennis with him at Rapallo in 1937 claimed that Pound took him aside, surreptitiously pointed at the surrounding hills and whispered that spies were watching him through binoculars up there—spies sent to Italy by the Wall Street bankers, who were afraid Pound's economic system would cut their stranglehold on all the world's resources.

Pound was kept in a cage by the United States Army at the Disciplinary Training Camp outside Pisa while awaiting trial for treason after World War II. The ungilded cage of wire, wood and concrete, one of ten for the most dangerous prisoners, stood in the middle of the prison yard, had a tar-paper roof, chain-link fence wire all around, no shades or other coverings, and was brightly lighted at night. For six months, from May to October 1946, Pound lived and wrote in his six-by-six-foot cage, a guard always stationed outside. None of the prisoners was allowed to look or listen while the caged bird sang. The poet finally collapsed with a complete breakdown. Remanded to a hospital for the criminally insane in Washington, D.C., after being indicted for treason, Pound remained there until the indictment was dismissed when Archibald MacLeish, Robert Frost, Ernest Hemingway and others interceded for him. Released from St. Elizabeth's, he went back to Italy, where he died 14 years later.

Leaving St. Elizabeth's Hospital in Washington, D.C., in 1958 after 13 years in custody, Pound replied to reporters: "How did it go in the madhouse? Rather badly. But in what other place could one live in America?"

There is no doubt that Pound's work deserved the Bollinger Award made to him in 1948, just as there is no doubt that he was given the first national prize for poetry as part of a plan his supporters hatched to free him from St. Elizabeth's mental hospital in Washington, D.C., where he had been committed for his broadcasts during World War II. Pound, however, had little use for the award, calling it the "Bubble-Gum Prize."

There has been much controversy about Pound's alleged anti-Semitism, as reflected in his bizarre economic theories. In 1967 poet Allen Ginsberg visited him and later wrote in a magazine article that Pound had expressed great regret for all the mistakes he had made. "But the worst mistake I made," he said, "was that stupid suburban prejudice of anti-Semitism. All along that spoiled everything."

Pound grew increasingly silent in his last years; in a German documentary made of him he refused to speak a word. In 1965 he told his French publisher Dominique de Roux, "I did not enter into silence, silence captured me."

▽ ▽ ▽

William Prescott (1796–1859)
While joking with other students in the Harvard Commons, Prescott was hit in the eye by a hard crust of bread and blinded. This did not stop him from becoming a writer. Able to use only one eye for brief periods, he would sit in a darkened room and jot down notes with a special writing apparatus called a noctograph while his assistant read books and historical records aloud to him. The notes were then read back to him and he arranged them in his head before dictating his work in progress. Prescott trained himself to retain some 60 printed pages of notes (25,000 or so words) at a time. He wrote most of his great histories in this manner. (See also FRANCIS PARKMAN.)

▽ ▽ ▽

Joseph Pulitzer (1847–1911)
Sure that his beloved *World* was the answer not only to earth's but also to all the *universe's* troubles, the egocentric American newspaper publisher, whose will established the Pulitzer Prizes in journalism and letters, once considered erecting an advertising sign in New Jersey that would be visible on Mars. He only abandoned his plan when an associate asked, "What language would we print it in?"

▽ ▽ ▽ ▽ ▽ ▽ ▽ ▽

Ellery Queen (Frederic Dannay, 1905–1982; and Manfred B. Lee, 1905–1971)
Frederic Dannay, then the surviving member of the mystery-writing team known as Ellery Queen (Manfred B. Lee had been his cousin and partner), told in *New York* magazine how the pseudonym was born, offering some insight into the varied ways in which authors choose pen names:

"Ellery" was the name of one of my oldest boyhood friends in the small town in upstate New York where I grew up. I had never heard the name before, and I never heard it again till I came finally to the big city and heard of Ellery Sedgwick, the *Atlantic Monthly* editor, and William Ellery Leonard, the poet. It was such an odd name and I liked it so much that I suggested it, and Manny agreed. The second name was arrived at after many experiments. We tried to get a combination of syllables that had a mnemonic value, that once heard or seen would be remembered. We were only 23 years old then; it was 1928, and we had no notion that the word "queen" had any other meaning. We've had some embarrassing incidents.

(Lee and Dannay also used the pseudonym Barnaby Ross, when writing of their detective Drury Lane—named after the famous London theater.)

The two cousins who became Ellery Queen changed their original names, Daniel Nathan and Manform Lepofsky, as young men. They first used the penname Ellery Queen (inventing it as described in the previous anecdote) when they entered a mystery novel contest sponsored by *McClure's Magazine* in 1928, the use of a pseudonym being required to ensure impartiality.

▽ ▽ ▽ ▽ ▽ ▽ ▽ ▽ ▽

John Randolph (1773–1833)

The fiery eunuch John Randolph of Virginia, known for his bitting soprano tongue on the floors of Congress and for his vitriolic pen, once actually fought a duel over the pronunciation of a word. But then Randolph of Roanoke was widely known for his eccentricity, which deteriorated into dementia in his last years. It was Randolph who made the famous remark about Edward Livingstone: "He is a man of splendid abilities, but utterly corrupt. He shines and stinks like a rotten mackerel by moonlight."

Commenting on words and the legal profession in one speech, he said in his high, shrill voice, "That it is by the dextrous cutting and shuffling of this pack that is derived one half of the chicanery and more than half of the profits of the most lucrative profession in the world..."

The great orator was an erratic freelance whose opposition to the Missouri Compromise led to his denunciation of Kentuckian Henry Clay on the floor of the U.S. Senate in a speech that was widely reprinted. The inevitable duel with

Clay that followed proved bloodless—Clay's second shot piercing Randolph's white coat—but the men were never really reconciled. Randolph was buried as he requested—with his face to the west so that he could keep his eyes on Henry Clay!

∇ ∇ ∇

Burton Rascoe (1882–1957)
Recalling the literary life in America before the revolution of the 1920s, the critic and columnist remarked, "There were only two things for an artist to do in those days—stay drunk or commit suicide."

"What no wife of a writer can understand," Rascoe once said, "even if she lives with him for twenty years, is that a writer is working when he's staring out the window."

∇ ∇ ∇

John Reed (1887–1920)
The wealthy Harvard-educated author of *Ten Days That Shook the World* (1919), a later edition of which has an introduction by Le..in, helped form the first Communist Party of the United States and fled to Russia when he was indicted for sedition. Later he died there of typhus and was accorded the great honor among communists of being buried in the Kremlin wall after an elaborate funeral procession through the streets of Moscow.

Reed never approved of the institution of marriage. When in 1918 he was appointed as Soviet consul to New York he worried that he would have to marry people. "I hate the marriage ceremony!" he exclaimed. "I shall simply say to them: 'Proletarians of the world; unite!'" (Before he ever performed a marriage ceremony he was removed from his post upon protest of the U.S. government.)

∇ ∇ ∇

Major John Richardson (1796–1852)
Richardson's frontier romance *Wacousta* (1832) was one of the first expressions of literary nationalism in his homeland, Canada, and his *War of 1812* marked the beginning of scientific Canadian history. Drifting to New York City, where he hung on the outside of the Bohemian circle, he was one of the "poor devil authors" Poe wrote about, eking out an existence. Richardson even had to sell his faithful little dog for a few bits of food. He was buried in an unmarked pauper's grave, forgotten by all.

James Whitcomb Riley (1849–1916)

The Hoosier poet's life wasn't an easy one. He is responsible for the saying "the life of Riley," a metaphor for a rich, joyous life of ease, because his simple sentimental poems often depict barefoot boys with no concerns, loafing in the summer.

In one of his first jobs he traveled with a quack doctor who sold patent medicine. While the "doctor" was giving his spiel to the locals off the back of the wagon Riley would sit there, scribbling on old envelopes what were to be his first published poems.

He was an alcoholic who would got to any length to get a drink. Before one speaking engagement his friends locked him in a hotel room to keep him sober. Riley bribed a bellboy to hold a water glass of whiskey up to the keyhole so that he could sip it through a straw.

Hamlin Garland called upon Riley one evening while he was dressing for a dinner engagement. "'Pears like I'm always dressin' fer dinner nowadays," Riley told him in his easy Hoosier drawl. "When I was young and had a good digestion, could eat anything at any time, no one asked me to dine, but now that I'm old and feeble, stomach all gone, can't eat a thing but crackers and milk—look at that! [He put his hand on a stack of invitations.] Don't it beat hell?"

Riley was an accomplished, or atrocious, punster. When he heard that a neighbor's cook had fallen asleep near her stove and caught fire and burned to death, he offered an epitaph: "Well done, good and faithful servant."

∇ ∇ ∇

Morgan Robertson (1861–1915)

Science fiction is usually cited as the literary genre where near-perfect examples of *promesia* ("memory of the future") are most often found. But it would be hard to find a better example of fiction's becoming reality than popular novelist Morgan Robertson's excellent short novel *Futility* (1898). Published 14 years before the *Titanic* sank in history's most famous marine disaster, it told of a great "unsinkable" luxury liner named the *Titan* that sank on its maiden voyage after hitting an iceberg, with the loss of almost all passengers because there weren't enough lifeboats aboard. More similarities between the *Titan* and *Titanic* are shown in the chart below:

	Titan	Titanic
Ship length	800 feet	882.5 feet
Ship tonnage	75,000	66,000

Speed at impact	25 knots	23 knots
Propellers	3	3
Number of passengers	3,000	2,207
Number of lifeboats	24	20
Month of sinking	April	April

▽ ▽ ▽

Edwin Arlington Robinson (1869–1935)

Early in his career Robinson had written to a friend: "You cannot conceive how cutting it is for a man of twenty-four to depend on his mother for every cent he has and every mouthful he swallows." He was 36 when President Theodore Roosevelt took an interest in his work. After Robinson had self-published a volume of his poems, one of the President's sons was assigned to read those poems by a prep school teacher who had bought a copy. The son recommended it to his father. Roosevelt persuaded his own publisher to publish the poet's work and also created a sinecure for him in the New York Custom House, a job that paid $2,000 a year and required him only to report to work every morning. Like Melville and Hawthorne before him, Robinson was employed for a time as a customs officials, but he lasted only four years in the job—until Teddy Roosevelt left office and it was rumored that President Taft might make Robinson work. "My chief duty as a pillar of the government," he complained almost as soon as he took the job, "appears to consist of remaining a prison in Room 408. This is particularly rotten just now, as I am in a mood for work (work with me means studying the ceiling and my navel for four hours and then writing down perhaps four lines—sometimes as many as seven and again none at all) …"

A newspaper reporter asked Robinson just what poetry was. "Poetry," he replied, "is a language which tells us, through a more or less emotional reaction, something that cannot be said." Another time he told a friend, "There are too many words in prose and they take up altogether too much room."

For weeks Robinson's Boston publisher, Small, Maynard & Company, tried to find the long poem "Captain Craig," included in the author's *Captain Craig* collection, which was to be published by the firm in 1902. Robinson searched his papers, the office was turned upside down, all to no avail. Finally the poem was recovered in a Boston brothel, where Robinson's editor had left it, and the book could go to press.

When a prolific novelist told him that she never wrote less then 5,000 words a day, the poet replied, "This morning I deleted the hyphen from 'hell-bound' and made it one word; this afternoon I redivided it and restored the hyphen."

The poet was a shy, unassuming, laconic man. Once an admirer exclaimed, "That's *the* Mr. Robinson." Overhearing her, Robinson said, "A Mr. Robinson."

∇ ∇ ∇

J.J. Rodale (1899–1971)
It is hard to think of a more ironic end than that of this author and publisher who did so much to advance the cause of organic farming and good health in America. Rodale died while appearing on the Dick Cavett television talk show, soon after stating, "I'm so healthy that I expect to live on and on." Just as the show ended, before he could leave his chair, he slumped over with a fatal heart attack.

∇ ∇ ∇

Will Rogers (1879–1935)
The homespun philosopher, a humorist in the tradition of Artemus Ward, came from an Oklahoma family that was part Indian. One time he was speaking to a group of women from the Daughters of the American Revolution, whose ancestors all came over on the first voyage of the *Mayflower*. "I can't claim my folks was *Mayflower* descendants," he told the women glumly, and then a gleam came into his eyes: "But I recollect they was here to meet the boat."

Rogers once presided as a toastmaster at a fraternal dinner. He introduced the principal speaker, who droned on and on, saying little. When the man finally finished Rogers arose and said, "You have just listened to that famous Chinese statesman, On Too Long."

While visiting Paris, Rogers sent a postcard of the Venus de Milo to his niece, writing on the back: "This is what will happen to you if you don't stop biting your fingernails."

∇ ∇ ∇

Eleanor Roosevelt (1884–1962)
The first lady's magazine and newspaper columns, her books and her other writings and personal appearances inspired people to write her as many as 300,000 letters a year, more than her husband Franklin received. She answered as many of these as she could, sometimes staying up all night to do so, and all the proceeds of her writing went to charity.

Franklin D. Roosevelt (1882–1945)

The American president, who wrote five or six books, inspired great hate as well as great love. When *The Public Papers and Addresses of Franklin D. Roosevelt* came out in 1938 a famous old Boston bookstore advised the publisher: "We'll buy as many sets of the Roosevelt papers as you can deliver bound in his own skin."

Bedded down with the flu in the fall of 1940, President Roosevelt woke to find the following headline staring him in the face: F.D.R. IN BED WITH COED. Instead of ordering the head of the anonymous editor, proofreader or typesetter who had created the blooper, F.D.R. ordered 100 copies of this early bulldog edition.

∇ ∇ ∇

Theodore Roosevelt (1859–1919)

Although Theodore Roosevelt died when only 60, he crammed more action into his lifetime than any two people. Surely America's most energetic president, he was celebrated for his Spanish-American War "Rough Riders"—who, incidentally, fought their most noted battle on foot—his big-game hunting, trust-busting, the books he wrote, and his colorful use of language. Among the words he coined or revived were *muckraker, square deal, weasel word, nature faker, mollycoddle, speak softly and carry a big stick* and *lunatic fringe.* One member of the lunatic fringe, John Schrank, tried to assassinate Roosevelt in 1912. The bullet struck the folded manuscript of a speech he was carrying in his breast pocket and failed to do fatal damage. The intrepid Teddy refused to be treated for his wound until after he had delivered his speech with the bullet hole in it.

While at Harvard Roosevelt was rehearsing a poem in a public speaking class. He could only get as far as the line "When Greece, her knees in suppliance bent" and then stood there dumbstruck, unable to say anything else, until the instructor suggested; "Roosevelt, suppose you grease her knees again, and then perhaps she'll go."

"I am a Democrat!" a drunken heckler cried out in the middle of one of Roosevelt's speeches.

"May I ask the gentleman why he is a Democrat?" Roosevelt replied.

"Because my grandfather was a Democrat, my father was a Democrat and I am a Democrat."

"But my friend," said Roosevelt, thinking he had the situation in hand, "suppose your grandfather had been a jackass and your father had been a jackass—what would you be then?"

"A Republican!" the man quickly replied.

One of the more literary of American presidents, the energetic Teddy wrote at least 17 books and corresponded with many contemporary authors, including Henry James, whom he thought a snob, but who considered him a windbag.

Novelist Owen Wister called upon Theodore Roosevelt in the White House only to have the president's daughter burst into his office three or four times with trivial interruptions. "Theodore, isn't there anything you can do to control Alice?" an exasperated Wister finally asked. "I can do one of two things," Teddy replied. "I can be president of the United States or I can control Alice. I cannot possibly do both." (Later in her life Alice became famous in her own right as Alice Roosevelt Longworth, Washington wit and hostess.)

∇ ∇ ∇

Harold Ross (1892–1951)
When only 14 years old the founder of the *New Yorker* worked as a reporter on the *Salt Lake City Tribune*. One of his assignments was to interview a bordello madam. He began by asking her, "How many fallen women do you have?"

Ross was perhaps the only private in the American army to have calling cards. His card read: "Pvt. H.W. Ross/CompanyC/Eighteenth Engineers Railway U.S. Army/United States Expeditionary/Force in France."

Ross ran the *New Yorker* on a meager budget in the early days. Once he asked Dorothy Parker why she hadn't come into the office to write a piece she had promised him. She had, Dorothy replied, but "someone else was using the pencil."

Brendan Gill writes in *Here at the New Yorker* that Ross had a firm rule for newly hired editors: "Don't fuck the contributors." The corollary to this was, "Moreover, we won't hire the people you *do* fuck." (Though Gill adds: "Certain exceptions to the edict spring to mind.")

Ross phoned author Robert Coates about his *New Yorker* review of Hemingway's *Death in the Afternoon*. "[Alexander] Woollcott tells me there's a hell of a bad word in the book—bathroom stuff," he told Coates. "What word is that?" Coates asked. "I can't tell you over the phone," Ross said.

"You can't quit," he told E.B. White when White threatened to leave the *New Yorker*. "This isn't a magazine—it's a Movement!"

"I'm a profane *** by nature," he told an inteviewer in explaining how he managed to avoid guest spots on radio programs, "and whenever one of those *** round tables or something called up, I'd say, 'Hell, yes. I'll be glad to sit in on your *** panel, or whatever the *** you call it!' The word soon got around that I couldn't draw a breath without cursing and the *** hucksters never bothered me again."

Ross wasn't noted for his erudition, but he did try to improve his mind. According to James Thurber, the *New Yorker* editor took the *Encyclopedia Britannica* with him to the bathroom whenever possible and "was up to the letter H" when he died.

Ross butted into a conversation about Willa Cather. "Willa Cather?" he said. "Willa Cather? Did he write *The Private Life of Helen of Troy?*"

Speaking to Sherwood Anderson one afternoon he happily advised him, "There hasn't been a good short story written in America, Anderson, since O. Henry died."

Dubuque, Iowa, is named for the first settler, a French-Canadian lead miner named Julien Dubuque. But what about the famous symbol of prudery, *the little old lady in Dubuque?* The phrase seems to have originated in this sense with Harold Ross, when he promised in a prospectus of the *New Yorker* that his magazine would *not* be edited for "the old lady in Dubuque." According to Brendan Gill, in his fascinating *Here at the New Yorker* (1975), Ross may have been inspired by "Boots" Mulgrew, a former Broadway musical comedy skit writer forced by drinking and financial problems to retreat from New York to his birthplace. Mulgrew soon after began contributing squibs to a widely read *Chicago Tribune* column called "A Line o' Type or Two." These pieces, describing "the provincial absurdities of Dubuque," were signed with the pseudonym "Old Lady in Dubuque," and Gill suggests that "Ross read them, admired them, and, whether consciously or not, got the old lady in Dubuque fixed in his mind as a natural antagonist."

∇ ∇ ∇

Damon Runyon (1884–1946)

The journalist and short story writer, noted for his tales of the New York underworld and New York City itself, requested that his ashes be scattered over Broadway. On his death his ashes were dropped on the Great White Way from a large transport plane flown by famous American aviator Eddie Rickenbacker.

Benjamin Russell (1745–1813)

Above editor Benjamin Russell's desk in the offices of the *Centinel*, a Massachusetts Federalist newspaper, hung the serpentine-shaped map of a new Essex County senatorial district that began at Salisbury and included Amesbury, Haverhill, Methuen, Andover, Middleton, Danvers, Lynnfield, Salem, Marblehead, Lynn and Chelsea. This political monster was part of a general reshaping of voting districts that the Democratic-Republican-controlled state legislature had enacted with the approval of incumbent Governor Elbridge Gerry. The arbitrary redistricting, a fairly common practice of the time, would have enabled the Jeffersonians to concentrate Federalist power in a few districts and remain in the majority after the (then annual) gubernatorial election of 1812, and was of course opposed by all Federalists. So when the celebrated painter Gilbert Stuart visited the *Centinel* office one day before the elections, editor Russell indignantly pointed to the monstrous map on the wall, inspiring Stuart to take a crayon and add head, wings and claws to the already lizard-like district. "That will do for a salamander," the artist said when he finished. "A *Gerry*-mander, you mean," Mr. Russell replied, and a name for the polticial creature was born.

▽ ▽ ▽ ▽ ▽ ▽ ▽ ▽

Augustus Saint-Gaudens (1848–1907)

The Irish-born American sculptor and author, whose *Reminiscence*s were published by his son six years after his death, is the prototype of Mr. Wharton in Henry Adams's novel *Esther*. He felt that all creative people—sculptors, painters, writers—had to at least be slightly peculiar. "What garlic is to salad," he once said "insanity is to art."

▽ ▽ ▽

Arthur Samuels (fl. 1920s)

The editor of *Harpers Bazaar* listened impatiently to Alexander Woollcott telling yet another of his how-it-was-in-the-theater-of-war tales. "If you were ever in the theater of war, Alec," he finally interrupted, "it was in the last row seat nearest the exit."

∇ ∇ ∇

Carl Sandburg (1878–1967)

A young playwright asked the American poet and biographer of Lincoln to evaluate his play at a dress rehearsal. Sandburg, however, fell asleep during the performance and the young man protested. "Don't you know how much I want your opinion?" he said. "Sleep *is* an opinion," replied Sandburg.

T. O'Connor Sloan III, long a book editor before retiring several years ago, tells the following story.

> Many years ago, when Robert Giroux was editor-in-chief of Harcourt, Brace, he told me this little anecdote. He was expecting a visit from T.S. Eliot one day, and he knew that Carl Sandburg was going to be in the offices at the same time. Mr. Giroux made what arrangements he could to keep the two from meeting face to face, because he knew that the poets were not mutual admirers. When he returned to his office from lunch, to his horror he saw Sandburg and Eliot there, glaring at each other from opposite corners. "Your face has deep lines," Sandburg was saying to Eliot. I later told this little story to Melville Cane, the lawyer and poet. He said, "If I had been Eliot, I would have said to Sandburg, 'I can't say the same for your poetry.'"

Why was Abraham Lincoln loved by so many diverse people, Sandburg asked an old Irish railroad flagman who had lived in the president's time. There came the best answer to the question the poet received in all his years of Lincoln study. "He was humanity," the flagman said.

He had a standard, rhymed reply for the thousands who wrote him over the years asking how to become a writer: "Solitude and prayer—then go on from there."

"Ordering a man to write a poem," he remarked, "is like commanding a pregnant woman to give birth to a red-headed child. You can't do it—it's an act of God."

His editor William Targ took him to 21, where a bowing headwaiter asked him, "Where would you like to sit, Mr. Sandburg?"
"I wanna sit where I can see the 'ceelebreeties,'" he drawled.

He was asked to describe his monumental Lincoln biography, replying: "It's a book about a man whose father could not sign his name, written by a man whose father could not sign his.

His love for the goats he raised was so great that one frigid Michigan night he herded 15 of the shivering animals into his house and played his guitar for them.

∇ ∇ ∇

William Saroyan (1908–1981)

When he began his writing career Saroyan kept his rejections in a stack beside his desk. It is said that before his first story was accepted the stack reached up even with the top of the desk.

Loyal to both America and his ancestral homeland, the Pulitzer Prize-winning author willed half of his ashes to be buried in his Fresno, California, birthplace and half in the Armenian capital of Yerevan, now in the U.S.S.R.

Saroyan made "a suggested posthumous statement" to the Associated Press five days before his death. "Everybody has got to die," he said, "but I have always believed an exception would be made in my case. Now what?"

∇ ∇ ∇

John Godfrey Saxe (1816–1887)

Saxe was strolling on Broadway when he met a friend who asked him what his plans were for the week.

"I'm bound for Boston tomorrow," the New England poet said, "God willing."

"What route is that?" his friend asked.

"By way of Providence, of course," Saxe replied.

∇ ∇ ∇

Delmore Schwartz (1913–1966)

Serving as an editor of the *Partisan Review* in 1945, the poet rejected a short story submitted by Calder Willingham, then a young, unknown author. Schwartz called the story "unrealistic" and when he received a long letter from Willingham denouncing the rejection, he answered it as best and calmly as he could. Several years passed and Willingham won fame with his novel *End As a Man*. Schwartz bought a copy of the novel in paperback and was startled to find a whorehouse in the novel named the Hotel Delmore. From then on he could read no more of Willingham's work, but he did tell a mutual friend that the hotel naming must have been a subconscious expression of deep resentment. Not so, Willingham told the friend; he had been completely aware of what he was doing when naming the house of ill fame after Schwartz, although the name had also been "exactly right from an artistic standpoint."

In his biography of the poet, James Atlas attributed these lines to him:

All poets' wives have rotten lives
Their husbands look at them like knives.

∇ ∇ ∇

Harry Scovel (fl. late 19th century)

While in Cuba during the Spanish-American War this little-known *New York World* correspondent, the son of a minister, covered the action wearing his rumpled suit and battered black derby. Coming to a village American troops had captured, Scovel went to hoist the Stars and Stripes in place of the Spanish flag but was reprimanded by Major General William Shafter, head of the American Army in Cuba. Scovel promptly punched the general in the jaw, considering his interference an insult to the *World*, whose owners stuck by him.

∇ ∇ ∇

Charles Scribner (1854–1930)

Reading the manuscript of *The Sun Also Rises* the conservative publisher grew concerned about the four-letter words Hemingway used. As he read, he recorded these words on a daily calendar, leaving it on his desk when he went out to lunch. While she straightened his desk that noontime his rather prudish secretary came across the calendar. It was headed "Things To Do Today" with the words "piss…shit…fuck" listed below.

∇ ∇ ∇

Edward Wyllis Scripps (1854–1926)

When his former mistress tried to blackmail him by making public their affair the publisher held a news conference, giving the story to rival papers and running it in his own *Cincinnati Post* the next day. Rather than lose circulation, as everyone had expected, *Post* sales increased.

∇ ∇ ∇

William Seabrook (fl. 1920s)

The adventure writer, whose *Jungle Ways* was a best-seller in the 1920s, was an alcoholic and sadist whose hatred of his mother, one psychiatrist claimed, compelled him to want to hurt all women. At a party he gave in Paris guests were startled to see a beautiful prostitute who had been hired to hang suspended by chains from a balcony. He was reportedly seen in New York's Greenwich

Village leading leather-masked women on leashes, their hands locked behind them in handcuffs studded with pearls.

∇ ∇ ∇

William Secker (fl. 1705)
Secker in 1705 wrote and published the first miniature book in America. Measuring 2 by 3.5 inches and containing 92 pages, the book has a title that explains its subject nicely: *A Wedding Ring Fit for the Finger, or the Salve of Divinity on the Sore of Humanity With directions to those men that want wives, how to choose them; and to those women that have husbands, how to use them.*

∇ ∇ ∇

Ellery Sedgwick (1872–1960)
The former *Atlantic Monthly* editor told of a short story class that met at Harvard:

> It was at a time when Russian literature of a particularly dismal type infested the minds of young men. The proletariat were called on to furnish all the characters, and the successive themes invariably represented deepening crises of poverty, illness, and general misery. The instructor was no doubt a kindhearted man (all teachers are), but the drab monotony of his students' stories overmastered his sympathy. "For Heaven's sake," he said, "give me variety. Mix in a few aristocrats with the populace and don't begin your story with some platitudinous affirmation of the brutality of life. Begin dramatically."
>
> The students took him at his word. When the class met again, the story first to be considered began with the dramatic note: "What insolence!" cried the Duchess, rising in alarm. "Take your hand off my knee!"

∇ ∇ ∇

Sequoyah (ca. 1770–1843)
This Cherokee Indian is one of the few people in history, and probably the first, known to have invented an alphabet for a living language. (Another was King Njoya of Bamun, in Kamerun West Africa, who devised an original writing system for his people around 1900.) It took Sequoyah 12 years to invent his 86-character alphabet or syllabary, all of the characters representing the sounds of spoken Cherokee. The alphabet was so logical and simple that it could be learned in a few days and it made an entire, illiterate population literate within a few months.

∇ ∇ ∇

Anne Sexton (1928–1974)
Out drinking with two fellow poets, Sexton parked in a "Loading Only Zone." "It's O.K.," she told her companions, "we're only going to get loaded."

Irwin Shaw (1913–1984)

The novelist waited and waited for a waiter to take his order in a French restaurant. Finally, the maitre d' appeared to advise him that snails were the specialty of the house. "I know," said Shaw, nodding his head, "and you've got them dressed as waiters."

▽ ▽ ▽

Charles Monroe Sheldon (1896–1978)

Sheldon's *In His Steps* (1896), which has sold 30 million copies is the best-selling novel of all time. The Topeka, Kansas, minister wrote a utopian fantasy of what the world might be like if people lived literally according to Christ's teachings, and then tested the novel by reading it a chapter at a time to his Sunday evening congregation. Unfortunately for him, he sold the book for only $75 to the *Chicago Advance*, which printed it as a serial. Only part of the serial was sent to the Copyright Office and thus the copyright was declared defective and Sheldon lost millions when numerous editions were released by various publishers. His novel has been translated into at least 23 languages.

▽ ▽ ▽

Benjamin Penhallow Shillaber (1814–1890)

Shillaber, a popular humorist, printed Mark Twain's first work in his *The Carpet Bag*, a weekly important in developing the new school of American humor. In 1847 Shillaber had created the character of Mrs. Partington, which he used in a number of books, beginning with his *Life and Sayings of Mrs. Partington* (1854). Critics charged Shillaber with lifting his character from English politician and author Sydney Smith. The American admitted that he took the name from Smith's allusion to the legendary Dame Partington, who had tried to sweep the flooding Atlantic Ocean out of her cottage and whom Smith had compared in an 1831 speech with the opposition of the House of Lords to reform. Although Shillaber denied using anything more than the Partington name for his gossiping, Yankee Mrs. Malaprop, his own name came into some disrepute and may have become the basis for *shillaber* and then *shill*. As a matter of fact, Mark Twain owes far more to Shillaber's Mrs. Partington (for Tom Sawyer's Aunt Polly) than Shillaber owes to Smith (for Mrs. Partington).

▽ ▽ ▽

Joseph Shipley (1894–1988)

The drama critic, teacher and etymologist published his last book, *The Origins of English Words*, at 91, and was still working three years later when he died of a stroke on a visit to London.

Christopher Latham Sholes (1819–1890)

The word *typewriter* was coined by American Christopher Latham Sholes, who patented the first practical commercial typewriter in 1868 (slow, difficult machines, intended primarily for the blind, had been invented as early as 1714). Sholes's "type-writer" had only capital letters. Manufactured by Remington, it was owned by Henry James, Mark Twain and Sigmund Freud, among other famous early experimenters. Mark Twain, in fact, typed *The Adventures of Tom Sawyer* on Sholes's machine in 1875, this being the first typewritten book manuscript (a fact that Twain kept secret in his lifetime because he didn't want to write testimonials or show the uninitiated how to use the machine).

∇ ∇ ∇

William Gilmore Simms (1806–1870)

Though he was called "a Southern Cooper," the South Carolinian author never believed he lived up to his potential. This is reflected in the melancholy epitaph over his grave, which he wrote himself:

> *Here lies one who after a reasonably long life,*
> *distinguished chiefly by unceasing labors,*
> *left all his better works undone.*

∇ ∇ ∇

Richard Leo Simon (1889–1960)

In promoting Simon and Schuster's children's book *Dr. Dan the Bandage Man* the publisher decided to give away six Band-Aids with each copy. "Please ship half million Band-Aids immediately," he wired a friend at Johnson and Johnson. He soon received the reply: "Band-Aids on the way. What the hell happened to you?"

∇ ∇ ∇

Upton Sinclair (1878–1968)

One of the most prolific of authors, the muckraking novelist and journalist, born in Baltimore, had to support his family with his writing from the time he was 15, when he began selling stories and jokes to the dime novel magazines. Sinclair's father, a heavy drinker, was unable to provide for the family. Moving to New York City at 17, young Upton continued to support them, and put himself through City College by writing novels. While he attended graduate school at Columbia he wrote six novels under various pseudonyms; he once estimated his output for the 18 months ending in November 1898 as 1 1/4 million words. His work written before 1900 is rarely included with the more than 100 works that followed.

Sinclair's larger purpose in writing his novel *The Jungle* (1906) was to protest "wage slavery" and attract people to socialism, but it was generally regarded only as an exposé of the meat-packing industry. The book caused a storm of indignation in the country that led to the Pure-Food Act of 1906. (Many papers printed the anonymous parody: *Mary had a little lamb, and when she saw it sicken,/She shipped it off to Packingtown,/And now it's labeled chicken.*) Sinclair wrote his book over a period of nine months in a little eight-by-10-foot board cabin near Princeton, New Jesey, and it was rejected five times as too controversial before it found a publisher. Less than a dozen of his 308 pages were about the gruesome details of meat production and he devoted most of his book to the exploitation of the Packingtown workers, but *The Jungle* made few converts to socialism. Sinclair was very disappointed, despite the book's success. "I aimed for the public's heart," he said, "and by accident I hit it in the stomach."

▽ ▽ ▽

Alfred E. Smith (1873–1944)
In the early days before he ran for president the noted politician, author and magazine editor was speaking at a political rally when a heckler interrupted him. "Go on, Al, tell 'em all you know," the man shouted. "It won't take long!"

The Happy Warrior smiled back at the heckler. "I'll tell 'em all we *both* know," he said sweetly. "That won't take any longer."

▽ ▽ ▽

Logan Pearsall Smith (1865–1946)
This American author spent most of his years in England studying the English language and is reponsible for the aphorism "People say life is the thing, but I prefer reading."

"Have you finally found any meaning in life," a friend half jokingly asked him shortly before his death.

"Yes," he replied, "there is a meaning; at least for me, there is one thing that matters—to set a chime of words tinkling in the minds of a few fastidious people."

▽ ▽ ▽

Red Smith (Walter Wellesley Smith; 1905–1982)
The esteemed sports columnist spent a night with several colleagues over a few bottles of scotch at his hotel bar. Late the next morning the desk called to say that a hat had been found in the bar, did it belong to him? "I don't know," Smith said. "Does it have a head in it?"

"There's nothing to writing," Smith told an interviewer. "All you do is sit down at a typewriter and open a vein." (See also GENE FOWLER.)

∇ ∇ ∇

Solomon Franklin Smith (1801–1869)
Smith's books and tall tales reflected the customs and characters of the early American Southwest. Once he told of a woman who was offered condolences on the death of her husband. "Warn't of much account, no how!" she replied.

∇ ∇ ∇

Winchell Smith (1871–1933)
Winchell Smith's 1906 dramatization of George Barr McCutcheon's *Brewster's Millions*, a perennial favorite, included among its cast members a "George Spelvin." This was a second name given to a member of the cast who played two parts. Since that day "George Spelvin" has had the same theatrical use.

∇ ∇ ∇

Jean Stafford (1915–1979)
When the novelist told an old cowboy in Colorado that she was a writer, he told her, "That's real nice work, Jean. It's something you can do in the shade."

∇ ∇ ∇

Lincoln Steffens (1866–1936)
The muckraking American author made a trip to Russia in 1919. Upon meeting American financier Bernard Baruch after his return, Steffens made his famous remark about Communist Russia, "I have seen the future and it works." Actually, his exact words were, "I have been over into the future, and it works." Steffens's companion on the trip to Russia, William Bullitt, claimed that Steffens's remark wasn't spontaneous, that he had invented it even before he set foot on Russian soil!

∇ ∇ ∇

Gertrude Stein (1874–1946)
Gertrude Stein was one of William James's favorite students when he taught at Radcliffe, and he went to absurd lengths to give her preferential treatment. One morning, after a night of partying, she wrote on an examination paper, "Dear Professor James, I am so sorry but I do not feel a bit like writing an examination paper on philosophy today." Wrote James in reply, "Dear Miss Stein, I understand perfectly. I often feel like that myself."

What Gertrude Stein really wrote in her poem "Sacred Emily" was "Rose is a rose is a rose is a rose," but her words have been misquoted as "a rose is a rose is a rose" so often that she may as well have written it that way. In her prose Gertrude Stein had no use for nouns: "Things once they are named the name does not go on doing anything to them and so why write in nouns." But in poetry, she felt: "You can love a name and if you love a name then saying that name any number of times only makes you love it more." And poetry is "really loving the name of anything."

Gertrude Stein hated commas and would have rid the world of them. Said she: "If you want to take a breath you ought to know yourself that you want to take a breath."

Explaining her *The Third Rose* to a friend she said, "The central theme of the novel is that they were glad to see each other."

After visiting Gertrude Stein and Alice B. Toklas, American critic Edmund Wilson wrote to John Dos Passos: "[Their relationship is] the most complete example of human symbiosis I have ever seen."

Stein's editor, A.J. Fifield, sent her a rejection slip in a style she had no trouble appreciating, though the content might have bothered her:

> I am only one, only one, only. Only one being, one at the same time. Not two, not three, only one. Only one life to live, only sixty minutes in one hour. Only one pair of eyes. Only one brain. Only one being. Being only one, having only one pair of eyes, having only one time, having only one life, I cannot read your MS three or four times. Not even one time. Only one look, only one look is enough. Hardly one copy would sell here. Hardly one. Hardly one.

"Une génération perdue," remarked Monsieur Pernollet, owner of the Hotel de Pernollet in Belley. He was speaking to Gertrude Stein and pointing at a young mechanic repairing Stein's car. Young men like the mechanic, Monsieur Pernollet said, had gone to war, had not been educated properly in their formative years, and were thus a lost generation. Gertrude Stein remembered Monsieur Pernollet's phrase and applied it to Hemingway and his friends. Hemingway quoted her in *The Sun Also Rises* (1926) and the words became the label for an entire literary generation.

Gertrude Stein posed 80 times for Picasso's famous 1906 portrait of her, but he wiped off the face each time, claiming that he just couldn't "see" her. Picasso finished her portrait from memory in Spain and when she complained that it didn't look like Gertrude Stein, he remarked that that was all right—someday she'd look like his portrait. And she did. (Picasso, perhaps not so incidentally, did not like Gertrude Stein, referring to her behind her back as "the hippopotamus.")

Members of England's Bloomsbury group, composed of writers and artists, thought highly of themselves. One member, asked during the Great War why he was not in uniform fighting for civilization, replied disdainfully, "Madame, I am the civilization they are fighting for." Gertrude Stein thought little of the group. It was, she said, "The Young Men's Christian Association—with Christ left out, of course."

While the sculptor Jacques Lipchitz did her bust, Gertrude Stein asked him, "Jacques, of course you don't know too much about English literature, but besides Shakespeare and me, who do you think there is?"

She never said that she taught Hemingway the "manly art," as she claimed about writing, but Gertrude Stein did take boxing lessons while attending Cambridge. There was no match with Hemingway, so far as is known.

Bennett Cerf prefaced this "Publisher's Note" to her *The Geographical History of America or the Relation of Human Nature to the Human Mind*:

> This space is usually reserved for a brief description of a book's contents. In this case, however, I must admit frankly that I do not know what Miss Stein is talking about. I do not even understand the title.
>
> I admire Miss Stein tremendously, and I like to publish her books, although most of the time I do not know what she is driving at. That, Miss Stein tells me, is because I am dumb.
>
> I note that one of my partners and I are characters in this latest work of Miss Stein's. Both of us wish we knew what she was saying about us. Both of us hope too that her faithful followers will make more of this book than we were able to!

When Cerf interviewed her on his national radio program, he commented, "I'm very proud to be your publisher, Miss Stein, but as I've always told you, I don't understand very much of what you're saying."

"Well, I've always told you, Bennett," she replied, "you're a very nice boy but you're rather stupid."

When a friend smuggled her manuscript novel *Mrs. Reynolds* out of France into England a customs inspector nearly seized it, the prose being so incomprehensible to him that he thought it was a secret code.

One time Pablo Picasso brought her some of his poetry to read. "I read his poems," she later recalled, "and then I seized him by both shoulders and shook him good and hard. 'Pablo,' I said 'go home and paint!'"

"What is the answer?" Gertrude Stein asked on her death bed. When she heard no reply from Alice B. Toklas, she murmured, as her last words: "In that case, what is the question?"

∇ ∇ ∇

John Steinbeck (1902–1968)

Steinbeck, like Newton before him, saw the only draft of a book destroyed by a dog. The novelist's setter pup Toby chewed into confetti half of the first draft of *Of Mice and Men*. "Two months' work to do over again," the author wrote at the time. "I was pretty mad, but the poor little fellow may have been acting critically. I didn't want to ruin a good dog for a manuscript I'm not sure is good at all. He got only an ordinary spanking." Later, when *Of Mice and Men* was panned in some quarters, Steinbeck felt even more strongly that the dog was a good critic. "I'm not sure Toby didn't know what he was doing when he ate that first draft," he wrote in another letter. "I have promoted Toby-dog to be lieutenant-colonel in charge of literature. But as for the unpedictable literary enthusiasms of this country, I have little faith in them."

Another of Steinbeck's novels was accidentally destroyed…by the thousands. Some 5,000 copies of *The Wayward Bus* (1947) went up in flames when the truck taking them from the bindery collided with a bus—yes, a wayward bus—traveling on the wrong side of the road.

He told of a reader so incensed about a Steinbeck book that he wrote a letter to him ending, "Beware. You will never get out of this world alive."

Playwright Jack Kirkland was so incensed at drama critic Richard Watts's review of Steinbeck's *Tortilla Flat* in 1938 that he punched the critic when he encountered him at a bar. Unfortunately for Kirkland, a good number of Watts's critic colleagues were in the bar and proceeded to attack him more violently than Watts's review.

While they were fishing in the Gulf of Lower California, the Nobel Prize winner and his friend Doc Ricketts noticed a little fish that lived in the cloaca of the sea cucumber and that kept darting in and out of the creature's anus. They named the hitherto unrecorded fish *Proctophilus winchilli*, after gossip columnist Walter Winchell.

"The profession of book-writing," Steinbeck told a friend, "makes horse racing seem like a solid, stable business."

Steinbeck confessed in a letter to a friend that whenever he heard writers, especially Nobel Prize winners, talking about "The Artist" he wanted "to leave the profession." Citing a recent Faulkner interview he noted, "Bill said he only read Homer and Cervantes, never his contemporaries, and then, by God, in answer to the next question he stole a paragraph from an article I wrote for the *Saturday Review* eight months ago."

Recalling what happened to Sinclair Lewis, Faulkner, Hemingway and many other writers, he feared that he would be unable to write after winning the Nobel Prize, in 1962. His fears proved justified, for he didn't publish another book in his remaining six years.

∇ ∇ ∇

Frances Steloff (1888–1989)
The New York bookstore owner and champion of avant-garde literature built Manhattan's Gotham Book Mart into a literary legend and continued to be involved in this hangout for the literati until her death at 101. "H.L. Mencken and Theodore Dreiser once came in here drunk," she recalled, in recounting one of the many literary anecdotes that originated on the premises. "They signed everything they could put their hands on. Not only their own books. All the religion books, including the entire stock of Bibles."

∇ ∇ ∇

George Sterling (1869–1926)
This melancholy poet was used by Jack London as the basis for Russ Brissenden, the socialist poet in his novel *Martin Eden* (1909). In the novel London has Brissenden commit suicide. In reality Sterling died the same way 17 years later, taking his life one night in San Francisco's Bohemian Club.

∇ ∇ ∇

Wallace Stevens (1879–1955)
In proposing to his future bride in 1905 the poet wrote: "Are you really fond of books—paper valleys and far countries, paper gardens, paper men and women? I live with them constantly."

Stevens's wife was the model for the head on the Liberty Head dime. When Stevens was introduced to Oscar Levant, the pianist and wit quipped, "Why shouldn't you be a great poet? I'd be inspired too, if my wife had little wings where her ears should be."

"Let's talk about politics," he told a friend one evening, "or law, or plays, but don't let us argue about poets or poetry."

He seemed able to face literary folk only when well in his cups. It is said that he invaded Hemingway's Key West house uninvited and began berating him. "You're a cad," he cried drunkenly, "and all your heroes are cads and you are all your heroes, so you must be a cad!" "Come now, Stevens," said an unusually indulgent Hemingway, "I'm really not so bad as all that, am I?" "Yes!" the poet said and left as abruptly as he came.

∇ ∇ ∇

Adlai E. Stevenson (1900–1965)
"An editor," the statesman and author observed, "is one who separates the wheat from the chaff and prints the chaff."

∇ ∇ ∇

Donald Ogden Stewart (1894–1980)
The humorist and several other writers were attending a party at Secretary of War Robert Lovett's home when the phone rang and Lovett answered it. Most were awestruck when they heard their host say in the course of the conversation, "Why, yes! Let Austria have eight million dollars." All but Stewart. The next morning he sent Lovett a telegram reading, "You have made me the happiest little country in the world." It was signed "Austria."

∇ ∇ ∇

Frank Stockton (1834–1902)
In Stockton's immensely popular short story "The Lady or the Tiger" (1886), which was even made into an operetta and is still anthologized today, an ancient king invents a system of justice that has the accused open one of two doors in an arena. Those who open the door behind which is a tiger are adjudged guilty and eaten alive, while those who open the other find a beautiful lady (more beautiful even than the king's lovely daughter), are adjudged innocent and must marry the lady. The king's daughter meanwhile falls in love with a handsome youth who is accused of a crime and sentenced to this form of trial. Finally, the princess, having learned the secret of the doors, signals her lover to choose the right-hand door. Here the story ends, with the words: "And I leave it with all of you. Which came out of the opened door—the lady or the tiger?" Needless to say, this inconclusive ending drew thousands of letters to Stockton. For the next 20 years,

until his death, the author was begged, tricked and threatened for the answer, which he never gave. One time even Rudyard Kipling ragged Stockton about the solution; their encounter was reported by the *San Francisco Wave* in 1896:

> Stockton and Kipling met at an author's reception, and after some preliminary talk, the former remarked: "By the way, Kipling, I'm thinking of going over to India some day myself." "Do so, my dear fellow," replied Mr. Kipling, with suspicious warmth of cordiality. "Come as soon as ever you can! And, by the way, do you know what we'll do when we get you out there, away from your friends and family? Well, the first thing will be to lure you out into the jungle and have you seized and bound by our trusty Wallahs. Then we'll lay you on your back and have one of our very biggest elephants stand over you and poise his ample forefoot directly over your head. Then I'll say in my most insinuating tones, 'Come now. Stockton, which was it—The lady or the Tiger?'"

Stockton received thousands of letters begging (sometimes threatening) him to reveal the ending of "The Lady or the Tiger." There, indeed, seemed to be no place in the world where people weren't interested in the fate of Stockton's hero. In her diary his wife recounted the following story about a tribe in northeast Burma:

> Miss Evans, our niece, wrote to us that a missionary who was visiting her mission station among the Karens told her she had just come from a distant wild tribe of Karens occasionally visited by missionaries and to her surprise was immediately asked by them if she knew who came out the door, The Lady or the Tiger? Her explanation of it was that some former visitor had read to them the story as suited to their fancy; and as she had just come from the outside world they supposed she could tell the end of it.

∇ ∇ ∇

I.F. Stone (Isidore Feinstein Stone; 1907–1989)

The radical political journalist was asked by the editor of a science fiction anthology to write the inscription for a plaque that might be left by astronauts when they landed on the moon. His proposal: "Their [mankind's] Destructive Ingenuity Knows No Limits and Their Wanton Pollution No Restraint. Let the Rest of the Universe Beware."

∇ ∇ ∇

Lucy Stone (1818–1893)

Use of the "Ms." form of address for a woman today recalls the all but forgotten *Lucy Stoners* active earlier in this century. A woman who refused to change her maiden name upon marriage was often called a *Lucy Stoner*. The term recalls American feminist Lucy Stone who deserves far greater recognition than she has received. On graduation from Oberlin, the only college accepting women at the time, Lucy Stone was 29, and she plunged headlong into the woman suffrage and antislavery causes. Her important work included helping to form the National Woman's Association, of which she was president for three years, and the founding of the *Women's Journal*, the association's official publication for nearly 50 years. An eloquent speaker for women's rights, Lucy Stone became well-known throughout the United States. In 1855 she married Dr. Henry Brown Blackwell, but as a matter of principle she refused to take his name, and she and her husband issued a joint protest against the inequalities in the marriage law. Lucy Stone would never answer to any but her maiden name all her married life, and the Lucy Stone League later emulated her, defending the right of all married women to do so.

Of the Lucy Stone League George S. Kaufman quipped, "A Lucy Stoner gathers no boss."

∇ ∇ ∇

Wilbur Storey (fl. mid-19th century)

What are the responsibilities of a newspaper? the *Chicago Times* editor was asked in 1861. "It's a newspaper's duty to print the news and raise hell," he advised.

∇ ∇ ∇

Rex (Todhunter) Stout (1886–1975)

The mystery novelist told of his mother's great passion for reading, despite all the time it took to raise nine children. Whenever she was reading a book, she placed a bowl of cold water and a washcloth on the table beside her. If one of the children interrupted her, he would have his face vigorously scrubbed. There were few interruptions.

The impeccable Alexander Woollcott had a fatal heart attack in 1943 while serving on the panel of a radio talk show. Suddenly, Woollcott slumped over his microphone and scrawled "I am sick" on a piece of paper. Stout and other members of the panel helped the stricken author to a couch. "I knew something was radically wrong with Alec," Stout said later. "A healthier Woollcott would have printed 'I AM ILL.'"

∇ ∇ ∇

Harriet (Elizabeth) Beecher Stowe (1811–1896)

"The Lord himself wrote it," Mrs. Stowe said of *Uncle Tom's Cabin*. "I was but an instrument in His hand." She later explained that the story "all came before me in visions … and I put them down in words" and confided that after the death of Little Eva she was so shaken that she "could not write a word for two weeks." She claimed that when the last pages were finished the book was sent to the publisher "without one word of correction or revision of any kind." In his biography of his mother Charles Edward Stowe reported that the conclusion of the novel, the death of Uncle Tom, was written first. Mrs. Stowe was seated at a communion table in the Bowdoin College church when "suddenly, like the unrolling of a picture, the scene of the death of Uncle Tom passed before her mind. So strongly was she affected that it was only with difficulty that she could keep from weeping aloud. Immediately on returning home she took pen and paper and wrote out the vision which had been as it were blown into her mind as by the rushing of a mighty wind."

She may have thought that no revisions were made on *Uncle Tom's Cabin*; but William Dean Howells later contradicted her:

> As for the author of *Uncle Tom's Cabin*, her syntax was such a snare to her that it sometimes needed the combined skill of the proofreaders and the assistant editor to extricate her. Of course nothing was ever written into her work, but in changes of diction, in correction of solecisms, in transposition of phrases, the text was largely rewritten in the margin of her proofs. The soul of her art was present, but the form was so often absent, that when it was clothed on anew, it would have been hard to say whose cut the garment was in many places.

Uncle Tom's Cabin was turned down by several publishers, including the Boston house of Philips, Samson and Company that later started the *Atlantic Monthly*, "for fear of alienating the southern trade."

John P. Jewett, the publisher who agreed to take *Uncle Tom's Cabin*, offered Mrs. Stowe a chance to share the printing costs with him and share the profits, or receive a 10% royalty. Unwisely, as it turned out, she chose the royalty. American sales were tremendous, the book selling out its first printing of 5,000 in two days and selling half a million copies in five years. Foreign sales were even greater, but most foreign editions were pirated, with no royalties paid. Mrs. Stowe made nothing on the many very profitable dramatizations of *Uncle Tom's Cabin*, for she disapproved of theatergoing and refused to grant her permission to dramatize the book.

A few years after her success with *Uncle Tom's Cabin* the author described herself in a letter to a friend: "I am a little bit of a woman—somewhat more than forty, about as thin and dry as a pinch of snuff, never very much to look at in my best of days, and looking like a used-up article now."

Uncle Tom's Cabin (1852) prompted President Lincoln to say on meeting the author, "Is this the little woman whose book made such a great war?" The book may be unpopular with some blacks today, but in its time it was anathema to slaveowners. One piece of hate mail Mrs. Stowe received contained the ear of a slave. (See also JOSIAH HENSON.)

It isn't widely known that Mrs. Stowe wrote many of her lesser works under the pseudonym Christopher Crowfield. Among the many women who used male pennames were the three Brontë sisters (*q.v.*), Mary Ann Evans (George Eliot), Olive Schreiner (Ralph Iron), Mary Noailles Murfree (Charles Egbert Craddock), Amandine-Aurore-Lucie Dupin (George Sand; earlier, Jules Sand), Blanche Marie Louise Barrymore (Michael Strange) and Ethel Henrietta Richardson (Henry Handel Richardson).

∇ ∇ ∇

Frank (Francis John) Sullivan (1892–1976)

When *Vogue* asked him for an autobiography to run with one of his pieces, the humorist supplied the following complete bio:

> Francis John Sullivan is that rara avis, a native of Saratoga Springs, where he was born in 1892, the son of Lotta Crabtree and Harold W. Ross. He made his first appearance on the stage two months later playing Fleance to Mme. Modjeska's Lady Macbeth. A promising stage career was terminated soon afterward when during a performance at Hamanus Bleecker Hall in Albany, Mme. Modjeska dropped the budding Fleance on his head. The next day Sullivan became a humorist and startled the literary world with his brilliant novel of a man's love for the woman he loves, *What Makes Martin Chuzzlewit Run?* ("Could not put it down."—Hamilton Wright Mabie. "Held me from start to finish."— Brander Matthews. "Perfectly corking but lacks an index."—James Gibbons Huneker.) Frank is five feet six inches high and about the same across and sleeps in the raw. His pupils dilate normally but his mainspring needs tightening. He spent the summer of 1910 pasting labels on bottles of Saratoga water. We shall see later how this affected the campaign of 1912.

"I wasn't a very good reporter," he said of his early newspaper days. "Once I wrote an obituary of a prominent woman that made the front page. It was an excellent obituary. The only thing wrong with it was that she wasn't dead."

∇ ∇ ∇

Herbert Bayard Swope (1882–1958)

The millionaire executive editor of the *New York World* was renowned for the parties he gave at his Great Neck estate, at which he often lavishly entertained the literati. Swope's food and liquor bills for his house guests came to thousands of dollars a week at his "almost continuous house party." He was a gambler and croquet addict, like many of the Algonquin Round Table group, but his greatest love was poker. In a 1923 game in Palm Beach that lasted 48 hours Swope won $470,000.

Genevieve Taggard (1894–1948)

One of the "socially conscious" American poets of the 1930s, Taggard wrote the poem "On Planting a Tree in Vermont," the last line of which read:

> Bloom for the people. Don't be a family shrub.

∇ ∇ ∇

Edward Thompson Taylor (1793–1871)

The crusty Father Taylor, who preached at Boston's Seaman's Bethel Church and was the inspiration for Melville's Father Mapple in *Moby Dick*, was a great friend and admirer of Emerson, even after the philosopher deserted formal Christianity. To a woman who asked if Emergson was going to hell for leaving the church, Taylor replied: "Go there!—why if he went there he would change the climate and the tide of emigration would turn that way."

∇ ∇ ∇

Albert Payson Terhune (1872–1942)

The popular novelist, best known for his stories of collies, claimed he had a conscience that wasn't powerful enough to keep him from sinning yet was powerful enough to keep him from enjoying the fruit of his sins. He first knew this in early childhood when he stood accused of eating a whole bowl of lump sugar.

"Did you do it?" his mother demanded.

"Yes," young Terhune sobbed, "but I cried all the time I was eating it."

∇ ∇ ∇

Ernest Laurence Thayer (1863–1940)

The mock-heroic poem "Casey at the Bat" was first published in the *San Francisco Examiner* on June 3, 1888, and *Casey at the Bat* has been popular ever since. Its initial popularity was due as much to the actor De Wolf Hopper, who included the 13-stanza poem in his repertory, as it was to the poet, a former editor of the *Harvard Lampoon*. Everyone knows that there was no joy in Mudville when the mighty Casey struck out, but few are aware that Thayer patterned his fabled slugger on a real player, Daniel Maurice Casey, who was still posing for newspaper photographers 50 years after the poem's initial publication. Dan Casey, a native of Binghamton, New York, holds no records worthy of recording—not even as a strikeout king. He was a pitcher and an outfielder for Detroit and Philadelphia, but his career was overshadowed by the exploits of his elder brother, Dennis, an outfielder for Baltimore and New York. Casey died in 1943, when he was 78, in Washington, D.C. As for Thayer, he was paid only $5 for his poem, which actor De Wolfe Hopper recited over 5,000 times, making a career of it.

∇ ∇ ∇

Henry David Thoreau (1817–1862)

Thoreau made no money at all from literature in his lifetime and himself paid for the publication of his first book, *A Week on the Concord and Merrimack Rivers* (1849). In his journal he noted that his publisher had no room for the unsold copies. "So I had them all sent to me here," he wrote, "and they have arrived to-day by express, filling the man's wagon—706 copies out of an edition of 1000 which I bought of Munroe four years ago and have ever since been paying for, and have not quite paid for yet. The wares are sent to me at last, and I have an opportunity to examine my purchase. They are something more substantial than fame, as my back knows, which has borne them up two flights of stairs to a place similar to that to which they trace their origin. Of the remaining two hundred and ninety and odd, seventy-five were given away, the rest sold. I have now a library of nearly nine hundred volumes, over seven hundred of which I wrote myself." Only *A Week...and Walden* (1854), which has never gone out of print, were published while he lived, but his published works number over 20 today.

"You may rely on it," Thoreau told a visitor he did not want to call on him again, "you have the best of me in my books."

Though Emerson was a great admirer of Thoreau, he did not completely understand him or his values, sometimes regarding him as an eccentric hermit living in the wild. "I cannot help counting it a fault in him that he had no ambition," Emerson once said of his fellow New Englander, "...instead of engineering for all America, he was the captain of a huckleberry party." Ironically, despite his criticism of Thoreau's lack of ambition, it is Emerson who is the more neglected of the two writers today.

When Thoreau was jailed in 1843 for not paying the unjust state poll tax Ralph Waldo Emerson visited him. "Why are you here?" Emerson asked his friend.

"Waldo, why are you *not* here?" Thoreau asked.

When Emerson's little son Edward spilled the basket of huckleberries he had harvested and began crying, Thoreau came to the rescue. Nature, he explained to the child, had to plant seed so that there would be future abundant crops of huckleberries; thus she provided little boys who would stumble and sow the berries. Edward stopped crying.

Although he wasn't the wildman of the woods some people still make him, Thoreau did not have much sympathy for the ordinary man or his problems. As Whitman observed in recollecting him, Thoreau could not make allowances for "why one man was so and another man was not so," he was concerned only with the abstract ideal man of mind's making. Thus few, if any, could show affection toward him. "I love Henry," a friend said of him, "but I cannot like him; and as for taking his arm, I should as soon think of taking the arm of an elm-tree."

Hawthorne described Thoreau as "ugly as sin, long-nosed, queer-mouthed," and others said his nose was so long that he could take it in his mouth. Yet, despite his apparent celibacy, he was hardly passionless or sexually abnormal. Early in his manhood he competed with his brother for the hand of the lovely Ellen Sewall, and it seems clear that he was in love with his friend Emerson's wife, his constant companion when he worked as a handyman for Emerson. Thoreau was not unattractive to women. Schoolteacher Sophia Ford wanted to marry him and pursued him for many years, certain that she and Thoreau were "twin souls" that would be united in the "other world." Sophia, however, did not kill herself because Thoreau rejected her, as rumor had it. She died of old age at 85.

"What do you think of the world to come?" an admirer asked the philosopher. "One world at a time," Thoreau replied.

"Have you made your peace with God?" a maiden aunt asked Thoreau shortly before he died.
"I don't know that we even quarreled," he replied.

Thoreau was more noted at Harvard for his poor, unfashionable country clothes than for his scholastic accomplishments, although he was an intelligent, well-read student. Refusing to take his college degree, he said that "It isn't worth five dollars." Another time he observed that Harvard taught "all of the branches [of learning] but none of the roots."

He always put his insomnia to good use. "I put a piece of paper under my pillow," he noted in his *Journal*, "and when I could not sleep I wrote in the dark."

∇ ∇ ∇

James Thurber (1894–1961)
"Write short dramatic leads to your stories," Thurber's editor told him during his early days as a newspaper reporter. Soon after he turned in a murder story that began:

> Dead. That's what the man was when they found him with a knife in his back at 4 P.M. in front of Riley's Saloon at the corner of 52nd and 12th Streets.

When a woman told him she found his work funnier in French than English, Thurber replied, "Yes, I always seem to lose something in the original."

According to screenwriter Nunnally Johnson, who told the story to Groucho Marx: "Some drunk dame told [Thurber] at a party that she would like to have a baby by him. Jim said 'Surely you don't mean by unartificial insemination!'"

A librarian asked Thurber if there was a model for the hero in "The Secret Life of Walter Mitty," and though biographers have claimed that Thurber based the character on his father or brother, the author replied: "The original of Walter Mitty is every other man I have ever known. When the story was printed in the *New Yorker*...six men from around the country, including a Des Moines dentist, wrote and asked me how I got to know them so well."

Leaving a Hollywood premiere, Thurber asked a friend what he thought of the movie.
"I thought it stank," his friend said. "What did you think of it?"
"I can't say I liked it that well," Thurber replied.

Handing him the completed screenplay of what he called "The Secret Life of Walter Witty," Samuel Goldwyn, in another of his malapropisms warned Thurber not to read the last hundred pages because they were too "blood and thirsty." Ignoring the warning, Thurber read the pages in question and reported to Goldwyn that he was "horror and struck."

"What seven-letter word has three *u's* in it?" Thurber quizzed a nurse in the hospital. "I don't know," she said, pondering, "but it must be unusual."

Thurber was sure from experience that "some American writers who have known each other for years have never met in the daytime or when both were sober."

"Word has somehow gotten around that the split infinitive is always wrong," Thurber once observed. "That is a piece with the outworn notion that it is always wrong to strike a lady."

When Thurber submitted his famous parody of Henry James, "The Beast in the Dingle" (which he first entitled "The Return of the Screw"), to Harold Ross, the *New Yorker* editor rejected it, commenting, "I only understand 15 percent of its illusions."

He wrote, or rather invented, fillers when he worked in Paris for the *Chicago Tribune* international edition. A typical one, supposedly reported from Washington, D.C., went like this: "'A man who does not pray is not a praying man,' President Coolidge today told the annual convention of the Protestant Churches of America."

"Ross gave me a job [on the *New Yorker*]," he once recalled, "because he convinced himself I was an old pal of E.B. White. I tried to tell him I had met White for the first time on the way in to his office, but he wouldn't listen. I thought I was hired to be a writer, but for three weeks all I did was sign slips of paper they thrust under my nose. Finally, I asked, 'What am I signing here, anyhow?' 'That,' said my secretary, 'is the payroll.' That's when I found Ross had made me managing editor. When I asked him why, he said firmly, 'Because everybody starts at the bottom here.' It took me eight years of solid writing to persuade Ross to make somebody else his confounded managing editor."

Thurber died of pneumonia contracted after an operation for the removal of a blood clot on the brain. His last words are said to have been: "God bless...God damn..."

∇ ∇ ∇

Henry Timrod (1828–1867)
"The laureate of the Confederacy," who wrote the famous "Ode Sung at the Occasion of Decorating the Graves of the Confederate Dead," died at a young age of the tuberculosis that earlier led to his medical discharge from the Confederate army. He eked out a living writing his poems, his last years so painful that he wrote to his lifelong friend, poet Paul Hamilton Hayne: "You asked me to tell you my story for the last year...I can embody it all in a few words: beggary, starvation, death, bitter grief, utter want of hope."

∇ ∇ ∇

Harry S. Truman (1884–1972)
Washington Post music critic Paul Hume had criticized the singing voice of Margaret Truman, the president's daughter, and Truman fired off the following famous piece of criticism to *him*:

> I have just read your lousy review buried in the back pages. You sound like a frustrated old man who never made a success, an eight-ulcer man on a four-ulcer job, and all four ulcers working. I have never met you, but if I do you'll need a new nose and plenty of beefsteak and perhaps a supporter below.

Henry Theodore Tuckerman (1813–1871)

The poet and essayist wrote extremely conventional Petrarchan sonnets and his essays, too, were marked by extreme propriety. Some wag coined the word "tuckermanity," formed on his name and on the analogy of "humanity," and meaning excessive propriety and conventionality in the literary treatment of love.

∇ ∇ ∇

Richard Walton Tully (1877–1945)

Tully's play *The Bird of Paradise* (1906), about an American man's love for a Hawaiian girl, was challenged as a plagiarism by a mysterious woman who was awarded a judgment of over $780,000 when she finally brought the case to court in 1924. Tully, a popular playwright who had collaborated with David Belasco, spent all his savings fighting this decision and it was finally overturned on appeal in 1930. *The Bird of Paradise* was made into a musical that year, but Tully, financially and psychologically exhausted, was never able to write again.

∇ ∇ ∇

Gene Tunney (1898–1978)

It is safe to say that Tunney, who took the world heavyweight title from Jack Dempsey in 1926, was the most intellectual of American boxers. Before their match Dempsey thought he had the fight won—after a spy in Tunney's camp reported, "It's a set-up. I seen the lug readin' a book."

∇ ∇ ∇

Mark Twain (Samuel Langhorne Clemens; 1835–1910)

Samuel Clemens, a former riverboat pilot, took his pen name from the pseudonym of another riverboat captain, who in turn had adopted Mark Twain from the leadsman's call "Mark twain!" meaning, mark two fathoms. But what of *mark twain* itself? The words are probably a mispronunciation and compression of "Mark on the twine, six fathoms!" called out when riverboat leadsmen sounded the river with weighted twine.

Shortly after Twain took his first job as a reporter he was told by his editor never to state as fact anything he couldn't verify by personal knowledge. After covering a gala social event, he turned in the following story: "A woman giving the name of Mrs. James Jones, who is reported to be one of the society leaders of the city, is said to have given what purported to be a party yesterday to a number of alleged ladies. The hostess claims to be the wife of a reputed attorney."

At the top of a letter he wrote in 1865 describing how he first decided to make his life's work "serious scribbling to excite the laughter of God's creatures," he scrawled this sentence as an apparent afterthought: "You had better shove this in the stove—for if we strike a bargain I don't want any absurd 'literary remains' & 'unpublished letters of Mark Twain' published after I am planted."

During his lean days as a reporter in San Francisco, Twain was approached by a lady friend who saw him gazing into a shop window, a cigar box under his arm. "I'm sorry to see you carrying that cigar box, Mr. Clemens," she said. "I'm afraid you're smoking too much." "It isn't that," Twain replied. "I'm moving again."

He was greatly disappointed when his article "Forty-three Days in an Open Boat," his first effort to win Eastern readers, appeared in the December 1866 edition of *Harper's New Monthly Magazine*. It was printed under the name Mark Swain.

Twain's knees were shaking so violently that few people in the audience believed he would be able to deliver his first lecture, but he won the day when he began: "Julius Caesar is dead, Shakespeare is dead, Napoleon is dead, Abraham Lincoln is dead and I am far from well myself…"

Only once did he fail as an after-dinner speaker. In 1877 he was asked to speak at John Greenleaf Whittier's 70th birthday dinner in Boston. His speech, in which he was supposed to represent the West paying homage to the East, centered on three overbearing tramps who visited a camp of California prospectors. The three tramps were Ralph Waldo Emerson, Oliver Wendell Holmes and Henry Wadsworth Longfellow—who sat dignified as ever in the audience. None of them thought this conception funny and their reaction spread to the other guests. Except for a solitary hysterical man there was utter silence, and Mark Twain stood there so embarrassed that for one of the few times in his life he was unable to think of anything funny to say.

Among his most famous speeches was his address on New England weather at a dinner of the New England Society in New York in 1876:

> There is a sumptuous variety about the New England weather that compels the stranger's admiration—and regret. The weather is always doing something there; always attending strictly to business; always getting up new designs and trying

them out on people to see how they will go. But it gets through more business in Spring than in any other season. In the Spring I have counted one hundred and thirty-six different kinds of weather inside of twenty-four hours.

He answered a "Toast to the babies" at a Chicago banquet in 1879: "We haven't all had the good fortune to be ladies; we haven't all been generals, or poets, or statesmen; but when the toast works down to babies, we stand on common ground."

Speaking to the Young People's Society of the Greenpoint (Brooklyn) Presbyterian Church in 1901 he advised: "Always do right. This will gratify some people, and astonish the rest."

When a friend invited him to dinner, Twain, just arrived home off the banquet lecture circuit, wrote in reply: "Dear Lee—I can't. I am in a family way with three weeks undigested dinners in my system, and shall just roost here and diet and purge till I am delivered. Shall I name it after you? Yr. friend, Sam'l L. Clemens."

The parenthesis goes back to at least the 16th century, when the "upright curves" (the marks enclosing these words) were sometimes called "halfe circles" and "round brackets." Twain had the last word on parentheses. "Parentheses in literature and dentistry are in bad taste," he wrote, comparing *parenthetical expressions* "to dentists who grab a tooth and launch into a tedious anecdote before giving the painful jerk." (See JOHN BARRYMORE on footnotes.)

When Twain wrote his satire on Sherlock Holmes stories, called "A Double-Barrelled Detective Story," he began the tale as follows:

> It was a crisp and spicy morning in early October. The lilacs and laburnums, lit with the glory-fires of autumn, hung burning and flashing in the upper air, a fairy bridge provided by kind Nature for the wingless wild things that have their homes in the tree-tops and would visit together; the larch and the pomegranate flung their purple and yellow flames in brilliant broad splashes along the slanting sweep of the woodland; the sensuous fragrance of innumerable deciduous flowers rose upon the swooning atmosphere; far in the empty sky a solitary oesophagus slept upon motionless wing; everywhere brooded stillness, serenity, and the peace of God.

The "solitary oesophagus" in the passage was certainly solitary, for it never existed outside of Twain's teeming imagination. He had, of course, invented the bird—which know-it-alls were quick to describe to friends—and later remarked that few readers ever questioned him about it.

A customs inspector found a bottle of bourbon in his suitcase. "I thought you said there was only clothing in there," he questioned.

"I did," Twain replied. "You're looking at my nightcap!"

"Don't you adore babies?" an elderly lady, holding her infant niece in her arms, asked Twain.

"No, I hate them," Twain replied, vastly enjoying his outrageous joke. He went on to tell her that when he was recovering from typhoid his little nephew had come into his room and kissed him. "I made up my mind," he said in his best serious manner, "that if I lived I would put up a monument to Herod."

He observed in his notebook: "Familiarity breeds contempt—and children."

Remarked American literary critic Van Wyck Brooks: "His wife not only edited his works but edited him."

Though he quipped that working in bed is dangerous, "because so many people die there," Twain did a lot of his own writing in bed, as photographs of him show. Large parts of *Huckleberry Finn*, *Tom Sawyer* and *A Connecticut Yankee in King Arthur's Court*, among other works, were written between the sheets, with pillows propped up behind his head.

On the road for one of his lecture tours Twain went to a barber shop in a small town.

"You picked a good time to come, stranger," the barber said, "Mark Twain's going to read and lecture tonight. I suppose you'll go?"

"Oh, I guess so."

"Have you got a ticket?"

"Not yet."

"Then you'll have to stand. Everything is sold out."

"How annoying," Twain sighed. "I never saw such luck! I always have to stand when that fellow lectures."

A group of scholars were arguing heatedly about whether or not Shakespeare had written the plays and sonnets attributed to him. Finally, Twain butted in. "It wasn't William Shakespeare who really wrote those plays," he explained, "but another Englishman who was born on the same day at the same hour as he, and who died on the same day, and, to carry the coincidences still further, was also named William Shakespeare."

Twain was asked his opinion of Edgar Allan Poe. "To me," he said, "Poe's prose is unreadable, like Jane Austen's—no, there is a difference. I could read his prose on a salary, but not Jane's."

Twain sent this letter to *The New York Times*, signing W.D. Howells's name to it:

> To the Editor: I would like to know what kind of goddamn government this is that discriminates between two common carriers and makes a goddamn railroad charge everybody equal and lets a goddamn man charge any goddamn price he wants for his goddam opera box.

Enclosing a copy of the letter, he then wrote to his friend explaining his action:

> Howells, it is an outrage the way the government is acting so I sent this complaint to *N.Y. Times* with your name because it would have more weight.
>
> Mark

"It could probably be shown by facts and figures," Twain once mused, "that there is no distinctively native American criminal class except Congress."

Twain took a rival publisher, Estes and Lauriat, to court when they printed *Huckleberry Finn* before even his own publishing company could print it. When Judge Le Baron Colt ruled against him in the Untied States Circuit Court in Boston, the author was so enraged that he publicly condemned Colt. The judge, he said, has allowed the defendant "to sell property which does not belong to him but to me—property which he has not bought and I have not sold." Therefore, he went on, "Under this same ruling I am now advertising the judge's homestead for sale; and if I make as good a sum out of it as I expect I shall go on and sell the rest of his property."

"Dear Charley," he wrote to his publisher Charles Webster in early 1885, "the Committee of the Public Library of Concord, Massachusetts, have given us a rattling tip-off puff which will go into every paper in the country. They have expelled Huck [*Huckleberry Finn*] from their library as 'trash suitable only for the slums.' That will sell 25,000 copies for us sure." (It sold 50,000 the first year.)

In a strange case of censorship, Twain *agreed* with the Brooklyn New York Public Library when in 1905 it banned *Huckleberry Finn* from the Children's Room as a bad example for youth. "I wrote Tom Sawyer and Huck Finn for adults exclusively," Twain said, "and it always distresses me when I find that boys and girls have been allowed access to them. The mind that becomes soiled in youth can never again be washed clean." It is worth noting that Twain's wife had censored *Huckleberry Finn* before it was published, removing all profanity.

In his *Memoirs of a Publisher*, F.N. Doubleday, dubbed "Effendi" by Kipling, reveals the "perfect recipe" Twain gave him for making a modern publisher: "Take an idiot man from a lunatic asylum, and marry him to an idiot woman, and the fourth generation of this connection should be a good publisher from the American point of view." Mark Twain, of course, later became a publisher himself.

While giving a speech on honesty he told this story:

> When I was a boy, I was walking along a street and happened to spy a cart full of watermelons. I was fond of watermelon, so I sneaked quietly up to the cart and snitched one. Then I ran into a nearby alley and sank my teeth into the melon. No sooner had I done so, however, than a strange feeling came over me. Without a moment's hesitation, I made my decision. I walked back to the cart, replaced the melon—and took a ripe one.

Like many authors Twain rebelled against autograph hunters. He used to send out this printed refusal:

> I hope I shall not offend you; I shall certainly say nothing with the intention to offend you. I must explain myself, however, and I will do it as kindly as I can. What you ask me to do I am asked to do as often as one half dozen times a week. Three hundred letters a year! One's impulse is to freely consent, but one's time and necessary occupations will not permit it. There is no way but to decline in all cases, making no exceptions; and I wish to call your attention to a thing which has probably not occurred to you, and that is this: that no man takes pleasure in exercising his trade as a pasttime. Writing is my trade, and I exercise it only when I am obliged to. You might make your request of a doctor, or a builder, or a sculptor, and there would be no impropriety in it, but if you asked either for a specimen of his trade, his handiwork, he would be justified in rising to a point of order. It would never be fair to ask a doctor for one of his corpses to remember him by.

A friend asked Twain why he had so many books piled all over his house but no books lined on shelves. "You see," Twain explained, "it's so very difficult to borrow shelves."

When Twain asked a neighbor for the loan of a book, the man said that he was more than welcome to it, but he had to read it there, as he made it a rule never to let any book out of his library. Some time later the neighbor asked to borrow Twain's lawnmower. "Certainly," Twain told him. "You're more than welcome to it. But I must ask you to use it here. You know I make it a rule."

Twain was in a foul mood one morning. Unable to find a clean shirt fit to wear, he unleashed a stable of expletives only he could have strung together. His wife Livy Langdon, standing in the doorway, decided to teach him a lesson and slowly repeated each vile curse he had uttered. But when she was done, Twain simply sighed and said, "My dear, you have the words, but you don't have the music."

Though his wife Livy was prudish (see preceding story) she loved and worshipped Twain as much as he did her. It was just that she felt he was a boy who hadn't grown up, like one of the wayward boys in his novels. This was reflected in her pet name for the novelist—"Youth."

A gushing fan seized Twain's hand and kissed it in admiration of his work. "How God must love you!" she cried. "I hope so," Twain said, smiling, but after the lady left, he added, "I guess she hasn't heard of our strained relations."

At a dinner party guests were discussing heaven and hell and how one must act to merit either place. One matron turned to Mark Twain and demanded to know his opinion on the matter. "Madam, you must excuse me," Twain replied gravely. "I am silent of necessity: I have friends in both places."

Twain, an agnostic himself, was asked if he was going to hear the celebrated agnostic Robert Ingersoll lecture at the Hartford Opera House. "No," Twain replied. "I understand that Ingersoll will talk about what he thinks of Moses. But I would be far more interested in hearing what Moses thinks of Ingersoll."

A Mormon arguing with Twain defied him to cite any Biblical passage expressly forbidding polygamy.
"Nothing easier," Twain told him. "No man can serve two masters."

After hearing a dramatic sermon one Sunday, Twain told the preacher it was a good one but that he had a book at home that contained every word of it. "Impossible," the peacher snorted. "I'd certainly like to see that book, if it exists." Within a week the preacher received a bulky package from Twain containing an unabridged dictionary.

"Before I die," said a ruthless businessman to Twain, "I mean to make a pilgrimage to the Holy Land. I will climb Mount Sinai and read the Ten Commandments aloud at the top."
"I have a better idea," Twain suggested. "You could stay home in Boston and keep them."

"Do you think it will stop?" William Dean Howells asked Twain as they were leaving church one Sunday and it began to rain heavily. "It always has," said Twain.

"Quitting smoking is easy," the great cigar-smoker remarked. "I've done it a hundred times."

An acquaintance told Twain she hadn't been feeling well for a week or so and he advised her to buy a certain magnetic health belt.

"I bought the belt and have worn it constantly," she wrote him a few weeks later, "but it didn't help me one bit."

Twain wired back: "It helped me. I own stock in the company."

"In a world without women what would men become?" Twain was asked.

"Scarce, sir," said Twain, "mighty scarce."

"My grandfather was cut down in the prime of his life," Twain told a haughty woman who had been bragging about her ancestors. "In fact, my grandmother used to say that if he had been cut down fifteen minutes earlier, he could have been resuscitated."

Several friends, not knowing where in the world Mark Twain had wandered, sent him a birthday card addressed: "Mark Twain, God knows where." Within the month, they received an unsigned letter postmarked from Italy and reading only, "He did."

"Mr. Clemens, I would give ten pounds not to have read your *Huckleberry Finn*," an Englishman who encountered him on a train told a startled Twain. When Twain looked up, he added: "So that I could again have the great pleasure of reading it for the first time."

While visiting James McNeill Whistler's London studio, Twain bent as if to touch one canvas. "No," Whistler warned, "don't touch that! Don't you see it isn't dry yet!"

"It's all right," Twain said. "I have gloves on."

Twain claimed a certain admiration for British empire builder Cecil Rhodes, who had made his fortune in the Kimberley diamond fields and later was forced to resign as prime minister of Cape Colony, Africa, after being pronounced guilty of serious breaches of duty. "I admire him," Twain remarked, "I frankly confess it; and when his time comes I shall buy a piece of the rope for a keepsake."

An arrogant Frenchman remarked to Twain that whenever an American had nothing to do he could endlessly amuse himself by trying to find out who his grandfather was. "And whenever a Frenchman has nothing to do," Twain countered, "he can amuse himself endlessly by trying to find out who his *father* was."

Weak French coffee was a Twain *bête noir*. After drinking a cup one time he told a friend it was made by "rubbing a chicory bean against a coffee bean and dropping the chicory bean in the water."

Twain was charged eight dollars, a good deal of money then, for a boat tour of the Sea of Galilee. "Do you wonder that Christ walked?" he asked.

"All you need in this life is ignorance and confidence," Twain wrote in an 1887 letter to Mrs. Foote, "and then success is sure."

Twain was a dismal failure as a businessman, due to both poor judgment and too good a heart. (He gave the bankrupt Ulysses S. Grant 70% of the net profits from the 400,000 copies he sold of Grant's autobiography and may have ghosted or entirely rewritten most of the book himself.) One estimate has Twain losing more than a million dollars (money he made writing) in business deals of one kind or another. He lost over a quarter of a million dollars alone in the ill-fated Paige typesetter, money that he almost invested in the Bell Telephone Company, an investment that would have made him a millionaire many times over.

A traditional story has it that in 1897 an American newspaper bannered Twain's death. When another paper sent a reporter to check the story Twain came to the door of his Connecticut home and gave him the following statement: "James Ross Clemens, a cousin of mine, was seriously ill two or three weeks ago, but is well now. The reports of my illness grew out of his illness. The reports of my death are greatly exaggerated." Nothing any scholar says will change this tale, which is by now part of American folklore, but the true story is that a reporter from the *New York Journal* called on Twain while the author was staying in England—to check out a rumor that Twain was either dead or dying in poverty. Twain explained to the reporter that his cousin had been seriously ill in London and that reports of his own illness grew out of his cousin's illness, that "the report of my death was an exaggeration."

"When I was younger," he confided toward the end of his life, "I could remember anything, whether it had happened or not; but my faculties are decaying now and soon I shall be so I cannot remember any but the things that never happened. It is sad to go to pieces like this, but we all have to do it."

Twain was born when Halley's Comet appeared in 1835, and he died—as he had predicted—when it appeared again in 1910. "It will be the greatest disappointment of my life if I don't go out with Halley's Comet," he once confided. "The Almighty has said, no doubt: 'Now here are two unaccountable freaks; they came in together, they must go out together.'"

He wrote his last memorandum on his deathbed:

> Death, the only immortal who treats us all alike, whose pity and whose peace and whose refuge are for all—the soiled and the pure, the rich and the poor, the loved and the unloved.

∇ ∇ ∇ ∇ ∇ ∇ ∇ ∇ ∇

UNIVAC 1108 (c. 1973–?)

In 1973 at the University of Wisconsin one of these computers was programmed to write "Murder Mystery," a 2,100-word piece that is the first short story known to be written by a computer ("poems" had been written before). The story opens: "Wonderful smart Lady Buxley was rich. Ugly oversexed Lady Buxley was single. John was Lady Buxley's nephew. Impoverished irritable John was evil. Handsome oversexed John Buxley was single. John hated Edward. John Buxley hated Dr. Bartholemew Hume. Brilliant Hume was evil. Hume was oversexed…" This sounds like it took about 20 seconds to write, which it did.

∇ ∇ ∇

Louis Untermeyer (1885–1977)

Untermeyer once returned his fee for giving a lecture to a small group of struggling writers and asked that they put the money to good use. Several months later the poet and anthologist inquired about just what good use the group had chosen. "We've used it to start a fund to get better speakers," he was told.

"Write out of love, write out of instinct, write out of reason," he advised a young author. "But always for money."

"I'm writing my third biography," he boasted on his ninetieth birthday. "The other two were premature."

Clement Laird Vallandigham (1820–1871)

The notorious Ohio Copperhead politician and newspaper editor was banished behind Confederate lines for the duration fo the Civil War for supporting the South and declaring that the war being fought was not to save the Union but to free the blacks and enslave the whites. After the war Vallandigham became a prominent lawyer in his home state. His unusual end came in 1871 when he was defending a man charged with murder. Vallandigham's defense was that the murdered man had actually killed himself while trying to draw his pistol. When he demonstrated his theory to his associates in his hotel room—rising from a kneeling position, drawing his pistol from his pocket and pulling the trigger—he shot and killed himself. He had inadvertently used a loaded pistol. His defense theory later worked in court, however, and his client went free. (See EDWARD EVERETT HALE.)

∇ ∇ ∇

Frances Jane Van Alstyne (1820–1915)

The world's most prolific hymnist was blinded when only six weeks old but wrote more than 8,500 hymns, at least 2,000 more than her nearest rival, Charles Wesley. Mrs. Van Alstyne is reputed to have written one hymn in 15 minutes.

∇ ∇ ∇

Thorstein Veblen (1857–1929)

The great economist had a reputation as a womanizer. "Professor Veblen, we can't have any of that at Harvard," the head of his department told him when he came to Cambridge. Veblen replied that he need not fear: He had seen the women of Cambridge and they offered no temptation.

∇ ∇ ∇

Carl Van Vechten (1880–1964)

Van Vechten began as a critic, renounced criticism for fiction when 40, and gave up fiction for photography at 52. In the 1920s, however, he and his second wife, actress Fania Marinoff, were always at the center of New York literary life, "The Splendid Drunken Twenties" he called the time, and many of his novels described the fabulous literary characters he and Fania entertained at their famous parties. His novel *Parties* (1930) has as its central characters Donald Westlake, obviously based on novelist F. Scott Fitzgerald, and Zelda Westlake, fictional counterpart of the novelist's wife, Zelda.

Jones Very (1813–1880)

Very's friend James Freeman Clarke insisted that this early American poet had "monosania," not monomania, and Emerson, among others, also believed him "profoundly sane." But the Harvard faculty questioned the sanity of the mystic poet, who claimed that his religious sonnets were supernaturally communicated to him, and Jones agreed to let himself be committed to an insane asylum. It is said that Jones' eyes "burned with a strange and intense light" and that he would startle students in his Greek class at Harvard with sudden cries such as, "Flee to the mountains, for the end of all things is at hand!" After his release from the asylum be spent most of the last 40 years of his life as a virtual recluse.

∇ ∇ ∇ ∇ ∇ ∇ ∇ ∇

De Witt Wallace (1889–1981)

Wallace didn't begin publishing the *Reader's Digest* until 1922, but he got the idea for the most widely circulated magazine in the world a few years earlier while recovering from shrapnel wounds in a French hospital after World War I. There Sgt. Wallace, with much time on his hands and many Red Cross magazines to read, also perfected his method of condensing articles he thought too long and complicated.

The founder of *The Reader's Digest* suggested the following epitaph for himself:

The final condensation.

∇ ∇ ∇

Lew Wallace (1827–1905)

A veteran of the Mexican War and a major general who successfully defended Washington against Confederate forces in 1864, Wallace was actually a lawyer by profession. However, he is remembered neither as lawyer nor as soldier but as the author of *Ben Hur* (1880), one of the most popular books of all time, with perhaps three million sales worldwide and two famous motion pictures based upon it. *Ben Hur* is said to be the only book ever to have been published both by Sears, Roebuck and the Pope. But he almost didn't write the romantic novel.

Before *Ben Hur* Wallace had written *The Fair God* (1873), a historical romance about Cortez. "The publication of my first novel was almost enough to ruin my law practice," he once told Booth Tarkington. "As soon as the jury of farmers and village merchants heard the word 'novel,' they uttered hearty guffaws…I might as well have appeared in court as a circus clown."

∇ ∇ ∇

Artemus Ward (Charles Farrar Browne; 1834–1867)

During the Civil War, the Down East humorist was traveling in the rear car of a painfully slow train.

"Does this railroad allow passengers to give it advice, if they do so in a respectful manner?" Ward asked the conductor as he bent to punch his ticket.

"I guess they do," the conductor said gruffly.

"Well then," Ward said, "it occurred to me it would be well to detach the cowcatcher from the front of the engine, and hitch it to the rear of the train. For, you see, we are not laible to overtake a cow; but what's to prevent a cow from strolling into this car and biting a passenger?"

Ward was one of the few authors—Truman Capote was another who comes to mind—who wrote most of his work while lying down.

The long-winded chairman who introduced Ward for a lecture on "American Wit and Humor" covered the subject so exhaustively that when the humorist rose to speak, he began: "The chairman has said all that needs to be said on 'American Wit and Humor,' so instead of speaking on that subject I shall lecture on 'Indian Meal.'" Which he did.

"I am saddest when I sing," he told a group of listeners. "So are those that hear me; they are sadder even than I am."

∇ ∇ ∇

Nathaniel Ward (c. 1578–1652)

Ward wrote under the pseudonym Theodore de la Guard one of the first American books, *The Simple Cobbler of Aggawam* (1647), which is a crotchety defense of the status quo. He did not believe in toleration, for example, holding that "He that is willing to tolerate any unsound opinion, that his own may be tolerated, will for a need hang God's Bible at the Devil's girdle." He moved back to England shortly after writing the book.

Booker T. (Taliaferro) Washington (1856–1915)

Tradition has it that the great American educator and author, the son of a black slave and a white man, received his unusual first name when a child because of his great love for books. In his autobiography, *Up From Slavery* (1901), Washington adds that he chose his own last name when he first attended school after the Civil War had brought him freedom. He had gone only by the name Booker before then and when the teacher called the roll:

> ... I calmly told him "Booker Washington," as if I had been called by that name all my life ... Later in my life I found that my mother had given me the name "Booker Taliaferro" soon after I was born, but in some way that part of my name seemed to disappear and for a long while was forgotten, but as soon as I found out about it I revived it, and made my full name "Booker Taliaferro Washington." I think there are not many men in our country who have had the privilege of naming themselves.

∇ ∇ ∇

George Washington (1732–1799)

The first American president was a colporteur, or book salesman, as a young man, once selling over 200 copies of *The American Savage: How He May Be Tamed by the Weapons of Civilization* in his travels through Virginia. (See also ALEXANDER HAMILTON; PARSON WEEMS.)

∇ ∇ ∇

Henry Watterson (1840–1921)

This outspoken journalist, when editor of the Louisville *Courier-Journal*, was rebuked for criticizing Kentucky's governor. Said Watterson in a reply that eventually reached his editorial columns:

Things have come to a helluva pass
When a man can't cudgel his own jackass.

∇ ∇ ∇

Daniel Webster (1782–1852)

A prodigy who memorized whole chapters of the Bible when a boy, the New England statesman and orator, whose writings and speeches take up some 20 volumes, always stood head and shoulders above his classmates. Dartmouth College, however, for some unknown reason failed to make him valedictorian on his graduation, though Webster deserved the honor. After the commencement exercises, young Webster gathered together some friends on the green and tore the diploma he had been given into tiny pieces, casting them to the wind.

As his last words before he mounted his horse for the long ride home, he said: "My industry may make me a great man, but this miserable parchment can not!"

One of the richest men of his day, he relished his reputation for enjoying good food and drink. He boastfully proclaimed that "It is not often that good wine is under any roof where I am without my knowing it." One would hope so since an 1830 beverage inventory of his own house revealed an upstairs closet of 3,200 bottles of wine as well as a cellar with hundreds of bottles of port, madeira, sherry, claret, whiskey, rum and champagne.

Webster supported the Compromise of 1850, continuing slavery. At the time Emerson bitterly said of him: "The word *liberty* in the mouth of Webster is like the word *love* in the mouth of a courtesan." Many at the time called him "Tricky Daniel."

∇ ∇ ∇

Noah Webster (1758–1843)

Webster's major fault sems to have been his prudery, the norm in those days. In 1833, the American lexicographer published a bowdlerized edition of the Bible, removing "offensive words" that might make young ladies "reluctant to attend Bible classes." "Breast" was substituted for "teat," "to nourish" for "to give suck," "peculiar members" for "stones" (testicles) and so on. This hardly fits in with the legend about his being caught kissing the chambermaid. "Why Noah, I'm *surprised!*" his wife is supposed to have said. "Madame," Webster replied most correctly in the strict usage of his time, "*You* are astonished; *I* am *surprised.*"

An apocryphal story about Webster, probably invented by his nemesis William Cobbett, has Webster meeting Dr. Benjamin Rush. "How do you do, my dear friend," says Rush. "I congratulate you on your arrival in Philadelphia." "Sir," Webster intones, "you may congratulate *Philadelphia* on the occasion."

∇ ∇ ∇

Parson Weems (Mason Locke Weems; 1759–1825)

Today's book salesmen follow an honorable calling, one that dates back hundreds of years to when their kind carried Bibles and other books in a basket or pack hanging from their necks by a strap. For this reason they were, and sometimes still are, called *colporteurs* from the French *col*, "neck," and *porters*, "to carry." Typical of these was Old Parson Weems, noted for his charming fabrication of George Washington chopping down the cherry tree, not to mention his bold Homeric yarns about Ben Franklin and General Francis Marion, "the

Swamp Fox." Weem's most famous book is his biography of Washington, *The Life and Memorable Actions of George Washington* (1800), in the 1806 edition of which he invented the cherry-tree tale. He peddled books door-to-door for more than 30 years, believing that "the selling of good books was a field for God's work." (See GEORGE WASHINGTON.)

∇ ∇ ∇

Orson Welles (1915–1985)

It was the director's intention to "modernize" the Lord's Prayer for a religious movie in which he was to appear as the deity. "You can't do that," one of his writers said, "it's God's word." "Don't tell me about God's word," Welles insisted. "I *am* God."

One time he stared out at a tiny audience from a theater stage in Wisconsin. "What a pity it is," he said, "that there are so few of you and so many of me."

Welles often defended his early theatrical experiments against radio ad agency executives. After one broadcast an account executive argued that background sound effects drowned out the dialogue. "You object to the fact that the background predominated in a certain scene," Welles countered. "*Well who told you it was the background.*"

He was particularly innovative in creating sound effects for his radio plays. In *The Count of Monte Cristo*, for example, to create the effect of a dank prison cell he had the scene played in the studio bathroom, "where the dripping toilet water created the desired ambience."

∇ ∇ ∇

Nathanael West (Nathan Wallenstein Weinstein; 1902–1940)

In the late 1920s the author of *Miss Lonelyhearts* (1933) worked as the night manager of New York's seedy Kenmore Hall Hotel in Gramercy Park, the job paying $35 a week plus free room and board and giving him plenty of time to write—both on and off the job. West allowed his needy writer friends free use of all the unoccupied rooms in the hotel. With Dashiell Hammett, who was in the process of writing a serial novel for *Black Mask* magazine and had run out of money, West was especially generous. He let Hammett register under the unlikely and untraceable name, "Mr. T. Victrola Blueberry," and moved him into the hotel's finest suite. Hammett stayed until he finished the serial a week or so later, when West let him skip out without paying the bill. As Hammett was leaving West asked him what he had entitled his novel. "I think I'll call it *The Maltese Falcon*," Hammett said.

In the 10 years before his too early death West wrote four novels that earned him a total of $1,280—less than a month's pay at his job as an RKO script writer.

West died in an automobile accident when at the height of his creative powers. There were those who saw it coming. Many of his friends considered him the worst driver they had ever seen. One time he drove through 11 red lights, narrowly missed a trolley and finally hit a taxi while driving in New York City. The man with him wouldn't get back in the car.

$$\nabla\ \nabla\ \nabla$$

Edward Noyes Westcott (1846–1898)
A successful banker and local government official, Westcott began writing his *David Harum: A Story of American Life* while trying to recover from the tuberculosis that ultimately killed him. The novel was the only thing he ever wrote, and it was turned down by at least half a dozen publishers, finally being published six months after his death. Westcott never knew that the book at once became a bestseller, eventually selling over one million copies, a phenomenal number at the time. It was later made into two motion pictures as well as a radio series.

$$\nabla\ \nabla\ \nabla$$

Edith Wharton (1862–1937)
Many considered the novelist, born to a distinguished New York family, something of a snob. One time she was asked why she had only eight chairs in her large dining room. "Only eight people in New York are worth dining with," she explained.

She was reared in the genteel tradition. When just 11 she wrote a story with the line, "If only I had known you were going to call, I should have tidied up the drawing room." Her aristocratic mother's only comment on reading the story was, "Drawing rooms are *always* tidy."

Sillerton Jackson in Wharton's *The Age of Innocence* (1920) is partly modeled on Wall Street broker William R. Travers, a socialite who moved to New York City from Baltimore and was later a founder of the New York Athletic Club. When Travers, a stutterer, first came to New York, a Baltimore friend noticed that he was stuttering more than he ever had. "Ha-h-have to," explained Travers. "B-b-b-b-bigger city."

After taking a tour of her mansion in Lenox, Massachusetts, a patronizing Frenchman told the author that he gave the place his stamp of approval, save for the terrible bas-relief in the entry hall. "I assure you," the quickwitted Mrs. Wharton said, "that *you* will never see it here again."

∇ ∇ ∇

Phillis Wheatley (1753?–1784)

The black American poet was captured and shipped as a child to the Boston slave market and there became a slave of merchant John Wheatley, who encouraged her talent. When her poems began to attract attention, many people, especially in England, questioned whether a young black female slave could have written them, even though Thomas Jefferson vouched for their originality (though he didn't like them). As a result, the 18-year-old poet was called before 18 of "the most respectable characters in Boston"—including John Hancock and the Massachusetts governor— who questioned her in order to decide whether or not she had written the poems. They satisfied themselves and the following year Miss Wheatley was freed and her *Poems on Various Subjects, Religious and Moral* (1773) was published, the first book of poetry or fiction by an African-American.

∇ ∇ ∇

Edwin Percy Whipple (1819–1886)

This Massachusetts author was ranked as one of the foremost critics of his time, though today he is throught to have erred too far on the kind side in his judgment of native authors. One would expect as much from the first critic to observe that: "[The American author, without dignity and enough to eat] is ready to write on any subject which will afford him bread—moral or immoral, religious or atheistic, solid or flash."

∇ ∇ ∇

James Abbott McNeill Whistler (1834–1903)

The great painter, author and literary wit, born in America but reared in Europe, attended West Point before he began his art studies. He was dismissed from the Point in 1854 because he failed chemistry. Looking back later in his life, he remarked, "Had silicon been a gas, I would have been a major-general." (See EDGAR ALLAN POE for another West Point dropout.)

Though Oscar Wilde lived only 46 years, he is remembered as one of the greatest wits in English history. Perhaps only Whistler consistently got the better of Wilde in the exchange of ripostes. Once Wilde remarked "Oh, I wish I'd said that!" on hearing a clever remark, and Whistler replied: "You will, Oscar, you will." Another time Whistler wrote: "What has Oscar in common with Art? Except that he dines at our tables and picks from our platters the plums for the puddings he peddles in the provinces, Oscar—the amiable, irresponsible, esurient Oscar—with no more sense of a picture than of the fit of a coat, has the courage of the opinions…of others." To which Wilde replied: "As for borrowing Mr. Whistler's ideas about art, the only thoroughly original ideas I have heard him express have had reference to his own superiority as a painter over painters greater than himself." Which inspired Whistler to retort: "A poor thing, Oscar!— but, for once, I suppose your own."

"Whatever possessed you to be born in a place like Lowell, Massachusetts?" a snobbish matron asked Whistler. "I wished to be near my mother," Whistler explained.

Whistler was perennially in debt and often pawned his furniture to obtain money to pay his creditors. But he never let the loss of his possessions bother him. He would simply draw a picture of a sofa where the missing sofa had been, the picture of a chair where a chair had stood, etc.

"I can't say I like the portrait you did of me, Mr. Whistler," a well-known celebrity told the artist. "You must admit it's a bad work of art."
"Yes," Whistler agreed, staring intently at the man thorugh his monocle, "but then you must admit that you are a bad work of nature."

"I just came up from the country along the Thames," an admiring woman told Whistler, "and there was an exquisite haze in the atmosphere which reminded me so much of your little things. It was really a perfect series of Whistlers."
"Yes, madam," said Whistler, very seriously. "Nature is creeping up."

A lady of his acquaintance asked Whistler to help her determine whether a painting she had bought was a genuine or an imitation Turner.
Replied Whistler, who hated the British landscape artist's work, "Now that's really a fine distinction."

"How much for the lot?" asked an American millionaire, indicating all the paintings in Whistler's Paris studio. "Four million," Whistler said. "What!" the millionaire cried. "My posthumous prices," said Whistler.

A boring patronizing young lord was seated next to Whistler at dinner. "Aw, y' know, Mr. Whistler," he drawled, "I pahssed your little house just this morning."

"Thank you," Whistler said, "thank you very much."

Whistler called in a distinguished throat specialist to treat his beloved French poodle. On learning that he had made the house call to treat a dog, the eminent doctor was incensed, but he said nothing, prescribed, and went home. The next day, however, he sent an urgent message to the artist summoning him to his home and the artist obliged, thinking it concerned his dog. When he arrived, the specialist greeted him gravely. "Good morning, Mr. Whistler," he said. "I wanted to see you about painting my front door."

"Do you think genius is hereditary?" Whistler was asked.

"I can't tell you, madam," he replied. "Heaven has granted me no offspring."

"It's a good thing we can't see ourselves as others see us," said a friend, fed-up with Whistler's bragging.

"Isn't it!" Whistler replied. "I know in my case I should grow intolerably conceited."

"How like you, Walter!" Whistler complained when his disciple English artist Walter Sickert dropped a plate he was working on. Soon after Whistler dropped a plate. "How *unlike* me!" he observed.

"You shouldn't say it is not good," he remarked in explaining how to criticize a work of art. "You should say you do not like it; and then, you know, you're perfectly safe."

"I only know of two painters in the world," an enthusiastic fan gushed, "yourself and Velasquez."

"Why," replied Whistler sweetly, "why drag in Velasquez?"

▽ ▽ ▽

E.B. (Elwyn Brooks) White (1899–1985)

"If we should ever inaugurate a hall of fame," the humorist and *New Yorker* editor said, "it would be reserved exclusively and hopefully for authors who, having written four bestsellers, *still refrained* from starting out on a lecture tour."

White, the youngest of his family was a short man who often complained of his health; his physician, according to Brendan Gill, said he had "a Rolls-Royce mind in a model T body." *New Yorker* editor Harold Ross, however, saw things differently. "Don't worry about White!" he explained to Gill one day. "White was the runt of the litter! Runts live forever!"

∇ ∇ ∇

William Allen White (1868–1944)
In 1923 the editor of the *Topeka Capital* charged that "*The Emporia Gazette* is the best-loved paper in Kansas because its editor never looks in yesterday's files to see if what he proposes to write today is consistent." Replied White: "Consistency is a paste jewel that only cheap men cherish."

∇ ∇ ∇

Opal Whiteley (b. 1897)
Opal Whiteley had her childhood diary published in the *Atlantic Monthly* when she was 22, after convincing *Atlantic* editor Ellery Sedgwick that it was the work of a child. Readers throughout the world were enchanted by the work, the *London Times* proclaiming it "the most complete picture of a child's inner life that can be imagined," though some critics have charged it was a hoax. Since her time there have been at least a dozen authors who have published books before they were 10, the youngest of them only four years old.

∇ ∇ ∇

Walt Whitman (1819–1892)
Whitman claimed that he wrote his temperance novel, *Franklin Evans, or the Inebriate* (1842), in three days, cranking out 20,000 words a day. Moreover, the great poet claimed that he had written this temperance tract in the reading room of Tammany Hall while drunk, "fortifying himself with gin cocktails in order to keep going" (another time he said he drank "a bottle of port or what not"). He wrote this early soap opera because the "cash payment … was so tempting—I was so hard up at the time …" and admitted "it was damned rot—rot of the worst sort …" Published for 12 1/2 cents a copy as a supplement to Park Benjamin's *New World* newspaper, the novel, padded with stories "Walter Whiteman" (as the title page read) had on hand, sold some 20,000 copies. The author later reprinted it, when he was editor of the *Brooklyn Eagle*, as *The Fortunes of a Country Boy*.

For three months in 1848 Whitman lived in New Orleans and edited the *New Orleans Crescent*. Several of his biographers have claimed that he had an affair with a woman of mixed black and white ancestry at the time, this affair "the chief force in altering his character" as a young man. While there is no proof of such a relationship, Whitman did write of a woman he loved in "Once I pass'd Through a Populous City" (1867):

Day by day and night by night we were together—all else
  has long been forgotten by me,
I remember I say only that woman who passionately clung
  to me,
Again we wander, we love, we separate again,
Again she holds me by the hand, I must not go,
I see her close beside me with silent lips sad and tremulous.

Whitman not only published the first edition of *Leaves of Grass* (1855) himself, he also anonymously (and enthusiastically) wrote three of the five contemporary reviews of the book that are known to have been published. Never one to miss an opportunity for promoting his work, he made sure to acknowledge the famous laudatory letter Emerson sent him about the first 12 poems in the second, 33-poem edition of *Leaves* that he published the following year. Only by the time the third edition was issued in 1860 did Whitman find a regular publisher for his ever expanding book.

Leaves of Grass received some of the worst reviews ever accorded a masterpiece. Said the *Boston Intelligencer*: "This book should find no place where humanity urges any claim to respect and the author should be kicked from all decent society as below the level of brute…it seems to us that he must be some escaped lunatic, raving in pitiable delirium." A column in *The New York Times* called Whitman a "half beast…who roots among the rotten garbage of licentious thoughts." Even Algernon Swinburne, who should have known better (considering his own critics, such as Thomas Carlyle), said of Whitman: "Under the dirty clumsy paws of a harper whose plectrum is a muck-rake, any tune will become a chaos of discords…Mr. Whitman's Eve is a drunken apple-woman, indecently sprawling in the slush and garbage of the gutter amid the rotten refuse of her overturned fruit-stall: but Mr. Whiteman's Venus is a Hottentot wench under the influence of cantharides and adulterated rum."

It was among Whitman's greatest regrets that not one of his immediate family really understood or appreciated his work; in his own words, even his "dear mother," who gave him great support, "stood before *Leaves of Grass*, mystified, defeated." Said his brother George of *Leaves of Grass*: "I saw the book, but didn't read it at all—didn't think it worth reading. Mother thought as I did."

Whitman wrote in his diary that while working in Washington he saw President Lincoln out riding with cavalry escort almost every day, so often, in fact, that he got to exchange cordial bows with the President. The poet admired the great man but never knew how great an admirer of his poetry Lincoln was. Soon after *Leaves of Grass* was published, when Lincoln was practicing law in Illinois, the book was being discussed in the office and Lincoln picked it up, enjoying the poems so much that he read aloud poem after poem "with a growing relish."

When Whitman sent Emerson, whom he did not even know, a copy of his self-published *Leaves of Grass*, the Sage of Concord wrote a letter of praise that made the young poet famous and has become perhaps the most famous letter in American literary history:

> Concord, Massachusetts, 21 July, 1855
>
> Dear Sir—
>
> I am not blind to the worth of the wonderful gift of *Leaves of Grass*. I find it the most extraordinary piece of wit and wisdom that America has yet contributed. I am very happy in reading it, as great power makes us happy. It meets the demand I am always making of what seemed the sterile and stingy Nature, as if too much handiwork, or too much lymph in the temperament, were making our Western wits fat and mean.
>
> I give you joy of your free and brave thought. I have great joy in it. I find incomparable things said incomparably well, as they must be. I find the courage of treatment which so delights us, and which large perception only can inspire.
>
> I greet you at the beginning of a great career, which yet must have had a long foreground somewhere, for such a start. I rubbed my eyes a little, to see if this sunbeam were no illusion; but the solid sense of the book is a sober certainty. It has the best merits, namely, of fortifying and encouraging.
>
> I did not know until I last night saw the book advertised in a newspaper that I could trust the name as real and available for a post-office. I wish to see my benefactor, and have felt much like striking my tasks and visiting New York to pay you my respects.
>
> R.W. Emerson

As David S. Reynolds points out in *Beneath the American Renaissance* (1988): "Whitman [whether or not he was telling the truth] firmly denied that he was a homosexual. When the British author John Addington Symonds, after years of probing, asked point-blank about Whitman's sexual status, Whitman replied that such questions 'quite daze me,' calling Symonds's remarks 'morbid inferences which are disavowed by me and seem damnable.'"

The poet had a genius for self-promotion unrivaled in his day. When in 1871 he read "After All, Not to Create Only" to a crowd of 200 to 300 people at the National Industrial Exposition in New York, most of the newspapers reported that he could not be heard because the carpenters were still building exhibits. Whitman, however, wrote an anonymous piece for the *Washington Chronicle*, making the audience two- or three-*thousand* and reporting that five- or six-hundred workmen laid down their tools, enchanted, when he began to read his poem.

Author and critic Logan Pearsall Smith, a friend of the poet, writes in his autobiography that one of Whitman's favorite songs was "Old Jim Crow," which he often sang when he stayed at Smith's Germantown, Pennsylvania, home. One can picture the gray-bearded poet singing and dancing to the song, which had been introduced by black-face minstrel Thomas D. Rice in 1828 and is probably the source for expressions like *Jim Crow laws.*

"I am as bad as the worst," Whitman once said in assessing his work, "but thank God I am as good as the best."

∇ ∇ ∇

John Greenleaf Whittier (1807–1892)
The New England poet believed in "plain living and high thinking," as he put it, admirable qualities, but the same qualities that caused him to throw his copy of Whitman's *Leaves of Grass* in the fire.

A volume of Burns's poems given to him by his teacher inspired Whittier to become a poet. His work was printed for the first time by accident when his sister sent his poem "The Exile's Departure" to William Lloyd Garrison's *Newburyport Free Press.* The great abolitionist published it in 1826.

Whittier's famous poem "Barbara Fritchie," in which a 96-year-old Mrs. Fritchie flaunts the U.S. flag in the face of Confederate troops marching through Frederick, Maryland, was based on a true incident, but Whittier gave credit to the wrong flag waver. That lady was the real-life Mrs. Fritchie's neighbor, Mrs. Mary Quantrell. Mrs. Quantrell in reality was not molested by the Confederates, who raised their hats as they passed by, saying, "To you, madam, and not to your flag." Whittier, who got *his* information from novelist Mrs. E.D.E.N. Southworth, later admitted his mistake.

A devout Quaker, the poet dedicated just as much of his life to the antislavery movement as to his poetry, often risking his life for the cause. In the fall of 1835 he and an English abolitionist were attacked by a mob in Concord, New Hampshire. Five years later, in Philadelphia, the offices of his newspaper *The Pennsylvania Freeman* were burned to the ground by an angry mob.

Whittier remained a bachelor all his life, due mainly to his constant involvement with social reform and his preoccupation with his Quaker religion. The famous couplet from his sentimental poem *Maud Muller* is said to refer to this circumstance:

Of all sad words of tongue and pen
The saddest are these: It might have been.

He was regarded by many as a gentle poet, despite his fiery abolitionist beliefs, and his last words seem to bear this out. To the friends gathered around his bed he looked up and said with his last breath: "My-love-to-the-world."

∇ ∇ ∇

Ella Wheeler Wilcox (1850–1919)

After Ella Wheeler Wilcox published her poem "Solitude" in 1883, John A. Joyce claimed that he had written it 20 years earlier. The poet offered $5,000 for any printed version of the poem dated earlier than her own, and none was ever produced. Joyce however, had the last word when he died in 1915, aged 72. The most famous lines from the poem are attributed to him on his gravestone in Oak Hill Cemetery, Washington, D.C.:

Laugh and the world laughs with you
Weep and you weep alone.

∇ ∇ ∇

Thornton Wilder (1897–1975)

There are many Thornton Wilders, he told *Atlantic Monthly* editor Edward Weeks:

There's a Wilder who loves to teach and who feels starved if he doesn't occasionally have the chance to do so. There's the Wilder who must write novels and plays. There's the Wilder who enjoys Hollywood and the torment of having his stories manhandled by Sam Goldwyn. And there is Wilder the scholar, who hopes some day to complete the bibliography of Lope de Vega, the most fertile playwright in the Spanish world.

The immense erudition of this universal man impressed everyone who worked with him. "Whenever I'm asked what college I've attended," director Garson Kanin once said, "I'm tempted to write, 'Thornton Wilder.'"

In his mid-seventies he was asked what he considered the ideal age. "I was an old man when I was twelve," he replied, "and now I *am* an old man, *and it's splendid!*"

Wilder thought fiction immensely superior to nonfiction. He argued about this with author Garson Kanin and in concluding their argument wrote something on a piece of paper that he told Kanin to study when he had the time. This proved to be the last thing that Wilder wrote, for he died the next day. The paper read:

"If Queen Elizabeth or Frederick the Great or Ernest Hemingway were to read their biographies, they would exclaim, 'Ah—my secret is still safe!' But if Natasha Rostov were to read *War and Peace*, she would cry out, as she covered her face with her hands, 'How did he [Tolstoy] know? How did he know?'"

∇ ∇ ∇

Oscar Williams (1900–1964)
Introduced at a party to a remarkably well-endowed woman in a remarkably low-cut dress, the American poet and anthologist smiled, said he was glad to meet her, and then proceeded to unbutton his shirt. "I too," he revealed, "have a perfectly hairless chest."

Edith Sitwell had disagreed with the anthologist over poems he had selected from her body of work and threatened "to claw his eyes out." Williams was on his way to a cocktail party at the Gotham Book Mart, honoring Sitwell, when he heard of her threat. Fearing that she would do as she said, he hid in a cafeteria across the street until the party was over.

∇ ∇ ∇

Tennessee (Thomas Lanier) Williams (1911–1983)
Though one of the greatest modern playwrights, Williams saw his second play, *Battle of Angels* (revised in 1957 as *Orpheus Descending*), hissed off the stage in 1940. His producers then took the unprecedented step of going up on stage and apologizing to the audience for the production.

Williams, who first explored a new terrain of freedom in the American theater, once tried to define the motivation behind his art. "I was brought up puritanically," he confided to a friend. "I try to outrage that puritanism."

The playwright's first published work was an essay that appeared in *Smart Set* when he was only 16. Its title: "Can a Good Wife Be a Good Sport?" His first published *fiction*, for which he was paid $35, was the short story "The Vengeance of Nitocris," in *Weird Tales*.

He first used the name Tennessee Williams on the short story "A Field of Blue Children," published in the August 1939 *Story* magazine. He had dropped Thomas Lanier (after Southern poet Sidney Lanier), he later explained, because "it sounds like it might belong to the sort of writer who turns out sonnet sequences to spring."

Asked why he had given up his psychoanalyst, Williams seriously replied, "He was meddling too much in my private life."

In his acceptance speech for the gold drama medal of the National Institute of Arts and Letters, he told the following story:

> One time, Maureen Stapleton received a phone call from a friend who said that so-and-so was getting married, and the caller said, "Why is she marrying that man? You know he is a homosexual," and Maureen said, "Well, what about the bride?" And the caller said, "Well, of course we know she's a lesbian. And you know they're not even being married by a real minister, but by one who's been defrocked!" And Maureen said, "Will you do me one favor? Will you please invite Tennessee Williams? Because he'll say, 'Oh, they're just plain folks!'"

After leaving the bathroom in Benjamin Sonnenberg's huge, ornate Gramercy Park mansion, Williams was heard to remark, "It looked so shabby when I took it out, I couldn't go."

The playwright's absurd accidental death came when he choked to death in his Manhattan apartment after swallowing the cap of one of his many medicine bottles.

▽ ▽ ▽

William Carlos Williams (1883–1963)

The bizarre artist's model Baroness Elsa von Freytag-Loringhoven (*q.v.*), who painted her shaved head purple, pasted postage stamps on her cheeks, and wore a cake with lit candles for a hat, among myriad eccentricities, took a kind remark Williams made to her as a declaration of love and offered to give him syphilis, which she said had been bequeathed to her by her father and would clear Williams's mind for his poetry. When Williams demurred she trailed him home to Rutherford and rang his bell, opening her fur coat to reveal herself naked when he answered the door. "Villiam Carlos Villiams, I vant you!" she cried, and when Williams cried "No! No!" she proceeded to assault him. The baroness, her real name Elsa Ploetz, died a suicide in Paris in 1927.

Williams was visiting Gertrude Stein in Paris when she asked him what he would do if he had such a large body of unpublished work as she did. "If they were mine," said the poet-physician glancing at the manuscripts, "having so many, I should probably select what I thought were the best and throw the rest into the fire."

"No doubt," said Gertrude Stein after a killing silence. "But then writing is not, of course, your *métier*."

In attempting to write a profile of the poet-physician for the *New Yorker* Brendan Gill followed him on his rounds through Rutherford. Gill found Williams, then in his late fifties, still a passionate man, despite his bad heart, a man "lacerated by sexual excitement" to whom "every young mother...seemed...a Venus." "Bill, tell me the truth," he heard the poet's adored wife, Floss, ask him one day. "Do you want to make love with every single woman you meet?" After considerable thought, Williams gravely replied, "Yes, I do."

▽ ▽ ▽

Alexander Wilson (1766–1813)
Famed ornithologist Alexander Wilson, whose nine-volume *American Ornithology* is a classic and who has the Wilson's petrel, phalarope, plover, snipe and thrush named after him, was an itinerant tinker and poet before he immigrated to America in 1794. Two years earlier he had been accused of writing a poem about a mill owner—the poem alleging that the man used false measures in determining the week's output of cloth—and then demanding five guineas to refrain from publishing the poem. Though he may have been innocent, he was fined and jailed several months for libel and blackmail.

▽ ▽ ▽

Edmund Wilson (1895–1972)
Novelist John Dos Passos recalled his first meeting with the eminent American man of letters in 1922, in the offices of *Vanity Fair*:

> There appeared a slight sandyheaded young man with a handsome clear profile. He wore a formal dark business suit. The moment we had been introduced, while we were waiting for the elevator, Bunny [Wilson's nickname] gave an accent to the occasion by turning, with a perfectly straight face, a neat somersault.

American poet Theodore Roethke virtually ignored Wilson at a party at the critic's house. Consuming great quantities of food from the buffet he finally took a large bunch of grapes in his hand and sat down next to his host on the couch, popping grapes into his mouth as Wilson talked. Finally, the big bear of a man leaned over and pinched one of Wilson's cheeks. "What's this?" he said. "Blubber?" Conversation halted. No one could think of anything to say except Wilson, who quickly recovered from the shock. "And just who are you?" he said, pointing at the grapes in Roethke's hand, "a half-baked Bacchus?"

When asked if he typed, dictated or wrote out his work, Wilson liked to reply, "I think with my right hand."

∇ ∇ ∇

Ellen Axon Wilson (1860–1914)

Woodrow Wilson's first wife assisted the president in writing his books and speeches, often sharing his proofreading with him. Once after a long morning correcting a book together they had the following conversation.

Said Wilson: "The soup comma my dear comma is delicious semi-colon Maggie is an excellent cook period No Wonder exclamation You taught her period."

Replied Ellen: "Thank you comma Woodrow period."

∇ ∇ ∇

Harriet E. Wilson (19th century)

Only recently was it established that a black woman wrote the first novel written and published by an Afro-American. Harriet E. Wilson has that honor for *Our Nig* (1859), rediscovered and reprinted in 1982 by Henry Louis Gates Jr., of Cornell University.

∇ ∇ ∇

Woodrow Wilson (1856–1924)

The 28th president of the United States, who authored many significant books and essays, was once invited to make a speech, the length of which was left to him. "If you want me to talk for ten minutes," he replied, "I'll come next week. If you want me to talk for an hour I'll come tonight."

∇ ∇ ∇

Thomas Wolfe (1900–1938)

A huge man who wrote huge novels, the author was unwilling or unable to cut his own work, which was usually pruned into shape by his editors. Often he would agree to a cut only if he were allowed to write what he called a "transitional sentence." The transitional sentences would turn into transitional paragraphs, pages and chapters.

Legend has it that the complete manuscript of *Look Homeward, Angel* that Wolfe sent to his editor Maxwell Perkins measured three feet high, or some 6,000 pages. Actually it was about a third of that, and the novel still had to be cut extensively.

In a letter to his editor Maxwell Perkins about *Look Homeward, Angel*, Wolfe wrote:

> ...although I am able to criticize wordiness and over-abundance in others, I am not able practically to criticize it in myself. The business of selection and revision is simply hell for me—my efforts to cut out 50,000 words may sometimes result in my adding 75,000.

Wolfe's handwriting was as confusing as his attitude toward women. "I can always find plenty of women to sleep with," he once said, "but the kind of woman that is really hard for me to find is a typist who can read my writing."

"Publishing is a very mysterious business," he wrote in a letter to his mother, trying to explain the financial side of the book trade. "It is hard to predict what kind of sale or reception a book will have, and advertising seems to do very little good."

"With money I'll throttle the beast-blind world beneath my fingers," he wrote in an early letter. "Without it I am strapped, weakened, my life is a curse and a care."

Wolfe, truly a giant man, had dined and wined with Sinclair Lewis in London and returned to his hotel early in the morning. Just as he got into bed the phone rang and it was Lewis asking him to hurry back—it was an emergency. Wolfe dressed and returned. When he entered the bar he heard Lewis turn to a man at his side and exult, "You see! Didn't I tell you he was a big bastard!"

∇ ∇ ∇

Alexander Woollcott (1887–1943)
The venomous humorist despised all things French. "Monty," Gerald Murphy once asked him, "just what is it you don't like about the French with their marvellous foods and wines and art...how can you find anything to dislike?"

"I'll tell you what I dislike," Wooley replied. "The trouble with the French is that they sit around twenty-four hours a day talking *French.*"

Though he tried to be in the middle of things, and usually succeeded, he was not popular in college. In fact, classmates nicknamed him "Putt," short for "putrid."

"Are you trying to cross me?" the more than ample Woollcott demanded in the midst of an argument with author Howard Dietz. "Not without an alpenstock," Dietz replied.

Of his dog Cocaud, named after the proprietress of a French brothel, Woollcott once said: "Considered as a one-man dog, she's a flop. In her fidelity to me she's a little too much like that girl in France who was true to the 26th Infantry."

Daisy Fellowes, heir to the Singer Sewing Machine fortune, had a flotilla of yachts, a string of horses and a long line of lovers, but no creative accomplishments to boast of to her literary and artistic friends. "You people are all so talented. You write or dance or sing or act. But I do *nossing*," she once said to Woollcott. "My dear," said Woollcott, with the trace of a leer, "I have heard different."

Moss Hart got the idea for *The Man Who Came to Dinner* (1939) after Woollcott spent a weekend at his house. After Woollcott left, Hart had remarked to George S. Kaufman, "Can you imagine wht would have happened if the old monster had fractured his hip and had to stay?" When Woollcott learned of his subsequent caricature as Sheridan Whiteside in the Kaufman-Hart play, he quipped, knowing a good thing when he had one, "The thing's a terrible insult and I've decided to swallow it." Later he toured in the part.

Woollcott had to take the management of the Shubert Theaters to court in 1915 in order to review plays in their houses. They had banned him from all Shubert productions for the "rancor and malice and venom" in his reviews.

After again reading his favorite novel *The Brothers Karamazov*, "the smartest of Alecs," as Heywood Broun called Woollcott, wrote to Cornelia Otis Skinner: "I have been weeping steadily because once again I had come to the great healing last chapter … It always chokes me up and fills me with a love of mankind that lasts till noon of the following day."

In her later years the English actress Mrs. Patrick Campbell, George Bernard Shaw's great love, needed financial help and moral support form her friends, but continually insulted and repelled them. "She was like a sinking ship firing on its rescuers," Woollcott said.

At a benefit performance in New York he played Henry VIII and Madge Kennedy portrayed Anne Boleyn. The audience of literati booed and hissed for a full five minutes when he made his entrance but he was incapable of getting the message. "I can't understand why Madge should be so unpopular," he remarked as he came offstage.

"I don't think you'd be very good as Lady Macbeth, do you, Peggy?" Woollcott said in trying to put down actress Peggy Wood. "No, Alec," she replied innocently, "but I think *you* would."

One afternoon he departed his villa in Antibes, leaving his poodle Cocaud in the care of Harpo Marx. A night and a day passed, until Harpo finally followed the eager dog into town, where it began scratching at the door of a nondescript house. A woman recognized the dog and let them in. She proved to be the madam of a plush bordello, where Woollcott lay on a couch between two half-naked prostitutes who were popping grapes into his mouth.

The bathroom in his apartment overlooking New York's East River was decorated with pictures of himself on the toilet. Charles MacArthur and Helen Hayes let one photograph of him suffice in *their* bathroom. They hung it directly over the toilet.

When Moss Hart stayed with Woollcott, Hart couldn't keep himself from reading Woollcott's unmailed letters, much to Woollcott's consternation. One day Hart picked up a letter that read in part: "I'll ask you up here as soon as I can get rid of that nauseating Moss Hart, who hangs on here like a leech, although he knows how I detest him." Hart was ready to do violence when his eye fell upon the postscript: "Moss, my puss; I trust this will cure you of the habit of reading other people's mail!"

He was not well liked, being called everything from Louisa May Woollcott, for his sentimentality, to a boorish foul mouth, and, not surprisingly, was the butt of many practical jokes. Playwright Charles MacArthur filled his bathtub with Jell-o, and friends once tricked him into delivering a basket of groceries to the home of "starving poet" Archibald MacLeish, a millionaire.

Woollcott's ashes were mailed by a friend to Hamilton College in Utica, New York, in accord with his wish to be scattered over his alma mater. Somehow they were mistakenly delivered to Colgate University and were forwarded to Hamilton. Woollcott's ashes arrived with 67 cents postage due. (See also REX STOUT and F.P.A.)

∇ ∇ ∇

Cornell Woolrich (1903–1968)

The suspense novelist may be the only author ever to dedicate a novel to his typewriter. In 1940 his famous *The Bride Wore Black* honored his machine with the following dedication [Chula was possibly a pet name, Spanish for "cute," for his mother]:

To
CHULA
And
Remington Portable No. NC69411
in
unequal parts

∇ ∇ ∇

E.V. Wright

Wright's novel *Gadsby* is among the most unusual ever written. Turned out in the Roaring Twenties at the height of a craze for pseudo-sophistication, the novel, which received a certain amount of critical praise, was written without the use of the letter *e*, the author tying down the *e* key on his typewriter and producing a work some 50,000 words long. E.V. Wright's feat was no mean accomplishment, as anyone will see who attempts to write even a paragraph under the same conditions.

∇ ∇ ∇

Richard Wright (1908–1960)

As a young black writer in Memphis the novelist had difficulty obtaining the books he wanted from the library, especially controversial works like those of H.L. Mencken. He solved the problem by borrowing a white friend's library card and forging a note in his name to the public librarian, which read: "Dear Madam: Will you please let this nigger boy have some books by H.L. Mencken?"

∇ ∇ ∇

Willard Huntington Wright (1888–1949)

The erudite Wright became addicted to drugs when blacklisted from New York literary life for several ill-considered acts during World War One, including his joking boast that he was related to the Kaiser. Eventually, he wound up in Paris, where he went into therapy with an analyst who virtually kept him in solitary confinement, with only mystery stories to read. He came out of this odd therapy cured and convinced that he could write much better mysteries than most of the trash he had read. The result was his intellectual Philo Vance mystery novels, which he wrote under the pseudonym S.S. Van Dine to keep his new career separate from his work as an art critic.

Elinor Wylie (1885–1928)

The novelist and poet had a high regard for her own work. Once she spotted a woman reading a novel of hers. Walking over, she said in all seriousness, "How I envy you reading that beautiful book!"

Her poetry and too-short life were characterized by a delicacy and fragility that led James Branch Cabell to call her a "Dresden china shepherdess." Not so her friend Katherine Anne Porter. Once, at four in the morning, she rang Miss Porter's bell, waking her from a deep sleep and advising: "Katherine Anne, I have stood the crassness of this world as long as I can and I am going to kill myself. You are the only person in the world to whom I wish to say goodbye."

"Elinor, it was good of you to think of me," Miss Porter replied. "Goodbye." Elinor didn't go through with it.

▽ ▽ ▽ ▽ ▽ ▽ ▽ ▽ ▽

John Peter Zenger (1697–1746)

Zenger was imprisoned for his scathing attacks on Colonial Governor William Cosby in his *New York Weekly Journal*. Alexander Hamilton defended him and won an acquital in what is regarded as the first important victory for freedom of the press in America. The German-born printer's paper was burned in public, and he was imprisoned for nine months awaiting his trial. Though he was denied pen, ink and paper, he all the while edited and published the *Journal*, outwitting the authorities, as he put it, by giving copy and instructions verbally "through the hole in the door to my wife and my servants." He missed publishing only one issue.

INDEX